Raising an Echo

Glyn Mathias

To my children, Mathew, Megan and Hannah
so they can hear the echoes from the past

Raising an Echo

My Autobiography

Glyn Mathias

First impression: 2014

Cover design: Y Lolfa
Cover photograph: Emyr Young

ISBN: 978 184771 820 4

Published and printed in Wales
on paper from well-maintained forests by
Y Lolfa Cyf., Talybont, Ceredigion SY24 5HE
website www.ylolfa.com
e-mail ylolfa@ylolfa.com
tel 01970 832 304
fax 832 782

I will pick up my boots and run around the shire
To raise an echo louder than my fear.

'The Flooded Valley', Roland Mathias

Contents

Preface

IT WAS A routine walk from the House of Commons to Downing Street. It was a walk which political journalists did most days to attend the briefing at No. 10 given by the Prime Minister's press secretary. Those briefings varied from the lively to the tedious, depending on how much information was being given out and how much the lobby journalists thought was being withheld.

It was always best to sup with a long spoon.

But this time it was far from routine. It was five o'clock in the afternoon on Monday, 5 April 1982. An international crisis had blown up out of nowhere with the invasion of the Falkland Islands by Argentina three days earlier. Parliament was in turmoil, the Foreign Secretary had resigned, the invasion had been condemned by the UN Security Council and the first ships of a task force ordered by the Prime Minister had left for the South Atlantic.

I was walking up Downing Street rehearsing to myself the questions I planned to ask Mrs Thatcher in the interview I was about to do for ITN. At that stage, it was still the hope of most people that the Argentines would leave the Falklands without resort to force. But the Prime Minister had set the wheels of war in motion. I was trying to settle on the wording of some of the key questions I wanted to ask. Was the country now at war – and, if Britain failed to expel the Argentine force from the Falklands, would she resign as Prime Minister?

A broadcast journalist should always try and put any personal opinions to one side, however difficult that might be. But I walked up Downing Street with some ghosts on my back. In my family there had been a disputatious difference of opinion about whether war was ever justified. My grandfather, Evan Mathias, had been in the army for most of his career, serving as a Nonconformist chaplain and rising to the rank of colonel. He had joined at the outset of the First World War, serving in the Dardanelles and on the Western Front. He was mentioned in despatches.

My grandfather never had any trouble reconciling his Nonconformism with his belief that military intervention could be and had been justified, as he made clear in his letters while serving with the British Defence Force in Shanghai. He was never remotely apologetic about his army career. My father, Roland Mathias, took a completely contrary view. For him, his religious conscience could not permit him to take any part in any military activity. His form of pacifism meant that nothing could justify the taking of human life, however great the provocation.

Both founded their views on war in their Christian belief. In my father's case, a refusal to undertake even non-combatant duties during the Second World War led to two spells in prison as a conscientous objector. He would not be associated with any form of work which might assist the war effort, however indirectly. It is difficult to imagine such a contrasting set of beliefs between a father and son.

My own views on the issue were far less determinate. To me, the war against Nazi Germany was a war which had to be fought, for moral as well as other reasons, and I could never imagine that I would have opted out of it. I would, however, have made a terrible soldier, and was always grateful that I was young enough to have escaped National Service.

To me, there was a line to be drawn between a just and an unjust war, and Britain has taken part in both. I always admired an old friend who had refused to respond to his call-up for the invasion of Suez in 1956 and wondered whether I would also have had the courage to refuse to serve in a war of such unjustified aggression. Blair's war in Iraq nearly fifty years later was another case of a war which lacked any adequate justification. Even if all the allegations about weapons of mass destruction had turned out to be true, it would still not have amounted to an adequate *casus belli*.

On that April afternoon in 1982, the arguments were less clear-cut. A British overseas territory had been invaded, and under international law Britain had every right to use force to regain it. On the other hand, it was a group of islands 8,000 miles away – about which the British had never seemed to care very much before – and there had been no time to prepare the public for what might lie ahead. The interview was therefore a vital platform for Mrs Thatcher to explain to the British people her justification for dispatching a task force to the South Atlantic.

I like to think that the ghosts on my back helped me formulate the right questions. We are all, in varying degrees, the product of our backgrounds. And the issues of war and peace, writ large on the battlefield, were also played out between the generations of my family.

GM

CHAPTER 1

Sennybridge, via Siberia

IT WAS THE envelope which first caught my attention. It was a small, discoloured envelope, with a red three-halfpenny stamp in one corner with the head of George V, and in the other top corner, the words 'Via Siberia' underlined twice. Then, in bold copperplate handwriting, the address:

Mr D. Mathias,
Emporium,
Senny Bridge,
Breconshire,
South Wales,
England.

It was a letter from my grandfather to his brother David, written from Shanghai in 1927 and was one of several letters from Evan Mathias discovered by my cousin Gareth in the attic of his house after his mother's death.

My grandfather was serving as a Nonconformist chaplain to the Shanghai Defence Force which had been dispatched by the Imperial War Committee to defend the city against a Communist takeover. Consisting of three brigades, it was the largest British force sent to the Far East up to that time. Chiang Kai-Shek, at that stage in alliance with the Chinese Communists, was marching his Nationalist army north from Canton, and had already overrun the British concession at Hankow.

Shanghai was the richest city in China, and the biggest prize in the struggle between the Nationalists, Communists and competing warlords. A large section of the city was controlled by foreign powers, who had created an international settlement outside Chinese jurisdiction. The primary fear for the British, the French and the Americans was that the valuable port of Shanghai would fall into Communist hands.

The city had become a revolutionary melting pot. For the Chinese Communist party, this was their main target, and they were already showing their strength through strikes, protests and street fighting. A number of foreign revolutionaries, such as Stalin's ally Borodin, had arrived on the scene. The foreign troops had turned the international settlement into an armed camp with barbed-wire barricades around it, and the tension was high.

Shortly after arriving in Shanghai, my grandfather wrote to his brother describing the scene. There were many more Chinese living in the settlement than 'white men' – *dynion gwyn.*

> *Yr oedd yn wybyddus fod nifer o "gunmen" mewn dillad cyffredin yn y Settlement, a phe bae cyfle yn dod ni fuasent yn brin o gymeryd eu rhan trwy saethu yn yr ystrydoedd (fel y gwnaethpwyd yn yr Iwerddon). Yr oedd y "Labour Union" hefyd wedi ychwanegu at anhawsderau'r awdurdodau trwy alw streic. Dychmygwch felly, weled strydoedd y Settlement yn ddu gan Chinese – ac yn eu mysg "gunmen" a "hooligans" yn disgwyl eu cyfle – tra yr oedd y "Cantonese" a'r "Northerners" y tu allan i'r ffin yn ymladd am yr oruchafiaeth.*

> [It was common knowledge that there were a number of gunmen in ordinary clothes in the Settlement, and if the chance came they would shoot in the streets as they did in Ireland. The Labour Union had added to the difficulties of the authorities by calling a strike. Imagine then, seeing the streets of the Settlement black with Chinese, and in their midst gunmen and hooligans waiting for their opportunity – while the Cantonese and the Northerners were outside the perimeter fighting for supremacy.]

By this time, Chiang Kai-Shek's army had reached Shanghai and had, with the help of the local Communists, captured all of the city outside the International Settlement. An assault on the Defence Force and the settlement itself seemed imminent.

> *Cerddais i fyny trwy Nanking Rd (y brif heol) y prynhawn dydd Mawrth hwnnw, a theimlais fod yr awyr yn wefreiddiol gan "excitement". Onibae fod y "police" yn cadw'r tyrfaoedd i fynd, a'r milwyr ni yn cerdded fel "patrols" trwy bob ystryd, buasai'r gwaethaf wedi cymeryd lle. Nid oes gronyn o amheuaeth yn fy meddwl fod danfoniad prydlon y "Shanghai Defence Force" wedi achub y ddinas hon.*
>
> [I walked up Nanking Road (the main street) on that Tuesday afternoon, and I could feel the excitement in the air. If it was not for the police keeping the crowds moving, and our soldiers patrolling every street, the worst would have happened. There is not the slightest doubt in my mind that the prompt arrival of the Shanghai Defence Force has saved this city.]

The foreign residents of Shanghai had little reason to distinguish between the forces of Chiang Kai-Shek and the Communists. Both seemed to threaten their comfortable and profitable expatriate life. But it turned out that Chiang Kai-Shek was more concerned to defeat the Communists, whom he saw as a threat to his power, than to take on the Western Defence Force. In April, Nationalist troops rounded up and murdered hundreds of Communist and union activists in Shanghai. And despite Chiang Kai-Shek's propaganda against the Western powers, he was content to strike a deal with them which left the International Settlement intact.

In his correspondence with friends and family, my grandfather was quick to rebut any suggestion that the British forces should not be there. The British soldiers were defending life and trade, and what he called the terrorists and Bolsheviks had left China in a wretched condition. Those whom he witnessed as prisoners in Shanghai looked like 'a bunch of highwaymen', he said. He was particularly concerned about the fate of the Christian missionaries, who had been warned to leave northern China for their own safety. Many were sheltering in Shanghai at the time, and my grandfather gave away the bride at one missionary wedding, representing her father who was back in Wales.

By August, my grandfather's main complaint was about the heat.

> *Y mae'r chwys yn byrbynnu allan ohono wrth ysgrifennu, a minnau yn eistedd yn "llewys fy nghrys" mewn ystafell gysgodol, a phob ffenestr a drws yn agored led y pen! Clywais rai dyddiau yn ôl fod Dean Symons (pen yr Eglwys Esgobol yn y ddinas) wedi danfon 24 o grysiau i'r golch yr wythnos ddiweddaf... Nid oes gennyf fi hanner cymaint a'r Dean o grysiau yn fy "wardrobe"; ond, pe bae, buasai eu heisiau bob un!*
>
> [The sweat is pouring out of me as I write and I am sitting in my shirtsleeves in a sheltered room with every window and door open wide. I heard a few days ago that Dean Symons, head of the Episcopal Church in the city, had sent 24 shirts to be washed last week. I haven't got half as many shirts as the Dean in my wardrobe, but if I had, I would have used every one!]

Initially, until he was joined by a Wesleyan chaplain from Hong Kong and a missionary, he was the only Nonconformist chaplain with the Defence Force. He was based with the 14th Infantry Brigade, but he was not attached to any one unit and his job was to minister to all the soldiers who had registered as Nonconformists – *'ac y mae gennyf gylch eang i fynd drosto'* [and I have a wide area to get around]. With the help of a schoolfriend from Llanelli, who was working as a ship's engineer in China, he bought a small car for £25, which 'was most useful to me in running about on my duties in that sweltering city'.

Apart from a few shots fired across the barricades, the Shanghai Defence Force saw no real action. And, in truth, life was not unpleasant for the visiting forces. My grandfather was lodged with the secretary to the British Chamber of Commerce, and receptions and dinner parties were the norm as the wealthy residents of Shanghai did their best to entertain the officers of the army which had come to protect them. Goods were cheap and plentiful, and my grandfather brought trunkloads back with him, including Chinese textiles, silks, brassware, pictures, ornaments and a large six-panel screen decorated with exotic oriental birds.

He returned home in 1928, and the Shanghai expedition became little more than a footnote in the history books.

*

Evan Mathias was born in 1885 in Rhos Llangeler, a village in Carmarthenshire. He was the eighth of nine children who survived early childhood, living in a small roadside cottage at Gât Bwlch y Clawdd. The cottage had one link to historical fame: the toll house which the name commemorates was twice destroyed by Rebecca rioters some forty years previously. My great-grandfather David came from a family who had lived in the area for several generations – impoverished people living hand-to-mouth. Described as 'a bear of a man', he was a carpenter by trade, as many of his forefathers had been. He married Mary, known as Mali, a determined woman who seemed to run the family.

Evan was a sickly child at first, with a weak digestion which was to plague him all his life. He was, by all accounts, slow to develop the usual skills of walking and talking. But when he was only five years old the family had an upturn in their fortunes. David Mathias got a job as a carpenter to the Stepney estate at thirty shillings per week, and he moved his family to Llanelli.

But with such a large family, life was still hard. My great-grandmother would sit at the table and work out how my great-grandfather's earnings would be spent – money for food, for school, for new books and so on. Such was her careful management that she could lend money to neighbours. One story had it that a family of steelworkers whose income was several times greater than theirs fell into temporary difficulties during a stoppage at the works. By the second week of the stoppage, the woman of the house asked to borrow money from my great-grandmother, and she had it to lend. But money was never plentiful. When my grandfather eventually went to university in Cardiff, family legend has it that his older brothers clubbed together to help pay his way.

The family were all *Annibynwyr* – Welsh Independents – and attended the Lloyd Street chapel in Llanelli. Every Sunday morning, my great-grandmother put the joint in the oven, timing it to perfection so that she could put it out ready for the table when she returned from chapel. No excuses from any of the family for non-attendance were ever offered. All who were at home attended every morning and every evening, an impressive witness to the solidity of Welsh Nonconformity at that time.

It was a tradition which my grandfather inherited and built on. After university in Cardiff, where it was whispered that he might have been enjoying himself a little too much, he studied for the ministry at the Memorial College, Brecon (in Welsh, *Coleg Coffa*), the training college for the Congregational Church. In 1909, he was appointed to his first ministry at the English Congregational Church, Edwardsville, Treharris. A report of the event said:

> Mr B.T. Evans, secretary of the church, gave the history of the call, and he showed that the call was a hearty and unanimous one. Following this, the Rev. Morgan Jenkins, Abercynon, put the usual questions to the young minister, and Mr Mathias replied in a clear and pithy statement. The ordination prayer was offered by the Rev. John Morris, Star Street, Cardiff, after which the congregation expressed their welcome to the newly ordained pastor by a show of hands.

It is a mystery as to why, as a Welsh-speaker, my grandfather chose to go to an English-speaking church. But gradually through his life, Welsh was overtaken by English as the principal language he used, to the extent that he eventually became reluctant to preach in Welsh because he felt he was too rusty.

Only two years later, he moved to take up a ministry in New Inn, Pontypool. It is not clear why he moved so soon, but it seems he was briefly engaged to the daughter of a minister at a neighbouring chapel to Edwardsville, an engagement which was broken off.

My father, who had his suspicions, wrote:

> A certain element of the risible may have turned the romance into farce. My father, after all, was a keen-eyed, lively, laughing and sociable man, but he was no more than five foot three and a half inches in his shoes. His lady love was probably five feet nine or ten at the very least.

As he entered the ministry, my grandfather came under some pressure to move to the United States. His uncle, Rhys Saron Jones (his mother's brother), had become a successful and prosperous minister in Scranton, Pennsylvania, the centre of a coal-mining and steel-manufacturing area which at one time had the largest Welsh immigrant population of any city in America. Rhys Jones repeatedly pressed my grandfather to join him there, but he decided against it. It would have established something of a preaching dynasty, and my father's generation sometimes speculated about what it would have been like to be brought up as Americans.

The advent of the Great War proved a turning point. Although he was about to get married, he applied for, and was granted, release from his church at Pontypool Road, New Inn, for the period of the war to take up duties as an army chaplain. It is difficult to understand at this distance what drove him to make that decision, but one event may have been a factor.

Nonconformist ministers had not hitherto been admitted to the ranks of army chaplains, and in the early days of the war the issue came to a head. There was an argument at a meeting of the cabinet in London in September 1914 between David Lloyd George, then Chancellor of the Exchequer, and Lord Kitchener, Secretary for War. Lloyd George pressed for Nonconformist ministers to be sent to the front as army chaplains alongside their Anglican counterparts. When Kitchener expressed his doubts, Lloyd George was reported as saying: 'If you intend to send a Church of England army to the front, say so, but you cannot fight with half a nation.'

Lloyd George's victory meant that my grandfather was among the first Nonconformist chaplains to serve in the army. By the end of 1914, he was at St Leonards-on-Sea with the Royal Welch Fusiliers. He told his New Inn congregation:

> I entered into my new world with all the bewilderment of a tyro. The metamorphosis was sudden and complete, for I went into one door of Messrs Harrods' stores a civilian, and came out the other a full-fledged chaplain; and the very ordinary man who an hour before had scarcely attracted notice from anyone now found himself an object of interest, and the recipient of numberless salutes from the soldiers who throng the streets of London. Such is the marvellous influence of a khaki tunic with big side-pockets and bestarred shoulder straps!

For my grandfather was now an army captain. Appointment as Chaplain to the Forces, 4th Class, gave him that rank. His job was to look after the spiritual welfare of those denominations which came under the United Board, which included Congregationalists and Baptists. He admitted that it was difficult to define exactly what constituted the duties of a chaplain.

At the camp on the south coast of England, he said that about 700 to 800 avowed Congregationalists and Baptists attended his Sunday parade, never mind the many Nonconformists who, through ignorance, had registered themselves as Anglicans. There were brief services on weekday evenings, and entertainments were organised for the men, usually in conjunction with the YMCA.

> When the men are free from the labours of the day, the chaplain has an opportunity of moving among them and chatting with them in their huts. But he will be wise to rigidly abstain from the "button-holing" methods of the American Revival evangelist, for they are often productive of resentment. The chaplain who is ever ready with a genial smile, friendly word and willing service is more likely to do good in this way than by any other method.

He frequently found himself writing to the families of soldiers who were unable to write themselves, and the chaplain of course visited the hospital.

> His presence is greatly welcomed by the soldiers who are lying there. I find it especially so in my case, for there are among them many Welshmen, and they are delighted with a visit from a fellow countryman and a chat in the language of Paradise.

By 1915, my grandfather was in the Dardanelles, serving with the South Wales Borderers. But the following year, he was shipped home suffering from dysentery. He was mentioned in despatches for his tending of the sick and dying on the hospital ship. On his recovery he was sent to the Western Front where he spent the remainder of the war.

There is, ironically, little record of his experiences there. He did not talk much about them, at least to his grandchildren. But apparently, like most who fought in the trenches, he saw death frequently and came close to it himself. He was marching with a replacement unit up to the front when he stopped to talk to a fellow chaplain who was accompanying a unit heading the other way. An incoming shell landed among them, and my grandfather was blown into the nearby ditch. When he got back to his feet, he could see the body of the man to whom he had been talking smashed into several different pieces on the ground.

He only talked about the war to me on one occasion that I can recall. A neighbour had come round to visit and, on spying me, said: 'My, he's a bit small, isn't he?'

My grandfather afterwards took me by the arm and said: 'Don't you worry, boy. In the trenches they used to say, "The taller they are, the further they fall".'

*

In 1919, my grandfather was stationed in Germany, working in the Chaplain-General's office. He was persuaded by his immediate superior, a fellow Welshman, to stay in the army despite the end of the war. He was said never to be fully at ease in the peacetime army, but having made his promise to stay, he kept it. He was stationed with the London Division of the Army of the Rhine at Marienburg, a suburb of Cologne. He had never seen such a beautiful city, and he wrote to his brother in some wonderment at the fine buildings, the tramcars and the boats on the Rhine.

> *Yma, mae'r ystrydoedd yn llydain bob un, a choed wedi eu planu ar ochrau'r ffyrdd, a bron pob tŷ yn balas yn sefyll ar ei ben ei hun. Mae gennyf fi letty mewn tŷ braf a gallwch farnu beth yw ei faintioli pan y dywedaf fod y teulu yn gallu fforddio rhoi "suite" o ystafelloedd – "bedroom", "sitting room", a "bathroom", un yn agor oddiwrth y llall – at fy ngwasanaeth i fy hun, ac ystafell arall i fy ngwas.*
>
> [Here all the streets are wide, with trees planted on both sides of the roads, and every house a mansion standing by itself. I have lodgings in a pleasant house and you can judge its size when I say that the family here can afford to give me a suite of rooms – with bedroom, sitting room and bathroom each opening out from the other – just for my use, and another room for my servant.]

Consequently, he was in no doubt where he stood on the vexed issue of reparations, the payments Germany had to make for war damage under the Treaty of Versailles.

> *Gwelaf fod llawer ym Mhrydain y dyddiau rhain yn amheu gallu Germany i dalu am y rhyfel. Yr wyf yn eithaf sicr na fydd neb sydd wedi gweld Marienburg yn coleddu y fath amheuaeth.*

[I understand that many in Britain these days are sceptical of Germany's ability to pay for the war. I am quite certain that nobody who has seen Marienburg would have such doubts.]

The recipients of the letter were David, his immediate elder brother, his family and his mother who had by this time gone to live in Sennybridge with them. David was a successful carpenter, working all over Britain, but at the same time a cultured man, winning Eisteddfod prizes. He had settled down and opened a shop in Sennybridge, called the Emporium, which was fondly remembered by my Aunt Dilys from her visits there.

Things I remember – riding on the gambo to the hayfield – picnics there, bottles of pop, bananas and sweets – riding home on the load – standing in the shop to sing to uncle and auntie and then some sweets as a reward – going into the back to watch Uncle David cutting up cheese or bagging brown sugar – the wonderful smell of it all – and all the interesting things down Auntie Ruth's end – the hats and tie ribbons and the boxes full of interesting things.

It was all in marked contrast to life in occupied Germany where in 1920, my grandfather's wife and children had joined him. There was a degree of suspicion and hostility from the inhabitants of the occupied Rhineland, particularly in the early post-war period. My father recounted an incident he was told by his mother which took place on a journey to the Saarland, outside the Occupied Zone.

In the railway carriage, my mother began to feel faint with the stuffy heat and asked my father to open the window a little. He did so, but immediately received a complaint from a German who said he felt a draught. The German then shut the window. My father then opened it again. The German shut it once more. How long this went on I cannot tell, but my mother was agonised about it and bade my father desist. But by this time things had gone too far. At the next station, the German called the guard and demanded that my father and mother be put off the train. This was done and

> a hostile crowd gathered which looked ready for violence at the least excuse. By good fortune, another train drew up on the other side of the platform and a Dutchman in it, sizing up the dangers of the situation, opened his carriage door and hustled my father and mother onto the train just as it was about to pull out. It was a narrow squeak.

My grandfather was a confident, strong-willed character, occasionally stern, but one who also got on well with friends and colleagues. He played rugby well into his thirties, captaining the British Army of the Rhine in several representative matches. He was a utility back, sometimes at outside-half, sometimes at centre or full-back. He brought an inventiveness and 'dodginess' to the game, or so it was said, which helped make up for his small physique.

He was subsequently posted to Salisbury, Aldershot and Catterick, reaching the rank of colonel. His period of service came to an end in 1940, and he declined the opportunity which presented itself of an extension of service and promotion to Assistant Chaplain General. He offered himself for other wartime duties, an offer not taken up, and at the age of 55, he retired to Brecon, the area where my grandmother had been brought up and where he could be close to his brother David.

Active in retirement, he became chairman of the local Welsh Society and treasurer of Memorial College in Brecon, the Congregationalist training college for ministers where he had qualified. It was an abiding sadness for him when the college was closed down and converted into flats. He was especially fond of Welsh musical evenings, which he often found himself organising.

As grandchildren, my sisters and I stayed in Brecon several times a year. We would wake up on a Tuesday or a Friday morning to hear the animals being brought in for the mart just below the house. We could watch the animals being led in to the auction ring from the bedroom window. My grandfather would take us to watch the auctioneers at work, warning us not to move a finger in case we ended up going home with a sheep. He taught us basic phrases in Welsh, so at least we could say *Nos da* before going to bed.

He continued to preach, often in remote country chapels, where sometimes the grandchildren would be brought along as well. In one letter, written in September 1942, he described taking services at Troedrhiwdalar – 'a real country church to which men still came on horseback and put up their ponies in the chapel stable. I like that sort of background: it belongs to the Wales of the day before yesterday.'

He was proud of being Welsh, but he was also a product of the age of British imperialism, as you might expect from someone who could remember the rejoicing in the streets when news arrived of the relief of the siege of Mafeking. His favourite trick was to put one of us on his knee and, with a twinkle in his eye, sing a music hall song from the early 1900s about an elderly cavalryman who could not get out of the habit of thinking he was still in the saddle. When it came to the chorus, my grandfather would suddenly start throwing us up and down on his knee.

Bumpity, Bumpity, Bumpity Bump, as if I was riding my charger
Bumpity, Bumpity, Bumpity, Bump, as proud as an Indian Rajah,
All the girls declare
That I'm a gay old stager
Hey, hey, clear the way
Here comes the Galloping Major.

CHAPTER 2

The Flooded Valley

MY GRANDPARENTS WERE married just before Christmas 1914 at Benaiah Chapel, Talybont-on-Usk. The bride was Miss Muriel Morgan, the youngest daughter of a farming family from Glyn Collwn, a few miles away. According to *The Brecon County Times*:

> The bride, tastefully dressed in Wedgwood blue satin and white toque, was given away by her brother, Mr Emlyn Morgan. She carried a magnificent shower bouquet, the gift of the bridegroom. After the wedding, the party proceeded in motor cars to Brecon, where the breakfast was partaken of at the Castle Hotel. The bride and bridegroom afterwards left for London for the honeymoon. It is interesting to note that the bridegroom has been unanimously released by his Church at Pontypool for the period of the war, though with many expressions of regret, to undertake the duties of army chaplain.

Glyn Collwn, usually known as 'the Glyn' (one of the many words in Welsh for valley), carries the River Caerfanell down from the Brecon Beacons until it flows into the River Usk. At the end of the nineteenth century, about 200 people lived in the Glyn, a largely Welsh-speaking farming community. It was here that in 1894, Joseph Morgan brought his family from Cardiff, renting a small farm called Tyle-Clydach, usually known as 'the Tyle'. The farm, which is still there, is a steep climb from the bottom of the valley, the Clydach being a small tributary of the Caerfanell. More than seventy years later, the farm was to achieve a brief fame as the base for a Tibetan farm school, training young Tibetan émigrés in self-sufficiency farming. It was closed down because the Dalai Lama declared the farming too primitive and refused to support it.

My great grandfather, Joseph Morgan, had been a stonemason and builder by trade, until his health gave way in his late thirties and he was advised to move to the mountains for the fresh air. He had been a man noted for his physical strength. Indeed, family legend has it that he once took up a 'Golden Guinea' challenge from the proprietor of a boxing booth, fought the professional fighter to a standstill and went off with the guinea prize. But the breakdown of his health left him a more uncertain man, and he got off to a bad start at the Tyle.

It was the custom to conduct the sale of the outgoing tenant's stock and goods in such a way as to maximise the sum for the departing widow. The neighbours rallied round to do what they could for Widow Evans, and the bidding took much of the stock above its market value. Joseph, who had no stock at all, thought he was being forced to pay above the odds to get what he wanted. Instead of realising that he had no need to do this, and better prices could be had elsewhere, he went in over his head, spending more than he could afford.

Furious about this afterwards, he preferred not to recognise his own folly but convinced himself of a plot by Welsh-speakers against a monoglot from Cardiff. For the rest of his life, he harboured anti-Welsh feelings, which, to a certain extent, my grandmother imbibed. It was Joseph's wife, Rachel, who was friendly with the neighbours, offering the help and mutual support which was characteristic of such a rural community. As his health declined, he became more withdrawn, and it was her brother Emlyn who gave Muriel away at her wedding instead of her father.

Life on tenant farms such as Tyle was hard. Like many of the farming wives in the Glyn, Rachel would take butter, milk, eggs and hens over the mountain ridge every week and down to market at Dowlais on the other side. The journey might have been by pony, or by train – because trains ran on the Brecon to Merthyr line up the east side of the valley and through a tunnel at the top, stopping at Torpantau station, then the highest railway station in Wales.

Muriel grew up a shy, if not timid, girl, but successful at her schoolwork. She was the first pupil from Talybont school to qualify for the new girls' school in Brecon. Many of the girls there were from 'the country' and were required to put up in approved lodgings if they lived too far away. The usual pattern was a train journey on Mondays and Fridays, but when my grandmother's family moved to a farm further up the Glyn, the train journey from Talybont meant she did not arrive at school until eleven o'clock in the morning. It was only six miles from Talybont, but the headmistress, Miss Davies, insisted that she board permanently in Brecon during term time.

For a shy, homesick girl like my grandmother, this was not easy. But there were others in the same boat. A contemporary of my grandmother's wrote about her 'dear little friend' Muriel Morgan:

> We lodged together at Mrs Boxhall's and she was just a year younger. I remember so well Miss Davies would not let us go home for the weekend if we couldn't get to school on time on Monday morning… At Mrs Boxhall's, we each had our space in the cupboard for our tea, butter, sugar and anything we brought back for the week – no fridges in those days and such a scrap of a backyard where the one W.C. was. But we were happy there.

In 1906, the family moved to Ffynnon Fawr, a 280-acre farm on the east side of the valley. In fact, the farmhouse was newly built, and spacious by local standards. The old farmhouse, just below it, had been uninhabitable for some time, used only for plucking fowl and other messy jobs. The family had moved up a little in the economic structure of the Glyn.

My grandmother worked briefly as a teacher at Talybont school where she had been a pupil. But, not helped by the fact that the headmaster was fond of slipping out of school for a pint, she found it too much of a strain. She earned a black mark when a governor of the church foundation school came to interrogate her class. She failed to address him as 'Sir'.

She returned to help her mother on the farm, mainly with the dairy work. She used to walk up the mountainside above Ffynnon Fawr, across the railway and the tramway above it, and over the top to the neighbouring valley to visit a friend. She was too nervous to ride a horse – a nervousness not helped by her brother Emlyn's habit of buying wild or bad-tempered horses and breaking them in. An early childhood memory of my father's was being driven in a trap by his grandmother, his mother being with them, when they encountered a steamroller at a narrow point in the lane. 'It was frightening enough to me, and to an imperfectly broken horse terrifying. In no time at all, we were sideways in the ditch, with the horse scrambling desperately about and intermittently beating a tattoo with its hooves on the trap bottom.'

It is not at all clear how Muriel met her future husband. The family was certainly Nonconformist, attending the chapel at Aber, the only village in the valley, and helping with the Sunday school there. There was something of a rivalry between church and chapel in the Glyn. The local vicar tried to disrupt a successful Nonconformist Sunday school at Abercynafon by holding an afternoon service in the church. Muriel's sister, Gladys, played the piano in the Sunday school, but she was also a teacher at the Talybont church school and so could not refuse to play the harmonium in the church.

Whether they met at a chapel service or elsewhere, my grandfather, a sociable man who was not short of female admirers in his congregation, chose to marry the shy girl from a distant farm. But his departure for the war meant that she was once again living at Ffynnon Fawr, where, on 4 September 1915, my father was born.

Ffynnon Fawr no longer exists. The valley was flooded in the 1930s to supply the town of Newport with water. The dam, completed by 1938, created the largest reservoir in

Wales up to that time. Ffynnon Fawr was now at the water's edge, empty and inaccessible. It was demolished in the early 1950s. As a child, I could still see the remains of the ruined walls, but now there is little more than a heap of moss-covered stones.

For my father, this gave him an overwhelming sense of loss. Many years later, already established as a poet, he described this sense of loss in his poem, 'The Flooded Valley':

My house is empty but for a pair of boots:
The reservoir slaps at the privet hedge and uncovers the roots
And afterwards pats them up with a slack good will:
The sheep that I market once are not again to sell.
I am no waterman, and who of the others will live
Here, feeling the ripple spreading, hearing the timbers grieve?
The house I was born in has not long to stand:
My pounds are slipping away and will not wait for the end.

To add insult to injury, the Brecon to Merthyr railway line was closed in the Beeching cuts of the 1960s. The trains no longer puffed their way up the valley and through the tunnel to Torpantau station and beyond.

My grandmother was never really comfortable with army life. The family moved to Cologne after the birth of her second child Alun, at Aber Farm in the Glyn, where they had moved after the death of her father in 1916. Her brother Emlyn was given the tenancy, despite his youth – a trust that proved justified. It was not long before he married and took a farm at Llangattock, ending up on valuable land on the outskirts of Gloucester. The last time I saw him was at my grandfather's funeral, driving a white Mercedes.

My grandmother's task was to manage the household, which she did in a patient, tolerant and equable manner. In Cologne, this was usually undertaken with the help of a German maid. By all accounts, she took little part in the social life of the army, encumbered as she was by two small boys. But there were trips on the Rhine, visits to Bonn and even Venice. Her daughter

Dilys was born in a nursing home in Southsea on their return from Germany.

At Bulford camp in Salisbury, the family acquired the services of a maid, a girl from the village, who apparently caused my grandmother a great deal of anxiety. The girl was pretty and good-natured, and was frequently to be found chatting at the back door with would-be admirers. The difficulty was accentuated by the presence in the house of my grandfather's batman, who seemed to have little else to do than clean my grandfather's boots and perform one or two odd jobs. He would often be found in the kitchen chatting up the maid, which disturbed my grandmother's puritan nature. She disliked any kind of gossip, bawdiness or any hint of immorality.

When my grandfather departed for Shanghai in 1927, my grandmother was left to run the household, now in Aldershot, on her own for a year or more. She did so, according to my father, without undue strain, rarely ever having to lose her temper with her three children.

She worked from time to time at the Percy Illingworth Institute in the camp, serving behind the counter in the canteen. Some of the friendships she made there lasted her lifetime.

But she was developing a horror of the army and all it stood for. Her conscience was telling her more and more that man had no right to kill his fellow man under the banner of patriotism. She found it hard to accept that Christians condoned and sanctioned such killing. She was wedded, through her husband and his status as an army chaplain, to institutions that she was growing to hate.

My father summarised her views at the time:

> By this time, there was in her a deep-seated conviction that the Christian church in all its denominations (I do not know how far she considered the Quakers) was the source of the greatest evil under which society suffered, in that it not merely condoned but actively supported war and the killing of fellow human beings.

It was not long before she ceased going to chapel, feeling called, she said, to oppose the church in all its denominational forms as the prime deceiver of the innocent of the world. She instead relied on a steadfast faith in her own relationship with God. She told me that at one time she felt so strongly that, shy as she was, she forced herself to speak on public platforms about the evils of war. As she got older, she acquired increasingly apocalyptic views about the conflict between good and evil in the world and an approaching Armageddon. I can remember her looking out of the window, indicating the dark clouds which signalled a coming storm and saying there was evil building up in the world.

She never sought to impose her views on her family or friends. But my grandfather was, quite naturally, upset and hurt. He had his Sunday services to take, his duties as a chaplain, his participation in army life. So there was tension and the occasional confrontation, of which the children were aware. My father recalled that, when defending her beliefs, her colour would rise and she would speak with a kind of dogged persistence quite unlike her normal conversation.

The advent of the Second World War dramatically increased the tension between the views of my grandmother and grandfather. 'This generation has again rejected Christ', she wrote, 'these terrible Christian leaders who are saying that the devil's will is God's will. The Christian cannot compromise.'

She believed that those who followed what she saw as God's will would be looked after by him. So she refused to wear a gas mask and occasionally had to be reprimanded by policemen or ARP wardens for a failure to observe the blackout.

It was, ironically, my grandfather's retirement from the army and their return to Brecon in 1940 which precipitated the crisis. Here, in a more close-knit community, it would be more difficult to keep her issues of conscience a private matter. On one of their first Sundays in Brecon, my grandfather had been to chapel services in the morning, afternoon and evening. My grandmother wrote that the Plough (the Congregationalist chapel) had been full of soldiers, and, in a letter to her eldest son, she did not disguise her view that the two things were incompatible. 'It is a thoroughly pagan and hypocritical little town, full of churches and church worship full of soldiers. The atmosphere has been pretty tense, as you can imagine – however I have destroyed all hopes [my grandfather] may have had of joining in the mockery of God by saying what I think of it all.'

The worst crisis came over the wartime evacuation of children from London and other cities. She, like other householders with room to spare, was approached by billeting officers and asked to take one or more children. She agonised over this but felt compelled to refuse. For her, it would mean that she was helping the authorities who were prosecuting the war, and she gave her son a surprisingly full account:

> It was Wednesday of last week that the Billeting Officer called because I refused evacuees on the grounds that it was not God's will for me to have them, for I said my God was a loving father and Almighty and able to take care of his creatures wherever they were and whatever circumstances prevailed, provided they trusted in Him and committed themselves to His keeping. The Billeting Officer said he feared it might mean prosecution. To my reason for not obeying, he said he didn't know about that. Certainly he didn't, because his God is certainly not my God, but the God of this world.

My grandfather was away for a few days at the time, but a letter arrived from the billeting officer informing him of her refusal to take evacuees even though they had sufficient room.

> A most painful struggle ensued. I've had lots of struggles in spiritual things, but this was the most terrible, for of course it involved so much... Seeing I'd give up my life rather than give in, he said he would go to the Billeting Officer and tell him that he disassociated himself from me altogether (this was what I had all

along wanted him to do and begged of him to tell the man I'd pay the penalty of my disobedience, whatever it was).

Whatever transpired at my grandfather's meeting with the billeting officer, no prosecution ensued, even though a further approach from the officer a few months later received a similar rebuff.

My grandmother went into town less and less, at least in part because of her anxiety about how local people now perceived her. But her anxiety on that score may well have been misplaced. By the time I was old enough to take notice, there were plenty of visitors at the house, whether it was neighbours and acquaintances, farmers' wives delivering eggs and butter, or occasionally people seeking help.

I can remember a visit from a woman to whom my grandmother was obviously giving some kind of advice and counsel. With her was a small boy about my age, and I could tell they were not well off. Partly to show off, I opened up my little cardboard suitcase to display the Dinky toys inside. I heard the boy give a gasp of astonishment, and realised that for him these were riches he could only dream about. I gave him some to play with and my grandmother's conversation continued uninterrupted.

For her grandchildren, like her children, it was a calm and secure household despite the theological disagreements: my grandfather smoking his pipe contentedly in the kitchen after breakfast; my grandmother drinking her glass of warm water every morning – all the medicine she needed, she said. Despite the fact that by the end of her life she was almost bent double, she continued running the house by herself and never went to see a doctor. That, too, was against her belief that she was in God's care, not her fellow man's. For forty years, she had no medical record.

I was sent to see my grandfather when he was bedridden after the stroke which was to lead to his death. He waited until my grandmother had gone out of the room and said: 'You know, she has been very good to me. She has looked after me all my life.'

At that moment, I was suffering from too much teenage embarrassment at the sight of his white fingers twitching at the bed sheet. But afterwards, I remembered what he had said.

Chapter 3

God's will

In August 1941, a police inspector called at my father's lodgings in St Helens in Lancashire. But my father was away on holiday from his teaching job, and news reached him by letter that the police were looking for him. His landlady wrote to him at his parents' home in Brecon, but he was in fact staying at a relative's farm just outside Cardiff.

A few days later, his mother wrote: 'One of the local police called this morning just after 10. Inquired if you were here. I told him you left on Saturday for Cardiff. We offered to wire you to get you back. However, he said to let you have your holiday for it was not till Sept 1st that you were needed up north.'

My father faced a summons, *Rex versus Roland Glyn Mathias,* 'to appear at Liverpool City Police Court in Dale Street, Liverpool at 11.15 o'clock in the forenoon on 1 September for failing to comply with the requirements of a written notice to submit himself to a medical examination'. The examination, under the terms of the Armed Forces Act, was to establish whether he was fit for military service. The court appearance was to lead him directly to a prison term.

It had been more than a year since my father had applied to be registered as a conscientious objector. Just as for his mother, the advent of the Second World War had created for him a moral crisis which was to put him at odds with most of society. In the application he set out his beliefs:

> I cannot engage in this or any other war, the aim of which is to take human life. In all circumstances I regard human life as sacred, and organised killing – even killing under extreme provocation – is murder. Nothing can eradicate that. Whatever the rights or wrongs of this war – and I believe that those who engage in it act sincerely according to their lights (the only difference being that their allegiance to their country overrides their allegiance to God) – it is one in which I can take no part.

But then came the reasoning which was to lead him ultimately to prison:

> For the same reasons, I must decline to engage with the R.A.M.C. or any other form of non-combatant service. Superficially a refusal to help the wounded sounds inhumane; but willingness to assist suffering humanity in general and to engage under the military regis to do it are entirely different things… In other words, the Medical Corps alleviates suffering for a military end; man is to be healed not as man pure and simple, but as a military being. To this I cannot contribute.

There is no doubt that my father had imbibed much of his mother's religious outlook. Her pacifism and Puritanism was embedded in the judgements which he made at this key time in his life. Two sentences stand out at the conclusion of his argument for being registered as a conscientious objector. 'Let me declare that humanity can only be raised by the maintenance at all costs of spiritual values by those who believe. Christ was never yet served by any man compromising with evil that good might result.'

My father had left Jesus College, Oxford, two years previously and, after a number of unsuccessful attempts, landed a teaching post at Cowley School, St Helens. He turned out to be a popular and successful teacher of history. The headmaster, Gerald Dowse, was soon to congratulate him on the results he was getting. He wrote: 'History tops all the results in both forms [of the sixth].'

It was a period of his life he was to remember fondly. He

acquired a lot of friends who were to last a lifetime, many of whom were subsequently called up and served on different fronts in the war. And he played rugby, usually as a wing forward, becoming secretary of St Helens Rugby Club. He would sometimes decry the unfitness of opposing teams, describing them as 'soft' and bemoaning the stoppages because they were winded every time they were tackled. One match report described his performance in the forwards as outstanding, adding: 'One scarcely expects to find a pacifist in a rugby pack.'

Extracts from a letter home written towards the end of 1940 give a flavour of his life at this time:

> Yesterday we had an enjoyable match against RAF Padgate, which we won 31–5. Our opponents had Horace Edwards, the Cardiff and Welsh centre, playing for them. I never did think he was much good, though he scored from an interception… We amassed a tidy total of points, and not even the steady dropping of passes by one or other of our centres could keep us out. In the second half, Horace Edwards picked up a dropped pass very neatly and was away: I got to him but was handed off square in the middle of the head despite my dive, and he ran in.
>
> I was just congratulating myself on coming off unscathed in the afternoon when I walked into a wall in the black-out… First time I've ever done that – my feet usually hit the thing first and I stop in time. Must have been in the middle of a step – immediate result, silence. Bob [Reed – a fellow schoolteacher] began fussing around like a frightened hen. Finally, it emerged that I was cut wide across the forehead and heavily swollen. Nose also a casualty. So my beauty is spoiled today – but I think it'll be alright in no time.
>
> I should have mentioned the 'blitz' in Liverpool on Thursday night. The noise was terrific, and things always seemed about to happen to us, but nothing did. Anyway, it awakened the fearful – many heavy eyes the next morning.

My father certainly discussed his pacifist views with his friends, and whatever the disagreements, he rarely lost their friendship. After an 'intimate discussion', one young friend,

Theo Barker, wrote to him to re-emphasise why he thought the pacifist attitude to the war was wrong: 'We must first prevent the evil forces arraigned against us from destroying the things which we hold most dear i.e. our liberty and freedom – our culture and our system of government, to say nothing of our homes and the lives of those we love.'

But nothing could shake my father from his refusal even to undertake non-combatant duties. His younger brother Alun shared his pacifist views and had also registered as a conscientious objector. But Alun was prepared to do agricultural work, which would exempt him from military service. And, by this time, he had found himself a position on a farm at Great Wolford, 'deep in the Cotswolds'.

My father did differentiate his views from those of his mother's, in general regarding his position as not quite so fundamentalist as hers. Whereas my grandmother believed, as in the case of the evacuees, that God would protect all his creatures who believed in him, my father accepted that others were entitled to think differently. He believed that he did not need to take shelter from bombs personally because he felt he was under God's protection, but others would feel otherwise and would expect his help in seeking shelter – especially if they were his pupils.

> I felt it my duty, therefore, to co-operate as a teacher when warnings sounded and to carry out my responsibilities fully in leading children into shelter. This I believed to be logical and not a compromise of my own position. During bomb alerts in Ruskin Drive [his lodgings] in 1941 I never went down to the shelter, though everybody else did. I stayed up and made cups of tea for those who were down below.

Such fine distinctions carried little weight with the local tribunal hearing his application to be registered as a conscientious objector and to be exempted from non-combatant duties. The findings of the tribunal on 6 June 1940 were caustic:

> The applicant has been guilty of much exaggeration. He has told the tribunal that in an air-raid he would not take cover. He has shown us that he has got a very elastic conscience. He tells us that his conscience will not allow him to be associated with organised first-aid, but it will allow him to teach children in his school A.R.P. exercises.
>
> The tribunal think that the man who can teach his children in his school A.R.P. exercises is not prevented from doing first-aid work in his local organisation. They feel that the most sympathetic view they can take of his case is that conscience prevents his taking life.

The order of the tribunal was that his name should be removed from the Register of Conscientious Objectors and that he should be liable to be called up for service, but to be employed only in non-combatant duties.

My father felt that his conscientious objection to non-combatant service had been misunderstood and he decided to appeal. His mother applauded his stand: 'Yes, my dear, you've been left by your Saviour until now so that you may take part in the most hectic period of spiritual warfare between good and evil, and that for the simple reason that you have the spiritual wherewithal to withstand the fierce onslaught of the enemy.'

A postcard from Southport which caught the five o'clock post on 5 December 1940 gave my father's account of the appeal hearing. It had taken the tribunal only two minutes to dismiss his appeal and uphold the decision of the local tribunal. 'I didn't have such a tough time of it because the chairman seemed to be deaf, and I feel much more at ease than I was before. Don't worry – I feel very calm about it.'

Calm he might have been, but the issue of conscientious objectors, including my father's case, became something of a cause célèbre in St Helens. The corporation came under pressure to sack all conscientious objectors on its staff. My father was concerned that the public stand he had taken would embarrass Cowley School where he was employed. To avoid any such difficulties, he had already decided to leave the school at the end of the term, and in the meantime he would fulfil his duties without pay. He had now been summoned to present himself for a medical examination to determine his fitness for non-combatant duties. If he submitted to such a medical examination, he was in effect accepting non-combatant service, and that he remained determined not to do. If he didn't change his mind, he would end up serving a prison sentence.

He decided to cast about for alternative employment, and here he had a curious, if temporary, change of mind. He applied to join the Auxiliary Fire Service. He had seen the devastation caused by the falling bombs, as he recorded in his poem, 'Blitz in Manchester':

Do you remember how the light dashed out,
The shuttered glass
Cracked right across,
And dressing-gowns lit up to dogged tea
Beneath the stairs
To the accompanying gallop of the guns?...
And in the morning how I picked a way,
Shambling through splinters to the station ramp,
Between the burning pillars, under sagging roof,
To see no trains...

Admitting that it was something of a change of heart, he had become convinced that this work would not run counter to his principles. His letter to the Ministry of Labour and National Service explained his position and ended with a rhetorical question: Would the government rather have me in prison, uselessly kept and fed, or doing useful work which I am willing to do?

In retrospect, it might seem that it was splitting hairs to argue that working for the fire service was different from other non-combatant duties. But his objection in principle was to non-combatant duties directed by the army. For his mother, there was no such distinction. She wrote that joining the AFS was not 'one bit in line with God's will' for him. In the event, this escape route was closed down by the minutiae of wartime bureaucracy. You had to be over thirty to work in civil defence organisations in lieu of military service.

By this time, he was getting into financial straits. He was working unpaid as a teacher (although the headmaster was helping out with small payments for various duties). He had his lodgings to pay for, and he was continuing to refuse to attend any medical examination relating to non-combatant duties. Furthermore, he was staying away from his parents' home in Brecon in order not to embarrass his father.

In February 1941, my grandfather wrote to him, saying he had not discussed the letter with his mother prior to sending it:

> Since I know you went back to face the music in St Helens (rather than here) mainly out of regard for my feelings, I feel that it is my duty to write to you to say that I think it would be wiser for you to come home than to dissipate your little stock of money to pay your lodgings up there... So I want you to understand that your return here will not be unwelcome, whatever betides. You are my son, and I cannot stand by and see you in difficulties.

My father did return to visit his parents later in the year. The machinery of the wartime state moved slowly, so slowly that it was not until August that the police inspector called at his lodgings to ensure that he turned up for the court hearing. In the meantime, he had been reinstated as a paid teacher at Cowley School, with the arrangement that he would resign as soon as he received a court summons. In early August, the headmaster, Gerald Dowse, wrote: 'Frankly, I never dreamed that we would have the good fortune to keep you till the end of term, and I have a fear that the good luck will not last.'

He was right. At his court appearance in Liverpool on 1 September 1941 he was sentenced to three months' hard labour. On his twenty-sixth birthday, he wrote to his parents from Liverpool Walton prison, giving an account of what happened:

> In Liverpool, I was caught in a very heavy shower: this soaked my mac through and wetted me a good deal. I think most of the proofing is gone! At Dale St, I was up with six other chaps, making three C.O.s, three Irishmen and one other. But I was the first case. Fined £3 and to be detained in custody till taken before a medical board.
>
> At the medical, only the odd man out submitted, and the rest of us were arrested and taken back to Dale St. The following day we were tried before the stipendiary and all pleaded guilty [to disobeying a court order]. The prosecuting solicitor demanded the maximum penalty as a deterrent to others, but the judge gave us three months each. And then we were brought here.

My father said little, then or later, about his time in prison. All letters were read by the prison authorities and any 'which were of an objectionable tendency' were suppressed. He reported that he was visited by a number of friends in prison, but the menace and monotony of prison life was evident in some of his poems. In 'Bars', he writes about:

... seven squared days that bleach and crack
Between the wells and balconies
And concrete exercise –
How can you give me back
Those gilded weeks and back
The breath of Wales...

His poem, 'Inter Tenebros (Even Here)', demonstrates that, even in the depths of Walton gaol, his religious faith was unshaken:

Here in the huddle of the lowest room
Prescribed for those with nothing in their hand,
... here in the pit, the nether lines
I feel thy penetration
Lord.

For reasons unknown, my father was moved to Stafford gaol the following month. He earned full remission and was out of prison on 2 November 1941.

Encumbered as he now was with a prison record, it was proving difficult to find a teaching job. He felt it was unfair to seek to return to Cowley School in St Helens, but cast about for other positions instead. It was the risk of re-arrest which was the main obstacle. The Central Board of Conscientious Objectors said it did not believe that the Ministry of Labour intended to proceed with a 'cat and mouse' treatment of COs in his position, but warned there was no guarantee.

Through the Society of Friends, he heard of a vacancy at a school in Reading, the Blue Coat School, which took both boarding and day pupils. The headmaster, Mr King, offered him a post at £100 per annum, together with 'board, residency and laundry'.

He did not agree with my father's views, but he said: 'I have a very great esteem for any man who will adhere to his opinion if he considers it to be right. I am quite prepared to take any risk there may be in your having to go to prison again, though I think it would be damnable to be "punished" twice for the same offence.'

My father was responsible for teaching history throughout the school, as well as teaching French, English literature and scripture. Once again, he quickly gained the approbation of his headmaster for the School Certificate results his pupils were achieving. His correspondence with friends, some of them now serving abroad, continued apace. He had been best man at the wedding of Maurice Clifton, a fellow teacher from St Helens, and when Maurice Clifton was posted to Aldershot, they met up at weekends.

Under the National Service Act of 1941, Parliament had given conscientious objectors a new procedure for appealing against tribunal decisions. To try and remove the threat of re-arrest and further imprisonment, my father decided to appeal against the original refusal of the tribunal in 1940 to exempt him from non-combatant duties.

In May 1942, the Appellate Tribunal dismissed his application out of hand, and, if anything, the failed appeal probably drew greater attention to his case. It was not long before he was being warned that the Ministry of Labour was after him again. Having failed at the Appellate Tribunal, my father was now liable to be directed to 'work of national importance' without any further notice or hearing. He was first directed to work as an agricultural labourer, which he refused. Then he was directed to work as a stores labourer with Great Western Railway at Didcot, which he also refused.

Some of his friends and acquaintances, while understanding his religious beliefs, failed to understand this unwillingness to take up the kind of work he was now being asked to do. They could not follow his reasoning for being prepared to do some kinds of work but not others. One or two described him as 'cussed' and 'extreme' in his views, but others accepted the strength of his conviction. His brother Alun, who by now was getting used to and enjoying farm work, wrote:

> Are you sure you are not just looking out for a cushy job? Manual work is of paramount importance – our education has been one-sided, we've not learned how to use our hands and we've rather tended to despise those who do... The thing one must do in life is to follow God's will and it may be that manual work is not for you, but even so you should have the complete willingness to do it even if you feel that your qualities would not be fully utilized in such occupations.

It was the failure to comply with the direction to work as a railway stores labourer that led him to his second prison term. He was summoned to appear in court at Reading on 14 December 1942. His mother's exhortations became even more apocalyptic in tone, urging him to stand up against the adversaries of Christ: 'Christ's work is nearly finished now and He and His forces will soon have completely overcome the devil and his forces – we are on absolutely the last lap and the consummation of Christ's kingdom is at hand.'

The evening before he was due to appear in court and knowing what was in front of him, my father said goodbye to his fellow staff at Blue Coat School. He tried to keep the news away from the boys, he said, asking the headmaster to make no reference to it at prayers. 'But there is not much that the big ears of the little pitchers do not catch, and I have no doubt that some of the frequent jokes at my expense at High Table were overheard – and interpreted. Anyway, when I was in my bedroom, packing my stuff, Miller (the senior prefect) crept up the stairs to wish me goodbye on behalf of all the boys.'

At 11.30 the next morning, he was in front of the magistrates' bench. He was told that his conscientious views were not relevant, and fined £20 or three months in prison. He refused to pay the fine, took the three months instead, and was taken by a detective to Oxford prison.

My father had been accompanied in court by his headmaster, Mr King, who himself offered to pay the fine, except that my father would not let him. But the headmaster was not willing to lose a good teacher so easily. He subsequently wrote: 'Within forty-eight hours, the boys of this school had subscribed the £20, asked me to go to Oxford and bring him back.'

On 16 December 1942, the following note was written on his prison papers: 'The fine was paid by the Scholars and Staff of Blue Coat School and he was discharged today.'

His friend Maurice Clifton, by this time serving in the Signal Corps in North Africa, wrote to him from the back of a three-ton Bedford truck somewhere in the desert, with the sound of guns blazing further up the line: 'Sorry about your predicament, though – believe me, Roland – I admire you for the way you stuck out for what you consider right.'

My father was now out of prison and back at Blue Coat School. But there was a misunderstanding about his liability to further prosecution. The headmaster thought that he would now be committing an offence by employing my father. In fact, according to a subsequent letter from the Central Board of Conscientious Objectors, the direction to 'work of national importance' had been withdrawn after payment of the fine. The mistake meant that for the next two years he was given free board and lodging but no salary – just 'occasional financial help' from the school's headmaster.

For the rest of the war, my father's career was not further 'disturbed' by the Ministry of Labour, and his life took off in other directions. He had showed enormous courage to take the stand he did for his religious convictions. But I am also struck by the tolerance and understanding of his friends, family and colleagues for the difficulties he caused for those around him.

One of Maurice Clifton's sons wrote to *The Times* on his death:

> Roland Mathias and my father were fellow members of the common room in the Lancashire grammar school where they taught before the war. He went on to be a brave pacifist; my father to be a brave soldier in North Africa and Italy. They exchanged many letters from their respective positions, prison and warfront, in which their mutual respect and admiration is self-evident. Roland was a fine and highly principled man.

Chapter 4

Yours hopefully

In February 1943, a lone Dornier bomber swept low over the town of Reading, dropping bombs and machine-gunning the streets. A total of forty-one people were killed and more than a 100 injured. The casualties might have been higher if it had not been a Wednesday afternoon and therefore early-closing day in the town centre. For reasons of national security, the newspapers could only report that a raid had taken place on a town in the Home Counties.

The hit-and-run attack, in reprisal for the Allied bombing of German cities, was the worst air raid on Reading during the Second World War. Unlike the large industrial cities, the town was not a significant target for German bombs. Government departments had been relocated to the town and children were evacuated from London to Reading for their safety.

For most of the population of Reading at this time, the main concerns were the shortage of food and coping with wartime bureaucracy. By early 1942, rationing had been extended to cover everything from meat to bread, butter, sugar and eggs – and even soap. The meat ration had been reduced to 1s 6d. per customer per week. White bread had been withdrawn. Private motoring was almost impossible unless the driver could show a special need for a petrol ration. Coal supplies had been reduced by twenty-five per cent, and in order to save paper, the throwing of confetti at weddings had been banned.

Civil defence precautions were vigorously, if erratically,

enforced. The local ARP wardens were constantly on the lookout for breaches of the blackout, checking up on any chink of light. Those refusing to take evacuees were liable to find themselves in court. A vicar at Wargrave declined the request of a billeting officer to take ten children into his eleven-bedroom house. He posted a notice on his front door saying 'Not in' and sent the billeting officer a telegram citing his conscientious objection to taking evacuees. He was fined £1 with £2 costs.

In early 1942, my father had just arrived in Reading after serving his prison sentence in Liverpool and Stafford gaols. He was living in at the Blue Coat School and was clearly feeling lonely. On 21 January, he sent the following letter which caught the 7.15 p.m. post:

> Dear Miss Hawes,
>
> I hope you will have heard of me before, or you are going to be very puzzled by this letter!
>
> My brother Alun at Great Wolford knows your cousin Dorothy very well, and he sent me your address. I am more or less a stranger in Reading – I have just got back for this term – and I should be very glad of your company occasionally, if you have time and opportunity of an evening. Living in, as I do here, leaves me with remarkably little chance of getting to know anybody outside. "Stone walls do not a prison make" – maybe not, but they give a mighty good imitation!
>
> Of course, I've no idea how you are fixed. You may be very busy or otherwise engaged, in which case I shall quite understand.
>
> But if not, can you manage any night this week? I am on duty tomorrow (Thursday), but Friday, Saturday, Sunday, Monday – any of them would suit me. If you can accept any of these, will you name the place and time of meeting (it's going to be difficult in this blackout) and we can go to the pictures or do anything else you like. I finish at 3.30 usually and will fall in with anything you can suggest after that hour.
>
> I am
> Yours hopefully,
> Roland Mathias

It was the beginning of a relationship which was to lead to a marriage of more than fifty years. My mother had indeed heard of my father before receiving his letter, because his brother Alun was friendly with – and soon to marry – her cousin Dorothy. Alun had written to my father about one Molly Hawes, 'one of the better cousins', teaching in a large elementary school in Reading.

The Hawes were a farming family in the Cotswolds, and indeed most of my mother's relatives were engaged in some aspect of agriculture. She was brought up at Fulwell Farm, near Enstone in Oxfordshire, one of four children. Although her eldest brother Cyril had died at the age of seventeen, it was a happy upbringing in what would now seem an old-fashioned and physically tough environment. My grandfather died when I was only seven years old, and my grandmother had died some years before that. But I can just recall my grandfather, dressed in a dark suit which he had apparently worn since before the war, meeting us at the station in an old, black car with the stuffing coming out of the leather seats. It was said that when the government brought in British summertime, my grandfather refused to change the clocks and insisted on keeping to the old time.

My grandfather may have been old-fashioned, but he did believe in educating his children. My mother went away to school at Thame, and she qualified as a teacher. Geography was her main subject, but her teaching career was brief as marriage and the arrival of children took over. An immensely practical woman, her qualities complemented those of my father.

My father's pacifist stance during the war had not put off a number of female admirers, one or two of them serving in the Auxiliary Territorial Service (ATS). One persistent correspondent had met up with him on a few occasions, and, apparently to his consternation, had gone to the extent of sitting on his knee. His cousin Sadie told him that the lady had thought he must be a bit on the slow side.

But from now on, privations of the war notwithstanding,

my parents' relationship deepened. My father's poems of love were bound up with the Oxfordshire countryside with which he associated her. In 'For M.A.H.' (although she was known as Molly, my mother's real name was Mary Annie), his tributes to her are intertwined with local references:

Walls cannot hold the wind against me now:
I am the one to walk the rows at Tew
Believing jasmine breathes the shape of you
And Lucius Cary makes you his first bow…

In September 1942, my father's first collection of poems, *Days Enduring*, was published. Arthur H. Stockwell, removed for the duration of the war to Ilfracombe, offered to print an edition of 1,000 copies on payment of £46 by the author. As his mother pointed out, they were asking a goodly sum and taking no risks themselves.

The terms were subsequently improved, but the publishers did little to publicise or market the book.

If this first volume received little public or critical attention, it was not due to the efforts of his parents. My grandfather wrote proudly that, although they might have been too dull to appreciate his work, they rejoiced that others did:

> Your mother went into F. H. Jones [then the principal bookshop in Brecon] ostensibly to buy a picture postcard but really to see her son's work exhibited on the shelves! She came back breathlessly to report that one copy had been sold since there were only five in stock, but I gathered that the remainder were not prominently displayed. So father strolled into the shop on the following day and, under pretence of looking at other books in their vicinity, removed those that were blocking the view and put yours so that the title etc. would be in full view.

At this time, my father was trying to learn the basics of the Welsh language, which he had never learned as a child because my grandmother did not speak it. My grandfather was setting him grammatical exercises, my father would complete them and then they would be returned corrected by the next post. 'I rejoice', my grandfather wrote late in 1942, 'that one, at least, of my children will know my mother's tongue'.

But, although my father professed in later life to have some knowledge of Welsh, it was an understanding of written Welsh rather than an ability to converse in the language.

By Christmas 1943, my parents had become engaged. A note from earlier in the year showed that my mother had already begun to look after him, getting things ready for his arrival: 'The bathroom is blacked out and there is enough hot water for you to have a bath if you wish. Your supper is in the kitchen as that is easily blacked out...'

At this time my father was once again not being paid a salary by his school (because of a misunderstanding about his liability to further prosecution), and this was a constant source of worry. Writing to him at the time of his engagement, my grandmother said she was glad that his finances had reached the height of getting Molly a ring. They married in April 1944 in Chipping Norton. His brother Alun was best man and my grandfather Evan helped to officiate. They could even afford a honeymoon in Llandudno.

In her last letter before the wedding, written from Fulwell Farm by the light of the fire, my mother told him not to worry too much about the ceremony: 'You will smile when I come in, won't you? It isn't a very long aisle fortunately, so I will soon be with you. Don't worry, we shall soon be leaving all that behind when we go on the 4.30 bus...'

My father's financial circumstances were further complicated by my mother's pregnancy. He could not continue at the Blue Coat School and would have to look for a better position. But his search for another post was complicated, not so much by his prison record, but the imminent end to the war and with it the return of servicemen seeking reinstatement in their former posts. He eventually obtained a temporary post at Carlisle Grammar School.

In February 1945, my mother was admitted to The Hill Nursing Home in Reading. She was issued with instructions to bring the following with her:

For baby
4 nightgowns
4 vests
1 ½ doz. Harrington squares
2 doz. Turkish napkins
1 crepe bandage (3 ins)
2 Shawls – 1 large and 1 small
1 pot Zinc and Castor Oil Cream (4 ozs) or White Vaseline
12 Safety pins
Baby's Hair Brush
Soap & Powder

But that turned out not to be enough. Much to mother's surprise, my emergence was followed ten minutes later by that of my sister Mary. Further supplies were required. Within days, my mother was telling my father about the difficulties of obtaining milk supplements, and asking him to inquire about a tin of Cow & Gate as well as a bottle and teat. 'Jonathan is now pushing his head back and bumping poor Mary's nose. But she remains unruffled.' (Throughout my childhood, I was known by my first name, Jonathan.)

Because no preparations had been made for the arrival of twins, the two of us were apparently put to bed in the drawers from a chest. My grandmother's letters were now full of helpful hints rather than the Christian exhortation which had dominated her earlier letters to her son. Commenting on some snaps of the babies, she wrote: 'I like the way little Jonathan is clasping his hands and trying to open his eyes – the sun is too strong for him, poor little fellow!'

CHAPTER 5

Six and out

THE MILESTONE HAS gone now. It was the last milestone on the road from London to the ferry at Hobbs Point. The double-sided stones had marked each mile along the former turnpike for more than a century and some can still be seen, with the clear lettering, black on white. This one, on London Road, Pembroke Dock, read:

1
MILE
TO
HOBBS POINT

The pier at Hobbs Point was originally built for the Irish packet service which ran from there from the 1830s. Now it served the ferry which took you across the water to Neyland at the point where the Cleddau flows into Milford Haven. As children, we would watch drivers nervously negotiate their way from the steep slipway onto the ferry deck with the aid of a small wooden ramp which occasionally slipped under the wheels of a car. Now, the ferry service is no longer needed, replaced in 1970 by the Cleddau Bridge.

We lived on the western edge of Britain, almost as far as you could go before you fell into the Irish Sea. It was more remote then, taking an hour to get to Haverfordwest and four hours to reach Cardiff. There was a sense of distance from events, a sense which often made me feel like an outsider looking in – a sense which never really left me.

We arrived in Pembroke Dock in 1948 when my father, at the remarkably early age of thirty-three (and despite his jail sentence only a few years previously), was appointed headmaster of the grammar school. We rented a terraced house in Argyle Street, not much more than a 100 yards from the school. The town had still not recovered from the war. There were gaps in some streets where the bombs had fallen, with the rubble of the houses still on the ground, and an estate of prefabs had sprung up just off the road to Pembroke.

Unlike Reading, Pembroke Dock – with its air station, naval oil depot and barracks – had been a frequent target for German bombers. Neighbours recalled only too graphically how they had sheltered under the stairs when the sirens sounded. In 1940, eleven giant oil tanks, situated not far from Hobbs Point, were bombed, causing a blaze which lasted for days and could be seen for many miles around. A decade and more later, local people were still talking about it.

Rationing was still in force, though on fewer items than in the depths of the war. I can remember queuing with my mother, complete with ration book, to collect concentrated orange juice. Much fresh fruit was still a relative rarity. I can just about recall my parents' disbelief when I refused to eat a fresh orange, a fruit of which they had been deprived for so long.

The town was still suffering from the closure of the naval dockyard in 1926. The whole town had been built around the docks, on the gridiron pattern common to other Victorian dock towns around Britain. Many people had left, unemployment remained high, and it was common to find families living hand-to-mouth with a little fishing, potato-picking and odd jobs.

Within three years, we moved up the hill to a brand-new semi-detached house overlooking the town, with a magnificent view all the way north to the Preseli Hills. We had watched it being built, taking regular walks up the hill to monitor its progress. When we moved in, I was given a bedroom which looked out across the town. From the window, I could see all the way from a reach of the Cleddau to the east, past Hobbs Point and Neyland, down the Haven to the west. Best of all, I could watch the Sunderland flying boats taking off over the town. They would start up their engines, propellers turning, with a growl which would shake the windows of the houses on the front. The growl would slowly build to a crescendo, until finally, let off the leash, they would lumber up into the air and head off to destinations I could only imagine. It was the last flying boat base in Britain and was closed down in 1956.

My sister and I used to play games of cricket on the strip of grass in front of the house with Terry, the boy who lived next door. On one side, was the road – fortunately a cul-de-sac, and on the other a steep drop to a field which ran at what seemed like a 45-degree angle down to the town's park. It was hopelessly laborious trying to retrieve a ball from the field, so we changed the rules to suit. If you hit the ball into the field, you scored six runs but were out at the same time. At the start of the game we would call: 'We're playing six and out.'

We had no television set at home. In fact, it was not until I was in my teens that I came home one day to find that my parents had at last agreed to have a television set in the home. But we could not miss out on the Coronation in 1953. We all went next door to watch the Coronation service, curtains drawn to help us see the flickering black-and-white screen. I remember thinking how strange it was for the curtains to be drawn during the daytime. Of course, as children we always wanted to go round and watch more television, but we were only allowed to watch *Whirligig* on a Saturday afternoon.

It was only rarely we were permitted to go to Haggar's cinema down in the town. An exception was made for *A Kid for Two Farthings*, the first film I had ever seen. It was a sentimental story, which doesn't bear watching now. But I was overawed by the big screen and it would not have mattered what the film was like. I also recall my father taking me to see *Battle of the River Plate,* which, given his record of conscientious objection, was surprising. I must have kicked up an awful lot of fuss about seeing it.

On the radio, my sister Mary and I loved the *Archie Andrews Show*. Unfortunately, it was broadcast at two o'clock on a Sunday afternoon, and we had to be in Sunday school by half-past two. So we would have to tear ourselves away before the end so that we could be at Trinity chapel in time. The family went to chapel every Sunday without exception, and as children that meant twice a day. In the morning service, there was the weekly ordeal of reciting verses in front of the congregation. Earlier in the week, my father would write out a verse from the Bible in his meticulous, but tiny, handwriting, and we would have to learn it in time for Sunday. We were tested on the Sunday morning before we went to chapel and it did not improve the atmosphere if we did not get it right.

On the way home from chapel, we would often call in at my father's office at the old school in Argyle Street. On one occasion, there on his desk was the biggest pile of water pistols, all confiscated, you could ever imagine. But, when we were about seven years old, he used the visit to his office to try, rather impatiently, to teach us how to find the hymn numbers in the hymn book. He did not seem to comprehend why we struggled to do it. More than fifty years later, it was my turn to help him find the numbers in the hymn book.

One Sunday, my mother collapsed in chapel. This was perplexing to us, because she had not seemed to be ill and she was always busy looking after us. In fact, it was she who did all the work around the house, because my father was totally impractical. He could not mend a plug and I cannot recall ever seeing him with a screwdriver in his hand. The centre of his life at home was his desk, which we were not supposed to touch. Apart from the usual domestic duties, my mother painted and decorated, she was adept at handicrafts and particularly good at making lampshades. She made marmalade and jam, and we had to be stopped from running into the dining room when a muslin sheet was stretched between two chairs, draining blackberry juice into a large saucepan ready to be made into blackberry jelly. She did most of the gardening, growing prize-winning chrysanthemums in the greenhouse. It was she who played games with us, took us for walks and taught us the little things in life. She even tried to teach me geography, the subject she had taught in her brief teaching career. And she was prominent in the local Women's Institute, a service which is still remembered.

So it was perplexing, the incident in chapel. We were taken out by a fellow member of the congregation, a local councillor, and ended up having Sunday lunch with his family. Only afterwards were we told that we were about to have a baby sister. We were six years old when Ceinwen was born. Mary and I were shipped off to our grandparents in Brecon, from where I wrote:

> Dear Mummy and Baby,
> I was very glad to have your letter and to hear Ceinwen is such a nice little girl. The ground is covered with snow and it is very cold here. Love and kisses from Jonathan.

Mary and I went to school first at Llanion, on London Road. But it was not long before we moved onto the primary school in Albion Square in the middle of town, about ten minutes' walk from home. The memory still lingers of the old-fashioned school desk with inkwells, dipping the nib of the pen into the ink and invariably getting it all over my fingers. I can remember nothing of the lessons, but I can remember the playground with the outdoor toilets, and the crates containing the bottles of free milk warming in the sun.

In 1955, the old grammar school site in Pembroke Dock was replaced by a brand-new school building a mile or so away on the old Bush estate near Pembroke. It looked so modern, a red-brick building with spacious grounds around it. Most unusually, there was a farm attached to the school where students could learn agriculture. The students were to lodge in the old mansion, Bush House, which first had to be renovated. Apparently, the workmen at one stage went on strike because they said one of their colleagues had seen a ghost – a lady in a crinoline dress coming down the main staircase.

'Nonsense,' said my mother. 'They just didn't fancy doing the late shift.'

Ever since, I have never believed in ghosts.

It was to the new Pembroke Grammar School that Mary and I moved up to at the age of ten-and-a-half after passing the eleven-plus. My father had quickly established a strong command over the school, imposing discipline almost effortlessly. He used to take the first year for Latin, and he was often late for classes, delayed on headmasterly duties. While waiting for him to arrive, the classroom would be bedlam, but the precaution was always taken of posting someone in the doorway to warn if he was coming. The second he turned the corner at the end of the corridor, the classroom was total silence.

The Latin classes were the only time I was taught by my father. They were well-ordered, quiet lessons, even if the subject was not every pupil's first choice. But one thing struck me as odd, even at that age. The first Latin verb most children are taught to conjugate is *amo*, to love. But my father chose the verb, *neco*, to kill. So the confirmed pacifist had the pupils in his class reciting *Neco, necas, necat, necamus, necatis, necant*.

There was one occasion when Latin was to prove to be more than just a dead language. In 1956, there were many Hungarian refugees arriving in Britain following the suppression of the revolt there by the USSR. One such refugee penetrated all the way to the far west of Wales. My father and I were waiting on the station platform at Pembroke Dock when we saw a man getting off the train, dressed in a shabby brown mac and carrying a cardboard suitcase. My father took him to his lodgings and afterwards I heard him describe the difficulties he had in communicating with the Hungarian. They tried English, French, a bit of German, and even some Italian with no luck. Then my father tapped the table and said '*mensa*'. The man's eyes lit up and thereafter they were able to establish some basic things in common.

My father, even when still in his thirties, was a dominant figure in the school, still remembered by former teachers and pupils. He was remembered in particular for encouraging the children of poorer families to continue their education and go to university, going round to their homes and trying to persuade the parents to let them carry on. He took part in school plays, held parties for old age pensioners, and even initiated an international summer school for foreign students.

Such was his reputation as a formidable headmaster, however, that it was difficult to persuade school friends to come round to my house to play. I was playing on one occasion with a friend in the dining room, when, to leave, he had to negotiate the kitchen where my father was sitting reading the *News Chronicle*. It was like a scene from a *Tom and Jerry* cartoon, with the mouse taking exaggeratedly silent footsteps around the cat in the hope that he would not wake up.

For my father, this was also a crucial and creative phase in his development as a writer and literary critic. In 1949, he helped to set up a literary magazine called *Dock Leaves* – the pun on the name of the town was deliberate. It was founded by a group of friends who met regularly to discuss literature, among them Raymond Garlick who used to live next door to us in Argyle Street. Raymond Garlick was the first editor of *Dock Leaves,* which subsequently transmuted into *The Anglo-Welsh Review,* which my father later edited for many years. He was to become a major influence in establishing Welsh writing in English as a recognised literary genre.

As children, we noticed the time my father spent at the desk in his study and occasional meetings which meant we had to stay out of the lounge. What we did enjoy were the trips in our green Jowett Javelin to the home of the group's treasurer Morwyth Rees at her house in the pretty seaside village of Manorbier. As my parents were conducted into the front room for the serious business, we were dispatched to the scullery to talk to the housekeeper Nellie and listen to *The Archers*.

For the three children, it was a privileged, middle-class upbringing, and I only slowly became aware how much better-off we were than most of those around. When Mary and I were only eight years old, we accompanied our parents, plus an uncle and cousin, on an Easter holiday to Switzerland. My mother kitted both of us out in identical plaid trousers and caps, which even at that age we were embarrassed to wear. We flew out of Blackbushe airfield just off the A30 (long since closed as a commercial airport) in what I think was a DC3 – I can remember the slope up towards the front of the plane.

It was our first visit to another country, but it seemed like another century as well. Everything seemed clean, sparkling and modern, with electric trains and modern roads. My abiding memory is sitting with Mary in several feet of snow and eating chocolate Easter bunnies. Further south, we had a trip in the Easter sunshine around Lake Lugano. At one landing stage, my mother told me that, if we got off there, we would be in Italy.

Back in Pembroke Dock we occasionally saw a Breton onion seller, and we had to watch out for Irish pennies in our change – but this was something else.

But it was the countryside around our home which defines my memory of this part of my childhood. We lived just a handful of miles from a coastline which is one of the most beautiful in the whole of Britain. On Saturdays, and during school holidays, the whole family would frequently go to the beach. There was not just one beach – we had a choice of beaches, most at that time with only a handful of visitors even in summer. And the variety – from Freshwater East with its wooden chalets in the sand dunes round to Freshwater West which faced the Atlantic and where we walked every Boxing Day. But our favourite destination was Barafundle, where we had to walk over the cliff top carrying our picnic, and in those days when far fewer families had cars, we were usually rewarded with a beautiful, empty stretch of sand.

Sheltered behind a string of Norman castles, this was Little England beyond Wales where the Welsh language was hardly ever heard. But for me as a child, it was a magical countryside which included old mansions (I am sure I saw Stackpole Court before it was demolished in the early 1950s), a smuggler's cove, a saint's chapel at the sea's edge, and a stunning stretch of cliffs to walk along. Our hearts would be in our mouths as our corgi ran to the edge of a fearsome drop, stopping only at the last moment to peer over at the sea far below. In his poem, 'Conversation on Stackpole Head', written at this time, my father described the scene:

No wind to speak of and the south-east roll
Flattening somewhat. If that hole
Goes past the immediate rabbit to the sea
This limestone headland and lee
Cliff landward are fretted further by the tide
Than one would think. This side
Is dangerous. See the rocks boiling at the jut
Where the race is. A slip would gut
One soon enough, and the sea feeding round the toe
Step quietly up.

Framed by the coastline, this part of south Pembrokeshire still calls to me as a haven of natural beauty, peace and personal security. But I was suddenly wrenched away and thrown into a very different world.

CHAPTER 6

Gwell dysg na golud

THERE WAS A silence in the school hall – an uncanny silence. Usually this was the moment when, after grace had been said, there would be a crescendo of noise as the boys from each table took it in turns to go up for their meal. Instead, there was a stillness around the bare, wooden tables, the boys not moving from the long benches.

I do not remember any elaborate plans to stage the food strike. But we all knew. A master stood up at the high table and tried to order one group of boys to go to the serving hatch. But no one moved. It was going to be macaroni cheese again, followed by tapioca pudding. Nobody went up for it. And, as the general hubbub gradually resumed, I could just see the cook being led away in tears.

In retrospect, conditions in the mid-1950s at Llandovery College – whose school motto *Gwell dysg na golud* proclaimed 'Better learning than riches' – were primitive. Nothing much had changed since before the Second World War. Bare floorboards, no heating, no hot water. During the first winter, I had never been so cold. We had to fill the washbasins with water before going to bed in case the pipes froze, and occasionally had to break the ice in the basin before being able to wash.

One of a handful of Welsh public schools, the college was set in the town of Llandovery in the middle of the rolling Carmarthenshire countryside. The uniform was a drab grey, with a black tie, because apparently we were still in mourning for some member of the royal family, although we were not sure which one. The only spot of colour was the cream boater we had to wear in the summer. Even then, it seemed slightly absurd walking the banks of the Towy in a straw hat. It did, however, make a passable Frisbee.

Both my sister Mary and I had been sent away to school. She went to Dr Williams' School, Dolgellau, which by all accounts was even more of a throwback and was closed down soon after she left. My parents felt that, with my father as headmaster, we were never going to be treated normally at Pembroke Grammar School. They were probably right about that, but for me it was like being thrown into a Dickensian world where you had to look out for yourself at every step.

I can still smell my life at Llandovery. The smell of boot-polish in the locker room, the smell of small boys in the dormitory, the smell of mud up my nose from the rugby pitch. Conditions did improve from my first year onwards, beginning with the introduction of new hot-water baths, although we still had to share two or three to a bath. Every morning, we had to line up in the school hall for inspection, holding out our hands in front of us. The warden (the head teacher) would walk up and down the line, dispatching any boy he deemed to have dirty fingernails or unpolished shoes.

When I arrived at the school, the warden was the Rev. G.O. Williams, who subsequently became the Bishop of Bangor. He walked with a spring in his step and so was nicknamed 'Bouncer'. The choice of warden was confined to Welsh-speaking clergy in the Church in Wales, which rather limited the field. His successor brought no particular educational skills to the school.

It did not help that I was the smallest boy in the class. I was pushed around a lot, and I suppose it would now be called bullying, but I did not think of it like that. I learned to fight back, and I was by no means bottom of the pecking order. That lot fell to the shambling figure of a boy who would now be termed educationally disadvantaged. He was bullied mercilessly, with the boy behind him in the class occasionally sticking the point of a protractor deep into his backside. When the boy left a few years later, his guardian told us how happy he had been at the school and how grateful he was to us for looking after him. I nearly cried.

Home seemed a long way away at that time. We received letters, of course, thrown at us from the gallery of the school hall by prefects. The name of the recipient was called, you shouted out and, with a flick of the wrist, the letter was sent in your direction. On St Valentine's Day, the calling of the names would be accompanied by catcalls and raillery. When my turn came, I did my best to hide it if, as usual, the letter was from my mother.

I can vividly remember the journey home at the end of the first term. The intense anticipation at getting up at around five o'clock in the morning to catch the train, the glow of cigarette ends in the dark as the older boys lit up on the way to the station, the joy at seeing the 'Coffee Pot', as it was nicknamed, puffing its way towards the platform. We scrambled into a compartment, lifted the window with the leather strap – and school was finally behind us.

I met up with my friend Terry from next door as soon as I could when I got home. We had used to wrestle on the grass in front of the house, neither able to prevail. It was not long before we were at it again. This time, I had him pinned to the ground within seconds. After twelve weeks away, I had become tougher. But I had also lost a certain innocence.

There were undoubtedly some good teachers at Llandovery. My love of history was instilled by Charlie Bell, a former army officer in a tank regiment. He could entrance his pupils with vivid accounts of historical events, and would then dictate detailed revision notes. A bachelor and something of a misogynist, he was also an inveterate smoker. His coughing would often get out of control and – with a wave of his hand to indicate we should get on with what we were supposed to be

Evan and Muriel with son Roland, 1916

My great-grandparents, David and Mali

My maternal grandfather, Sidney Hawes

Evan Mathias in Shanghai, 1927

Joseph and Rachel Morgan with their family at the Tyle – Muriel is second from the right

The Tyle farmhouse today

Ffynnon Fawr before the flooding

Site of Ffynnon Fawr today

Twins, 1945 – I am the one with the hair

Muriel with her great-grandson, Mathew

My father as headmaster, 1950s

My parents in retirement

Cub reporter in the Merthyr office of the *South Wales Echo*

In ITN's Westminster studio, with Pat Harris, David Rose and Julian Haviland

The new political editor, 1982

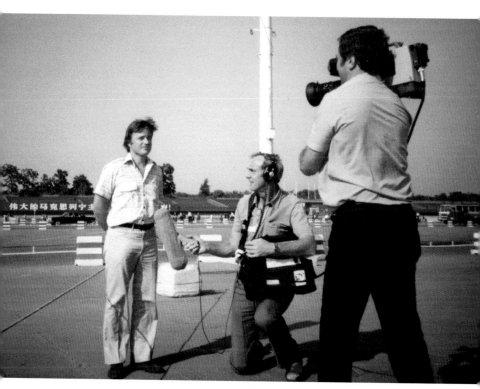

Piece to camera in Tiananmen Square, Beijing, 1982

Interviewing Mrs Thatcher, 1983

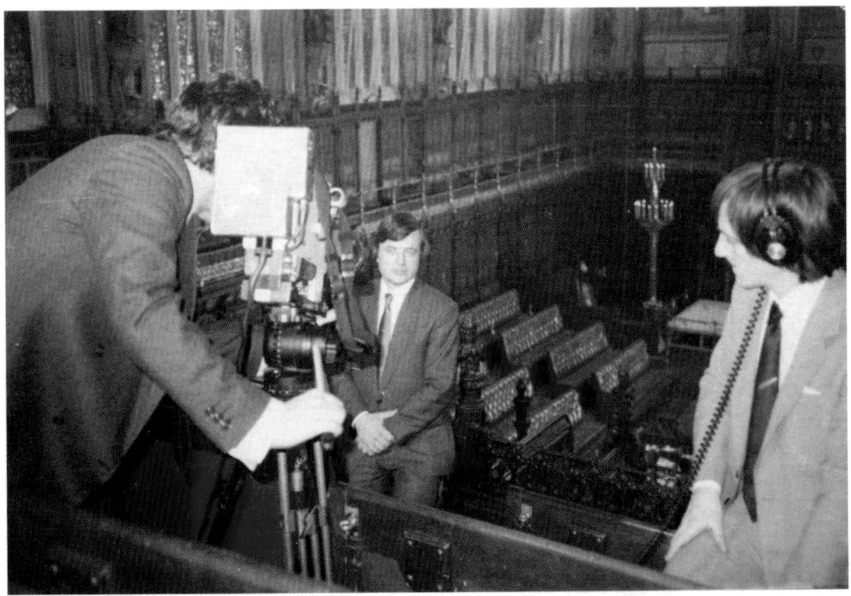

Explaining the televising of the Lords, 1985

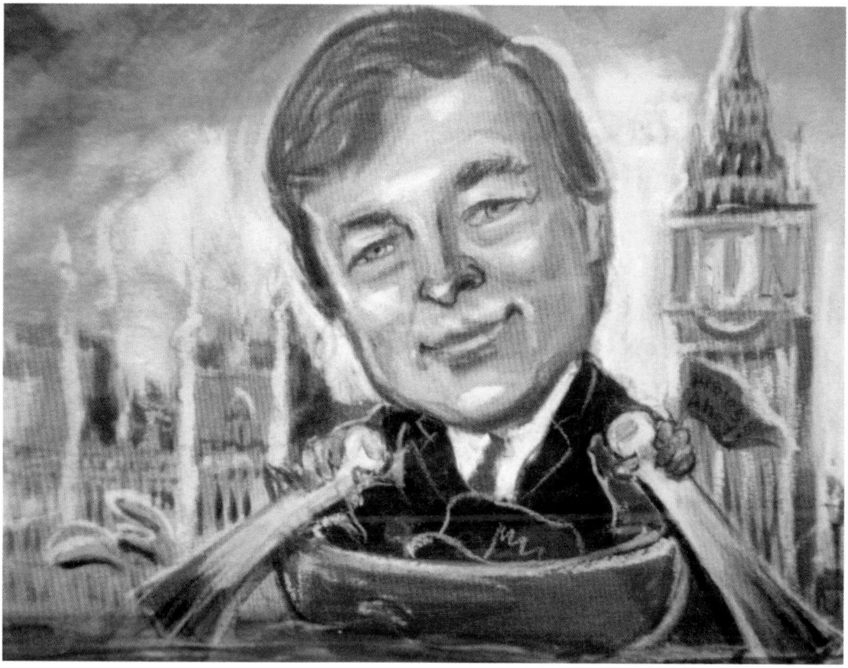

Cartoon on leaving ITN

Gagging Lloyd George for a PR stunt, 2003

Four generations, 2005

Megan and Hannah, 2013

doing – he would leave the classroom, sometimes for extended periods.

Then there was Archie Moore, who subsequently became head of a Midlands comprehensive. He taught us English and made the mistake of trying to treat us as adults. We quickly discovered that he could be easily distracted from the lesson he had planned. There would be a quick conspiracy before his lesson about how to divert him, and as soon as he entered the room, one of the boys would ask what he thought of the latest film we had seen or a book which someone had read. It was then the job of the rest of the class to keep the discussion going as long as possible. But we still learned more about English literature in the remaining time than we would have from most teachers.

The classics were taken by the elderly Mr Pie, whose first name I do not think I ever knew. He was highly respected in his field but something of a traditionalist. I had opted, under parental advice, for Greek instead of physics, and that, not unsurprisingly, was a very small class. But, even with the O level cribs we sneakily sent off for, I still struggled to unpick the Greek verse. Only rarely did I feel that my education was in any way futile, but I felt it overwhelmingly one summer afternoon, looking out at the blue sky over the rugby pitch, as Mr Pie tried to get us to understand the aorist tense. He made clear his disappointment when I told him I was not going to do classics at A level.

The school was Welsh in outlook, but the curriculum was broadly the kind you would find in any English public school. Many of the boys were Welsh-speaking, quite a few the sons of clergy. But the language in and out of the classroom was invariably English.

This did not stop a degree of anti-Englishness among the boys. The pupil who probably suffered the most in my latter years at the school was a boy with an upper-class English accent who, rather bravely, refused to tone down his pro-English sentiments.

To teach us Welsh and rugby we had the legendary Carwyn James, who had played fly-half for Llanelli and subsequently coached the Lions. He took the junior teams at rugby, and, since by tradition scrum-halves tended to be small, I was always picked in that position. Carwyn would take the junior team on away fixtures, some of us occasionally travelling in his car. But my rugby career was short-lived. I did not much enjoy being regularly flattened by the opposing wing forwards, and was soon replaced.

It was the influence of Carwyn which led the school to enter competitors for the Urdd National Eisteddfod. He coached us in in *cydadrodd* (choral recitation) and I can still remember painfully learning the words of *'Ystrad Fflur'*, by T. Gwynn Jones. We travelled to Mold for the eisteddfod, where the boys were parcelled out among home-owners willing to take them. I ended up sharing a double bed in a vicarage with Potso Stephens. But the words still come back to me:

Mae dail y coed yn Ystrad Fflur
Yn murmur yn yr awyr
[The leaves on the trees in Ystrad Fflur (the abbey of Strata Florida)
Murmur in the breeze]

Carwyn was an approachable and popular teacher, with no hint yet of the iconic status he was later to achieve in the Welsh-speaking world. For a couple of years, I was in his class for Welsh learners, but at that time it was a subject which was scheduled to be dropped the year before O level. A small group of us approached him to ask if we could carry on and take it for O level, as we felt we had the capacity and time to do so. But Carwyn turned our request down. The reason, I suspect, was that he did not want to increase his workload.

Boys who were from Nonconformist backgrounds were permitted to opt out of Sunday services in the school chapel. Along with one or two other boys, I went instead to a Methodist chapel in the town, the William Williams Pantycelyn Memorial

Chapel (William Williams was one of Wales's greatest hymn writers and a leader of the eighteenth-century Methodist revival). I was never convinced of the Nonconformist credentials of my companions. It seemed more of an excuse to duck under the nearby bridge on the way to the service in order to enjoy a Sunday morning smoke. Once in the chapel, we ensured that we were right at the back so that nobody could see us reading the comics – or 'bloods', as we called them – when our heads went down for prayers. It was here that I first heard the kind of extempore preaching for which Welsh Nonconformity had been renowned. There was one Sunday in particular when the visiting minister failed to turn up and one of the deacons offered to take the service in his place. From a standing start, he preached for nearly an hour, one of the longest sermons I have ever sat through.

One of the deacons owned a general merchant's store just down the street, and he and his wife would invite the college boys who attended the chapel for Sunday tea once a term. They lived above the shop, and in the spacious lounge the tea and cakes would be placed on small tables by the armchairs. But we had spotted fairly quickly some interesting-looking magazines nearby. They turned out to be *Men Only,* not just one copy but every copy published for the previous few months. *Men Only* was not at that time the garishly lubricious publication it subsequently became, but it was obvious enough. After some desultory conversation, our heads would disappear into the magazines. Amid the silence, the deacon's wife would sit knitting, occasionally murmuring: 'Naughty boys, naughty boys.'

My father had strongly urged me not to join the school's Combined Cadet Force. This was, of course, consistent with the pacifist views which had taken him to prison during the Second World War. Indeed, he had never allowed me to join the Scouts, which he regarded as a paramilitary organisation. The handful of boys who did not join the CCF were warned that they would have to pick stones off the school rugby field instead. But nobody could be bothered to supervise us on such a boring task and we were quickly left to our own devices. I did not miss all the Blanco-ing of kit and polishing of brass, and I could sit with my feet up reading a book and watching my classmates' square-bashing out in the school yard.

There was a problem about what to do with the boys on a Saturday night. It was not long before a film night was instituted in the school gym, and I can still see the copious dust swirling up through the beam of the projector as the grainy picture and scratchy sound filled the cold hall. The film was always interrupted as we waited for the reel to be changed, and occasionally the projector simply broke down. One film I remember simply because the projector broke down at such a vivid moment, just when a test pilot was apparently heading for a fatal crash as his plane dived out of the sky. It was half an hour before we got to see the last fifteen minutes of the film when the pilot at last managed to push the joystick in the opposite direction and the dive became a climb.

As sixth-formers, we were finally allowed to watch television, if only once a week. We would crowd into the lecture room in the science block by six o'clock on a Saturday in time to watch *6.5 Special*, the first pop music show on BBC television:

The 6.5 Special's steaming down the line,
The 6.5 Special's right on time...

The picture was projected from the television set onto a screen at the front of the room, and the loudest cheer was for the appearance of Adam Faith, swinging his arm over his shoulder as if he was warming up for a trapeze act. By this time, there was quite a bit of secret listening to Radio Luxembourg and ready discussion about favourite songs. It is perhaps a suitable verdict on my musical taste that I would walk out of the dormitory singing to myself the lyrics of an early Cliff Richard hit:

Got myself a crying, talking, sleeping, walking, living doll
Got to do my best to please her, just 'cause she's a living doll...

But what gave me most pleasure was the long summer afternoons when there was no requirement to check in for tea in the middle of the afternoon and the lessons did not begin again until half-past-five or six o'clock. We could go swimming in the Towy – in 'Shallows' for the non-swimmers and then, after a rudimentary test, to 'Deeps', although we had to watch out for the lampreys. But what I enjoyed most were the long walks into the countryside. There were permitted routes, designed to avoid passing any shop or, above all, pub. So we could walk out to the Dolau Bridge, a beautiful old hump-backed bridge further up the River Towy.

But the long afternoons meant we could often be more adventurous. We were always wandering off the road so that Dave Carter could smoke his pipe. I remember the smell of pipe smoke under damp trees and the slight feeling of furtiveness. I was not tempted to smoke myself – it just did not seem to be an attractive thing to do. One bright afternoon, a small group, led by Geraint Eckley, headed down the bank of the river and onto the railway line. Because it was a Sunday, it was unlikely there would be any trains. Geraint had found a guards van, which we cheerfully occupied for several hours, playing at living in the real world for a while.

Events outside the walls of the school gradually penetrated my consciousness. One evening on the way into dinner, I found a small boy crying his eyes out. Which was unexpected, because the boy, the son of a vicar, was a boisterous child whom the prefects found difficult to control. Indeed, it was rumoured that he had been sent away to school because he had thrown a stone though the east window of his father's church. But on this occasion, he was inconsolable. 'He thinks the world is coming to an end,' said his friend. 'That's what he's been told by one of the seniors, and he won't listen to me.' It was 1962, and the Cuban missile crisis was reaching its climax.

By this time, I shared a study at the top of the tower, where one of my colleagues concealed his bottles of ale beneath the floorboards. I was enjoying history, in particular, in the sixth-form, where I shared a small class with Deian Hopkin, who was to make his career as an academic historian, and ended up as Professor Sir Deian Hopkin. I was no use at rugby, poor at cricket and hopeless at music, but I was good enough academically to secure a place, like my father, at Jesus College, Oxford. Sometimes I was nicknamed Gunga Din (from Kipling's poem, which ends with the line: 'You're a better man than me, Gunga Din'). It was not that I had developed a superiority complex. Rather, as a strategy for survival I had developed a carapace within which I could hide what I really felt and thought. My time at Llandovery had made me self-contained and given me an ability to endure, but as a way of life it seemed unrelated to the world outside.

More than thirty years later, I was reminded of how much I had forgotten about my life at Llandovery. I had just returned to Wales to work, and at a reception at a Conservative Party conference I was introduced to a Member of Parliament who turned out to be a fellow Llandoverian. He was Rod Richards, subsequently to fall into considerable notoriety after a number of incidents involving women, money and drink. Corporal punishment was still, during our schooldays, administered by prefects, and he said that, after some misbehaviour in the dormitory involving him, I had given him a 'tanning'.

I was relating this story one day to my father and his friend Raymond Garlick, a fellow poet. There was a short pause before Raymond Garlick, slowly stroking his beard, said: 'At least you can die knowing you've done something worthwhile!'

CHAPTER 7

I like it

IT WAS GETTING rowdy at closing time in the Pig and Whistle. Even my bodyguard seemed to be getting a little nervous. In my new summer job at Butlin's, I was carrying the bag for the daily cash run. The trick was to get me in behind the bar before anyone noticed. As we went in, I could see two large groups facing up to each other, the Glaswegians against the Brummies, and the contents of a few pint glasses were being flung around.

My bodyguard was himself a Glaswegian, barely more than five feet tall, and a former paratroop sergeant. Without hesitation, he walked into the middle of the lurching crowd, straight up to the biggest man he could find. Bunching his fists, he shouted: 'Are you looking for a fight, Jimmy?'

It had the intended effect. Nobody wanted that kind of fight, and the place calmed down in a matter of minutes. Meanwhile, I was safely in through the locked door of the bar, and had started emptying the till. It was hot and sweaty, and I was wearing what I imagined were fashionably tight trousers. As I bent down to pick up the cash bag, which was the size of an old-fashioned Gladstone bag, I heard a loud ripping noise; my trousers had been torn apart all down my backside. I had some peculiar looks as I tried to sidle out of the pub with my back to the wall.

I was employed for the summer as an assistant cashier at Butlin's Holiday Camp in Skegness. It was an attempt to discover the world outside the middle-class, public-school education I had so far lived through. I was to find that, for many of those who came there, it was their first experience of life away from their home or work.

In the early 1960s, car ownership was a fraction of the current total, and that freedom to move about the country was not available to many working-class families. The opportunity of working at Butlin's was not just an opportunity for teenagers to leave home for the first time, it was often their first visit to the seaside. For girls in their late teens, it might be their only chance of adventure before getting married, which many fully expected they would have to do by the time they reached the age of twenty. The Swinging Sixties had not quite arrived in Skegness in the spring of 1963.

There were others, usually older, who clearly drifted through such temporary communities hoping nobody would catch up with them. On the train from Derby (my parents had by this time moved to Derbyshire, where my father was head of the Herbert Strutt School, Belper), I fell in with a man wearing a smart blazer and tie and a very plausible line in chat. He disappeared from the camp after less than a week when the police checks caught up with him. The manager of the hotel on the site – it was really just another pub – also suddenly vanished. An imposing man, he had been running the hotel with his 'wife', but he turned out not to be her husband or even who he said he was.

My job as a cashier was to collect the money from the tills in the shops and bars all over the camp. The bodyguard was only necessary for the late-night runs. I wrote in the diary I occasionally kept:

> One is taken up in the daily round of accounts to be balanced, money to be counted, tills to be cashed, till-girls to chat up or chasten, as the case may be, wages to be counted out and bagged up and then paid out to the grumbling queues of worried old ladies and docile old men, cheeky girls and stroppy young men

("Why can't we have our money now?" "Look mate, why have they stopped me £2s 10d. tax this week – I done nothing wrong?").

The morning would be occupied with the counting and tallying up, and, like my handful of colleagues, I would often end up staring at the blur of numbers in front of me, unable to work out where I had gone wrong. The chief cashier was, fortunately, bluff and good-humoured, and after a brief glance over my shoulder, a stubby finger would immediately point out where the mistake had been made. The day's takings always hit the midday bank-run dutifully reconciled.

Most memorable were the Saturday afternoons when the visitors arrived for the week. The queues would form at the reception desk, waiting to check-in and pay for their holiday. Each cashier would take one of the queues, and payments were almost always in ready money. These were the savings hoarded over previous months, sometimes longer. A few even paid in old white fivers. When I had taken more than about £1,000, which took little more than an hour, I would be replaced so that I could do a tally, one of which looked like this:

BUTLIN'S LIMITED
RECEPTION CREDIT NOTE

Date 11/7/63 Code week H Camp Skegness
This credit note covers the period on duty
From 2 p.m. To 3 p.m.

£10 notes	£10.0.0d.
£5 notes	£1,050.0.0d.
£1 notes	£133.0.0d.
10/– notes	£0.0.0d.
Silver	£15.0d.
Nickel	£0.0.0d.
Copper	£0.0.0d.
Postal orders	£11.5.0d.
British money orders	£187.5.0d.
Cheques	£207.10.0d.

Savings stamps	£46.5.0d.
Vouchers	£6.5.0d.
Green Shield stamps	£0.5.0d.

Total of balances per posting slip	£1,652.10.0d.

In my diary, I described Saturday afternoons on the counter:

> ... sweating through receipt form after receipt form and counting the money thrust forward out of quivering, aged hands when the money smells of mothballs and the feeling can't be resisted that they've kept these old fivers in the wardrobe over the past ten years; out of the quiet hands of the typical middle-aged family man backed up fiercely by his wife, just daring you to count that money wrong; out of the friendly hands of the smiling woman in her fifties, who must keep a boarding house; out of the fidgeting hands of the fretful mother who is trying to watch her innumerable children and prevent them clambering on the counter, as well as attempting to keep her eye on the preciously stored money, and to make sure her husband doesn't get lost behind the crowd...
>
> And out of the hands of leather-jacketed, and what's-the-talent-like-then youths, who come in groups and ask to pay altogether and produce odd bits of money out of side-pockets which I invariably get wrong, before I get riled by their sarky comments and tell them to add it up their bloody selves.

Since the day was broken into shifts, we often had the afternoons free. The beach was invariably too bracing, but we were free to use the billiard hall, the swimming pool and tennis courts, and go to the shows where they introduced 'stars of stage, screen and television' of whom we had never heard. We used the summer afternoons to cycle out into the flat Lincolnshire countryside, stopping at the occasional village church, before swooping back into the camp to sample a knickerbocker glory in the ice-cream parlour. And there were the visits to the tiny village pubs, where the bar was just the front room of the house and the beer was served in earthenware jars.

The camp and the countryside around were two different worlds. Every morning we were woken up in our cramped chalets by the Tannoy system blasting out songs such as 'The corn is high as an elephant's eye', and we were driven out of bed mainly because we could not stand the music any more. But there was one song which stuck in the mind, one of the early hits by Gerry and the Pacemakers:

I like it, I like it
I like the way you run your fingers through my hair
And I like the way you tickle my chin
And I like the way you let me come in
When your mama ain't there...

I did not envy the jobs of the famous Redcoats, who had to organise the 'knobbly knees' competitions and judge the most glamorous grandmother. And the continual bingo competitions, from which we also had to collect the takings. On one occasion, I found the bingo-caller snaffling some of the prizes. 'Here,' he said, 'have one yourself,' and threw a pack of playing cards in my direction. At which point, the manager came in and I instinctively thrust the illicit goods into my pocket. The manager did not spot anything, but I was so disgusted with myself that I threw the pack of cards into the nearest bin.

There were some tensions in the accounts office. One young man, slightly older than myself, stopped speaking to me and became very irritable whenever I was around. I couldn't work out what grievance he had against me. The only grievance I had against him was that he seemed far too well-off, driving an MG TD sports car and constantly flashing five-pound notes around.

It transpired that it was all about a girl. Not just any girl, but the chief receptionist who was the object of much admiration. Much to my surprise, she invited me one evening to join her on a ride on a merry-go-round, and even I could work out that this was intended to throw us together. Margaret was from Coventry and had come to Butlin's for the season with her friend, Gloria, and the attraction was immediate.

The holiday camp afforded little privacy, but we went on long walks when we could. All fairly innocent by the standards of today, but a wonderful new world for someone who had been locked away in a public school for most of his teenage years. My diary, which promised rather pompously not to 'descend into Pepysian licentiousness', was full of it.

At the age of nineteen, Margaret clearly felt under pressure to get married. She had already, she told me, been proposed to by the lodger in their Coventry home. But I had yet to go to university and there was a world out there waiting for me. From my encounter with the lives of so many different kinds of people at Skegness, I realised that I wanted to experience as much of the world as I could. I was determined not to 'sit in some provincial backwater and let most of life pass over me'.

In my first term at Jesus College, I invited Margaret to a college dance. I was not sure whether she was coming until I heard her voice in the quad asking her way to my room. She was wearing a broad, pink hat and a short dress which, in retrospect, she must have worried about a great deal before she came. I introduced her to my room-mate, Rod Morgan, and he could not stop talking in front of her. The evening passed in a blur, and it was the last time I saw her. Our lives had moved on.

*

The contrast could not have been greater between the mellow seventeenth-century Oxford stone and the brash, 'kiss-me-quick' style of the Butlin's holiday camp. I had swapped the cashier's office for the college library, the cafeteria for the dining hall with its Latin grace before the meal, the Pig and Whistle for the college bar.

At that time, newly arrived students of history were plunged into preliminary examinations at the end of their first term. In a matter of weeks, we had to get to grips with the Venerable Bede, de Tocqueville and Gibbon's *Decline and Fall of the Roman Empire* – all in the original languages. If you survived that daunting challenge, there were no further exams until finals at the end of the three years. It was easy to lose your way during that extended period, and it made the prospect of finals all the more terrifying.

Attendance at lectures seemed to be entirely voluntary, and indeed there seemed to be no requirement on the lecturers themselves to ensure they were relevant to the syllabus. The lectures, organised under the aegis of the university history faculty rather than the college, were invariably packed out to begin with, but with numbers rapidly dwindling to handfuls by the end of the course. The only requirement on the student was to attend a weekly tutorial, preferably with an essay completed often late the previous night. Here I was immensely lucky. John Walsh, an expert on the history of Methodism, was kind, always encouraging and showed a genuine interest in the progress of his students. John Hale, a historian of the Italian Renaissance, was effortlessly brilliant, even if he could not quite remember what you were supposed to have written an essay about and sometimes was still dressing as the tutorial began.

It was disappointing to me that, as far as Oxford was concerned, history stopped somewhere in the nineteenth century. We were able to choose one special subject, and I chose the most recent topic on the list, which was the American Civil War. I probably spent too much time in the library, but I was no good at sport. I tried my hand at coxing a rowing eight, but it was only a matter of minutes before we hit the nearest bridge.

I was something of an idealist at that age, firmly believing that some form of world order should be established to prevent the kind of war which was then raging in Vietnam. Like many others at the time, impressed with the likes of Dag Hammerskjold, I thought the United Nations was the best vehicle for such a new world order, and I got heavily involved with the university branch of the United Nations Association. Student opposition to the war in Vietnam was building up, and when the American Ambassador to South Vietnam, Henry Cabot Lodge, came to speak at the Oxford Union, I managed to slip past the police cordon and in through a side door to get one of the last seats in a packed house. Cabot Lodge had not seemed to expect the level of hostility he faced, and seemed a little shaken. In his wake, the British Foreign Secretary, Michael Stewart, who was speaking at the same debate, got a rough time as well. I watched as he left, protected by police and looking strained.

As long as I could remember, I had been interested in politics. At the age of eleven, I had drawn a cartoon depicting Sir Anthony Eden waving from the deck of a ship as he left for the West Indies. He had been forced to withdraw from the disastrous Suez campaign, and, suffering from ill-health, was being waved off by a rather gleeful Harold Macmillan. But I did not see myself as a participant in politics (though briefly tempted when in my thirties) and did not warm to the student politics of the Oxford Union.

My room-mate in college, Rod Morgan, was always ready for a political argument, and one such, I remember, we were engaged in while visiting his parents' home above a shoe shop in Carmarthen. Over the traditional high tea, we started arguing about Lloyd George, and I guess we were showing off a bit too much. During a brief pause, his mother suddenly intervened: 'I never liked that man Lloyd George,' she said. 'Myself, I'm an Asquithian Liberal.'

It was a wonderful throwback to political divisions from a different era. Rod went on to become chief executive of Carmarthenshire County Council, before dying of cancer at a tragically early age.

I shared digs in my second and third year with, among others, Geraint Talfan Davies, who was studying history in the same year as myself and an influential figure I was to come across at various other stages of my journalistic career. Many years later, he admitted that he had found several copies of my essays tucked into the university textbooks which he had kept all those years. I cannot imagine why he had them...

I was particularly friendly at that time with a fellow historian, John Slatford, with whom I went on a number of holidays, not least a fascinating trip hitch-hiking around the west coast of Ireland. A first-class hockey player, he went on to a career in local government, and I still meet up with him and a group of other college friends for the occasional lunch.

As I reached my final year, I increasingly felt that I was missing out on studying modern-day politics as opposed to the politics of the past. I decided to try and postpone the world of work for one more year and landed a place at Southampton University to do a postgraduate degree in international politics. It was a different environment to Oxford, with far more lectures, seminars and coursework than I had been used to. It was different also because I now had an old Ford van, which I had bought from a local garage in Worcestershire (where my parents now lived – my father having become head of King Edward VI Five Ways School in Birmingham), and where I had worked serving petrol for most of the summer. The van was difficult to start, and my exercise on cold winter mornings was to lunge at the starting handle in order to crank up the engine.

The head of the politics department at Southampton was Professor Joseph Frankel, who had encouraged me to join the postgraduate course. Eminent in his field, he seemed somewhat eccentric to the students, and we did not see a great deal of him. Perhaps the most colourful lecturer there was Geoffrey Williams, whose twin brother Alan subsequently became a Labour MP. In fact they looked identical, and Geoffrey used to speculate how easy it would have been for him to get into the Commons chamber and make a speech, because nobody would have known the difference.

Geoffrey was a specialist in defence studies and made a

significant contribution in that field. But he was also something of a Walter Mitty character, and began to style himself as Dr Williams, even though he had never completed his Ph.D. He was eventually shopped by someone who saw him on the BBC *Nine O'Clock News*. The problem went right back to his O levels, when he had failed to pass biology and had therefore failed to acquire the five passes then required to progress further up the academic ladder. By now in his forties, Geoffrey had to go back and study O level biology before he could then go on and acquire a genuine doctorate. The irony was that he was still the best lecturer there.

I enjoyed the more relaxed academic environment at Southampton. I enjoyed the fact that there were far more girls around than in the male-dominated colleges of Oxford, and I enjoyed in particular the beginnings of a long and fruitful friendship with my fellow postgraduate Bruce Reed, whose career took him through journalism to lecturing and consultancy. But this was a hiatus on the road to the real world, and it was time to get a move on.

CHAPTER 8

Veering not backing

IT WAS TO be my introduction to the world of paid employment. At three o'clock on an April afternoon in 1967, I was waiting outside the office of the editor of the *South Wales Echo* in Cardiff. I had decided that I wanted to take up a career in journalism, and this was where I wanted to start – as a trainee journalist with the Thomson Organisation. It was not as if my credentials were particularly relevant. A degree in history from Jesus College, Oxford, a prospective postgraduate degree in international politics, but no particular involvement with student newspapers. This did not amount to a track record that would encourage an editor to believe I was suited to local journalism.

I had conjured up an image of a newspaper editor from films I had seen, but Jack Wiggins did not fit the image at all. A man of rather military bearing, with a greying moustache, he conducted the interview in brisk fashion, and he did not sound impressed by the pompous young graduate sitting in front of him.

'What is the verb you use when the wind is changing direction clockwise round the compass?' he asked.

My mind went blank. Nothing struggled to the surface. He waited.

'Well,' he said, 'the word is veering. So the wind veers from north to east. If it's changing direction east to north, it's backing.'

He had made his point. A university degree was not going

to be adequate preparation for working on a local newspaper. But, to my surprise, I got the job, and it was not long before I had started work at a monthly salary of £84 1s 4d.

There was one decision I had made before I arrived in Cardiff. I was going to stop using my first name, Jonathan, and use my second name instead. I felt that Glyn had a better ring to it. But it was not just that. I was never particularly comfortable with Jonathan, and disliked it being shortened to Johnny. At school, I was frequently nicknamed after the American singer, Johnny Mathis.

I was surprised how easy it was. In a completely new environment, I just introduced myself as Glyn, and that was it. When the training officer at Thomson House, who remembered me from the interview, called me Johnny, my fellow trainees laughed and said my name was Glyn. My family had more difficulty with the change, and my mother in particular carried on calling me Jonathan. But I had no problem with that.

I found myself staying in a lodging house run by three elderly ladies, with a number of lonely-looking men occupying the other rooms. Dinner was at six o'clock sharp, or you missed it. Afterwards they would sit in a circle in the lounge, spending all evening admiring a large ginger tomcat. The sanitaryware had been manufactured by a local firm called Mathias, so I spent the first few weeks of my working life urinating on my own name.

The large newsroom in Thomson House was split between the morning and evening newspapers, the *Western Mail* to one side and the *South Wales Echo* to the other. I shared one of the reporters' desks, which was usually strewn with old newspapers, massive typewriters, half-empty coffee cups and the other detritus of office life which nobody ever seemed to clear. The rest of the room was filled with copytakers, sub-editors and the news desks for both papers. The smell of the newsroom was unforgettable, a smell composed of newsprint, tobacco and a lot of (mostly male) bodies.

A reporter was allocated to show me around the various

parts of the building I needed to know. It was Michael Buerk, who had been working on the paper for a year or so already, and exuded the confidence which was to make him one of the best BBC TV correspondents and, later, newscasters. Among my fellow trainees was Sue Lawley, who, as Mike himself put it later on, was 'just making a pit stop on the racetrack to stardom'. Also on the *Echo* was Alun Michael, with whom I worked quite closely in the local chapel of the National Union of Journalists. He was later to become Secretary of State for Wales and then the first leader in the new Welsh Assembly. Geraint Talfan Davies I had shared lodgings with at college, and he was already propelling himself up the hierarchy at the *Western Mail*, and was to end up as controller of BBC Wales. Also there was the most talented writer of them all, Chris Potter, who tragically died from cancer in his forties while working at *The Sun*.

The 8.30 a.m. start was something of a shock after university days. I would crawl out of bed not much before eight o'clock, put on the nearest clothes, and tear down to the office in my Morris Minor, hoping desperately not to be too late. The *Echo*, still a broadsheet paper, had the largest circulation in Wales, a readership across the city and up into the Valleys. I soon got used to the daily round of court cases, inquests and council meetings. And there were always the calls that came in about breaking stories, a fire or a car crash, or the calls to go down to reception because someone wanted to give a reporter some information.

I drew the short straw one day and found myself going down to talk to a man in a scruffy raincoat who produced a weather-beaten leather pocketbook filled with dense handwriting in green ink.

'There's absolute proof in here,' he said, 'that it's going to happen soon.'

'What's going to happen?'

'The Italians,' he said with absolute conviction. 'They're about to invade Britain.'

The first real story for which I was given the responsibility of reporting on my own came from a series of complaints by people living in Gabalfa, an area just to the north of central Cardiff. A large number of houses had been compulsorily purchased to make way for the new flyover that was to be built there. But the houses had not yet been demolished, and some of them were being used by tramps. I joined the local Labour MP, Ted Rowlands, who had been elected only the previous year. We spent some time listening to the neighbours' grievances, and Ted Rowlands promised to try and get the tramps removed. He got his publicity and I got my first story.

It was seeing the conditions in which so many people lived that shaped my political outlook. Working for a local newspaper meant you saw it day in and day out. If politics was to be about anything, it had to be about improving the lot of those least able to look after themselves. I knew it on the day when I was standing in a terraced house in central Cardiff, listening to the tenant of a private landlord angrily point to a gaping hole in the bedroom ceiling through which pigeons were scrabbling in and out. I knew it standing on the doorstep of a house in Aberfan, the disaster not two years past, and hearing the grief of the bereaved. I could always separate my personal views from my journalistic duty, and it did not stop me coming to my own conclusions.

It was not long before I was sent to Merthyr Tydfil to work as a district reporter. You could still see how Merthyr had once been called the crucible of the industrial revolution. There were still a number of deep coal mines in the area and the Dowlais ironworks were still there. Dominating the town was the big white tip, a mountain of slag from the furnaces of Dowlais (it was removed in the 1970s). It was my own beat, and I was determined to show that I could do it, working through a bad bout of flu on my first week.

The first call was usually to the police station, where I would be presented with a list of incidents over the previous 24 hours. It was usually sheep wandering onto the nearby mountain road and being killed by a passing car. I would call on local union officials, who usually knew which factories were opening or closing or where jobs were on their way in or on their way out. And for a local authority which was so dominated by the Labour Party, the politics was lively. The dissenting minority on the council were mostly to the left of Labour, stalwarts of the old Independent Labour Party, Labour defectors or Communists.

One of the most passionate debates I have ever listened to arose out of a small item on the agenda of a council meeting – the siting of an RAF recruiting van in a council car park. One after the other, councillors rose to argue that public property should not be used to foster support for a military cause. Mostly in their sixties or seventies, these men – from memory, all the councillors were men – were retreading the International Socialist and pacifist arguments of the 1930s. Their passion was in vain; the recruiting van was voted through by a huge majority.

Just down the valley was Aberfan, still overwhelmed by the very recent disaster when coal tips slid down the mountain and on to a junior school, killing 116 children and twenty-eight adults. By 1968, the government in the person of the Secretary of State for Wales, George Thomas, had promised that the Aberfan tips would finally be removed. The small print of that pledge, however, quickly revealed that a substantial part of that cost was to come from the disaster fund which had been built up from voluntary donations intended to help the bereaved and rebuild the community. The veteran local MP, S.O. Davies, described it as 'the meanest thing he had seen in all his thirty-four years in Parliament'. The bitterness of the people I spoke to in the village was obvious. It was as if raw wounds had been rubbed with salt. It was not until 1997 that a different Secretary of State, Ron Davies, restored the money to the fund.

Relaxation in Merthyr usually meant a visit to the Lamb Inn in Castle Street. It became famous through its association with the poet Harri Webb, but had its own strong tradition before then. It was the kind of pub which locked its customers in at closing time and had a colourful cast of characters. My favourite was a young man who admitted to being a Welsh Nationalist, so they promptly nicknamed him 'The Colonel' – on the basis that if he was a nationalist he must be in the Free Wales Army, which was a paramilitary nationalist organisation achieving considerable publicity at the time. A nationalist was then still a rare commodity in Merthyr, but in reality 'The Colonel's' views were moderate. I accompanied him on a visit to the local post office where he demanded the right to have an application for a driving licence in the Welsh language. He was refused, although sympathetically, and it gave me a story.

In the first few weeks of my time in Cardiff, I moved into a house in the Penylan area of Cardiff which I shared with an interesting bunch of other young men, all very different. There were a couple of lecturers, one of them Roy Thomas, teaching economics at the university in Cardiff. Several were fighting their way up the ladder in their respective businesses, including Martin Taylor, who worked for Monsanto. It was a useful antidote to my working life that I was the only journalist. We had a number of parties where we just cleared the front room of all the furniture and pulled up the carpets to create the necessary space. We would come down in the morning to find the lino swimming in beer. We all had professional careers, and it was a very different world from the one I went back to every week in Merthyr.

My next stint was as a sub-editor in the *Echo*'s features department, which was separated from the newsroom by a glass partition. It was, by comparison, drearily quiet, and I became impatient with the work. One of my duties was to prepare the horoscopes for inclusion on the television page, under the heading 'Follow the Stars'. The horoscopes were syndicated a week or so in advance, and I was astonished at how boring, repetitive and badly written they were. So I often tried to improve them, just a bit of sharpening up here and there.

Until I was found out, that is. I often wondered afterwards how many people's lives I might have changed.

One morning, the editor walked into the room and asked me to write a piece about Britain's gold reserves. Jack Wiggins had an unstated interest in such matters. He had been appointed by Jim Callaghan, then Chancellor of the Exchequer and local Cardiff MP, to the Decimal Currency Board – an interesting piece of patronage. Decimalisation did not take place until 1971, but the board had been appointed to supervise the process.

What I knew about the gold reserves could have been written on a postage stamp, and there were only two hours to go to the deadline for the features pages. All I was aware of was that, despite the recent devaluation of the pound forced on Harold Wilson, the balance of payments was weak and the pressure on sterling was still acute, with worries about a drop in the gold reserves. The editor wanted all this explained – in what was now less than two hours. I telephoned my friend Roy Thomas, the only person I knew who was likely to have the answers. Mercifully, he answered the phone and I wrote down just about everything he told me and reproduced it as nearly as I could in the article. By the time I got home, the *Echo* had been on the streets for a couple of hours. I asked Roy what he thought of the piece. He gave me seven out of ten.

I was soon writing about a growing range of subjects. In 1969, under the heading 'Timetable for the gogglebox revolution', I wrote about the imminent arrival of colour television in parts of England and complained that it was not going to reach south Wales until well into the following year. Not long afterwards, in a front-page splash, I warned that the Springbok rugby touring team, due in south Wales that winter, would face anti-apartheid demonstrations. I quoted the leading campaigner, Peter Hain, that this was just the beginning of their campaign against apartheid in sport.

Throughout this time I was gravitating towards writing about politics. It was not a conscious process, just an inbuilt tendency. I was fascinated by the changing face of the Labour Party. The 1966 general election had been the high water mark for Labour's Welsh hegemony, with thirty-two out of the thirty-six seats. But the party was losing its cloth-cap image. It had been the proud boast of the National Union of Mineworkers that they would 'send a man from the coalface to the floor of the House of Commons'. With the closure of pits in every south Wales valley, I noted the decline in the influence of the NUM and the rise of 'the classless intellectual' in the ranks of Welsh Labour MPs. A barrister, Denzil Davies, had just been selected in Llanelli to replace the former Secretary of State for Wales Jim Griffiths, a former miner.

I rang Conservative Central Office to ask what sort of candidates they were looking for in Wales. A press officer rang back with a facetious one-liner. 'We have three kinds of candidates: men, women – and those prepared to stand in Wales.' It was recognition, of a kind, of Labour's dominance.

There was one miners' MP who refused to follow the trend. S.O. Davies, by then eighty-three years old, had represented Merthyr since 1934. He was under pressure from inside his constituency party to stand down, but absolutely refused to budge. To find out more biographical details, I went to interview him at his home in Merthyr. He had total recall of his early life, beginning with going underground at the age of twelve, and talked in such vivid detail about it that I could not move him on to his later political career. I had arrived at his house at two o'clock on a Sunday afternoon, and by six o'clock we had only got as far as 1934. I had to glean the rest from other sources. S.O. seemed to regard himself as the incarnation of the working people in his area, above the machinations of other mortals. When he was eventually deselected, he stood against the Labour Party in the 1970 general election. To most people's surprise, except his own, he won.

Much more serious for the Labour Party – and a harbinger of things to come – had been the victory of Gwynfor Evans for Plaid Cymru in the Carmarthen by-election of July 1966. With a backdrop of protests over the Welsh language, and intermittent bomb explosions in the build-up to the investiture of the Prince of Wales at Caernarfon Castle, I was commissioned to produce a series of articles on the rise of nationalism. I went to see Gwynfor Evans, Plaid's first-ever MP, in the immediate aftermath of an explosion at the Temple of Peace in Cardiff. Over coffee in the Strangers' Cafeteria in the Commons, he was keen to distance his party from the violence which, he felt, was discrediting the nationalist cause. He then made the claim that the bombs were the work of agents provocateurs. 'I suspect,' he said, 'that they may be the agents of Whitehall'.

This was an extraordinary allegation, clearly calculated on his part and, by any standards, it was worth front-page treatment. But the word came down from the editor that it was to stay buried in the feature article. The newspaper management were clearly uncomfortable with such an attack, however outlandish, on the established order, and it passed with scarcely a ripple.

As for myself, I could not get worked up about the investiture, either for or against. For me, it was just a pageant, a bit like the one my father had helped to write and produce at Pembroke Castle a decade earlier. And at that stage, I was sufficiently republican to refuse to stand for 'God Save the Queen' at the end of cinema showings. I regarded, and continue to regard, the royal family as a stage army of curious characters who in a modern age were irrelevant to the body politic. My view chimed exactly with Dafydd Iwan's satirical song of the time:

O Carlo, Carlo, Carlo'n whare polo heddi,
Carlo, Carlo, Carlo'n whare polo gyda dadi,
Ymunwch yn y gân, daeogion fawr a mân,
O'r diwedd mae gyda ni Brins yng Ngwlad y Gân.

[Oh, Carlo (Charles), Carlo, Carlo, he play polo today,
Carlo, Carlo, Carlo, he play polo with daddy.
Join in the song, serfs great and small,
At last we have a Prince in the Land of Song.]

My failure to understand the popular appeal of the monarchy was at times to get me into journalistic trouble.

For George Thomas, the investiture was the high point of his time as Secretary of State for Wales. An ardent anti-devolutionist, he was using the monarchy to make a political statement about the union of the United Kingdom. But his party was, as ever, divided over the issue of devolution, and George Thomas was a divisive figure who exacerbated the rather excitable mood across Wales at the time. But it is worth remembering that George was a popular politician on his own patch. At one dinner of the Cardiff Rhondda Society, he held the floor for the best part of an hour.

'Who's from Maerdy?' he would ask with a rhetorical flourish.

As the hands went up, he would tell a story particular to that village. And he would go down through every village in the Rhondda Fach before doing the same for every village going up the Rhondda Fawr, including his own birthplace of Tonypandy. He could not do the same, however, for Welsh-speaking Wales.

Despite George Thomas, sentiment in the Labour Party was shifting back towards a pro-devolutionist stance, prompted primarily by the nationalist threat. I was soon reporting an announcement by Emrys Jones, secretary to the Welsh Council of Labour, that the party was once again looking at ways of devolving more power to Wales. When it gave evidence to the Crowther Commission (later the Kilbrandon Commission on the Constitution), Labour had renewed its call for an elected council for Wales. By the time the commission reported, I was working for ITN in London.

CHAPTER 9

Information of a secret nature

THE DENNIS FIRE engine was racing along the dual carriageway in Hampshire with its lights flashing. I was enjoying the ride in the cab and the growl of the big Jaguar engine pulling us along. The cameraman, rather more perilously, was hanging onto a ladder on the back of the vehicle, trying to get a shot of the onrushing road with the lights flashing in the foreground. I persuaded the driver to ring the fire engine bell for added effect. Gradually it dawned on us that there was another siren going, and it was closing in on us. A police car flagged us down, and the driver of the fire engine pulled into the side of the road.

'What's the incident you're attending?' asked the police officer. 'We haven't been told of anything.'

We had to explain that we were filming for the BBC, and there wasn't any emergency. The police officer was not amused and ordered us to switch off the emergency warnings. We drove back more sedately to the factory where the fire engines were being built. The manager of the works seemed unconcerned. For him this was an exciting day in his life, a day when his work was recognised on television, a day he would not forget. We filmed the bodywork of the fire engines in various stages of construction, and the manager gave a rather faltering interview. After a couple of hours, we left.

It was about two decades later that I had a telephone call

from the manager's son to say that his father had died and inviting me to attend the funeral. The afternoon I had spent with his father had apparently been an important moment in his life and he had never stopped talking about it. The memory had clearly developed into an imaginary relationship with me of which I, of course, was unaware. It was a salutary lesson in the power of the broadcasting profession which I had now joined.

I had got into broadcasting by a somewhat roundabout route. I had failed to get a job with the BBC in Cardiff, and so decided to head for London. But I made a massive strategic error. I was persuaded that it would be a good start to get a job with the Central Office of Information, the role of which was to provide publicity services for the government. There was a vacancy for a journalist on the COI's European desk, and it sounded interesting. I had visions of reporting European politics, of which I had learned something from my time at university.

The reality was infinitely more prosaic. My job was, for the most part, to rewrite stories from the British newspapers and help compile them into a regular bulletin which British embassies abroad could then feed out to the press in those countries. By the time the material reached any newspaper likely to use it, several days had gone by and it was usually out of date. The bureaucracy was unbelievable. Since most of my work turned out to involve cutting up newspapers, I asked on my second day for a pair of scissors. I was told I would have to go to the administration office at the end of the corridor, and there I had to explain why I needed them.

'Because I have to cut up newspapers,' I said.

'Well, you'll have to fill in this form, and put your reasons in writing.'

It took several days for my scissors to arrive. But if my job was fairly pointless, there were others which were even more so. In a little room next door there was a man with thick pebble glasses whose main job appeared to be to write down in a ledger all those stories which were accompanied by photographs. I never discovered why.

The room was managed by a fearsome lady whose authority was so absolute that grown men would keep their conversations to a whisper so as not to irritate her. Even the plants on the window sills seemed to wilt when she came in. One of the few people there who did not seem cowed in her presence was a young man called John Walton. Together we formed an escape committee, which met every lunchtime in the local pub, the Hercules. I took just over four months to get out. John took a little longer, but also managed to resume a proper journalistic career.

There was an additional reason why I needed to sort out a longer-term move. Earlier in the year I had married Sian Davies, the daughter of a Welsh-speaking Nonconformist minister. She was a RADA-trained actress, who had appeared on a number of well-known programmes, including *Z-Cars*, and was now working at the BBC in Cardiff. We had met at one of the parties in our house, brought by her friend Valmai, who lived just around the corner.

While I was going out with Sian, she had a regular part in *Ryan and Ronnie*, an iconic comedy series produced by BBC Wales. I spent many hours hanging around the set waiting for the rehearsal or recording to finish. The production always seemed to overrun, and I could never understand how such brilliant shows were created out of this apparent chaos. But it gave me a chance to see Ryan Davies in action, one of the best comic actors Wales has produced. But now things were far less glamorous. We were renting a seedy flat on Battersea Rise, where the garden was little more than a rubbish heap with the largest rats I had ever seen. Before we could buy a house, I needed to decide where I was going to be working.

By the end of September 1970, I found myself with two job offers. One was to work in the BBC newsroom at its regional studios in Southampton. The other was the post of leader writer on the *Evening Standard*. For reasons that were not particularly logical, I wanted the job at the BBC. The problem was that I had not quite been offered it. They were, they said, seriously interested in my candidature, but there would be 'some delay' in reaching a final decision. I stalled the *Evening Standard* as long as I could, but then in desperation, rang the BBC to find out what was going on. What I learned was that, before being accepted by the BBC, I had to be positively vetted by the security services. In other words, MI5 had to decide whether or not I was a security risk. I pointed out that I had already been vetted for the job at the COI.

'Quite,' came the reply, 'so it shouldn't be a problem.'

I gambled on this information, turning down the job in Fleet Street. In reality, it was a laughable idea that I could have been a security risk at either the COI or the BBC. What information could I have possibly passed to a foreign power – the wilting flowers on the COI window sill or the quality of the food in the BBC cafeteria? More seriously, it was scandalous that the government's security services should have the final say over the appointment of a BBC journalist. I had, in addition, to sign a declaration under the Official Secrets Act:

> If any person having in his possession or control any note, document, or information of a secret nature which he has obtained, or has had access to, owing to his position as an employee of the BBC, communicates such note, document or information to any person other than the person who is authorised to communicate it... that person is guilty of a misdemeanour...

Such 'misdemeanours' were, of course, a stock-in-trade of journalistic life, and the Official Secrets Act had no practical relevance and indeed no ethical relevance, to working as a journalist for the BBC. It was some years later that it became publicly known that such vetting was taking place, and the outcry that ensued put an end to the use of the Official Secrets Act at the BBC.

I knew Southampton well from the postgraduate year I had

spent there at the university. It was a quiet, unexciting city, but with the coast and the New Forest close by, it was a pleasant place to live. We bought a house in Bitterne on the side of the hill looking across the city. It was small, up a steep drive, but detached, and it cost, unbelievably, just £6,000. You had to cross the river Itchen to reach the city centre, and my favourite route was by the floating bridge, long since replaced.

The BBC offices in Southampton were located in the former Cunard building, just a stone's throw from the waterfront. Indeed, the office car park was on the old railway station platform, with nothing to stop you driving over the edge. The whole area was a bit run-down, although a new Berni Inn had just opened on the other side of the road. The menu of prawn cocktail, overdone steak and Black Forest gateau now epitomises the early 1970s, but we were grateful for it at the time because there was little else on offer.

My job as a news assistant was very much back-room stuff, putting news bulletins together and producing items for the regional programme, *South Today*. One of the main problems was that we covered such an amorphous area, from Bournemouth to Brighton and beyond. Defining what was news and what was not news was a more difficult task than in an area like south Wales with much more of an identity. It was a daily struggle to create news bulletins which did not consist entirely of road accidents, murders and court cases.

The programme was still in black and white and the technical resources were primitive by modern comparisons. But I did learn the basics of television production, if sometimes the hard way. One day, in an increasingly desperate attempt to fill the programme, I invited a group of schoolgirls to perform a song and dance number for which they had won some prize. They were already in the studio when the programme director, with a look of panic on his face, said that of course I should have known that the studio did not have the facilities for them to sing and dance at the same time. So the children quickly had to learn the art of miming to their previously recorded song.

I was able to pick up a few other tips along the way. The presenter of *South Today* was Bruce Parker, a past master at interviewing on any subject at a moment's notice. One day I asked him how he did it.

'Well,' he said. 'There are only really four questions... *How? Why? Just how serious is it?* and *What happens next?* All interviews are a variation on the same questions.'

A frequent task was to organise items for programmes in London, and I soon learned the metropolitan disdain for the geography of the rest of the country. I was trying to arrange for the dispatch of some film from the Isle of Wight. The man from network centre told me to organise a bike, a despatch rider, to collect it. I had to point out there was a rather large stretch of sea in the way.

The worst job of all was to be allocated the task of finding interesting items for *Nationwide*, the programme which purported to reflect the different regions of Britain. Whatever madcap theme the producers in London had picked on, we had to try and find an example in the south. It was usually a downward chase to the most ludicrous idea, and that shift usually ended in despair at the nature of our trade.

By this time, the family had grown with the birth of our son, Mathew. And we had an enjoyable circle of friends, including Martin Taylor, who had moved from Cardiff with his wife Eve and family to live on the edge of the New Forest. Life here could have been comfortable enough, but it was slowly dawning on me that I had a major domestic issue to contend with.

I had not realised when I married Sian that she had a drinking problem. I may have been particularly innocent about it, but as an actress she was exceedingly good at disguising the symptoms. At our home in Southampton, it became substantially worse – perhaps because of the tedium of looking after a child at home. I had a panicky phone call from her one day just before I was due to read a lunchtime radio bulletin. Unsure of the problem, I raced home after the bulletin was over and found her passed out on the sofa with one-year-old Mathew running around the room unsupervised.

It did not take much ingenuity to discover how bad it had become. Strange patterns of behaviour in the bathroom led me to investigate. Unscrewing the panels around the bath revealed a cache of several dozen wine bottles. Other cupboards revealed many more. Thanks to a stupidly compliant bank manager, she had been running up a huge overdraft. Very few knew about her drinking or its causes. There were the insecurities of her acting career, but it was more than that. Underneath a sophisticated exterior there was a constant sense of fear and guilt about her parents, instilled by her mother – an emotion she never really outgrew.

There had to be a break-point, if only for Mathew's safety. The legal advice I had received was clear that I had few grounds to take Mathew with me if I left, but that is what I threatened. Amazingly it worked. Sian accepted she had a problem, agreed to go for treatment and remained free of drink for a decade. Gradually life returned to a more normal pattern, except that Sian's health remained poor.

*

The BBC newsroom in the old Cunard building was a friendly place, where Mike Buerk soon joined us from HTV at Bristol. In fact, Mike stayed with Sian and myself at our house in Bitterne for several weeks while he and his wife, Chris, moved house.

On a rare occasion when I was allowed out of the newsroom, I accompanied Mike on a reporting assignment which I had arranged. It was an unexciting story about a caravan site, but I learned what a single-minded operator he could be. In those days, the film had to be processed before it could be edited, and the less time it took 'in the soup', the quicker you would be. So it paid to keep down the amount of film you shot. Mike knew exactly what answers he wanted from the man who ran the caravan site, but he knew he had to soften him up a bit first. He held a handkerchief behind his back and told the cameraman to start filming only when he dropped it. He got the answers he needed in the can, while saving several minutes of film.

For me, the BBC newsroom in Southampton was always going to be just another stop on the way to reporting politics, and my chance came in a peculiar way. Somebody in the newsroom had a spare invitation to a press lunch on the QE2, at that time docked not far from the BBC offices. So I went along, and sitting opposite me at this rather plush event was the industrial correspondent from Southern Television, the ITV station covering the south of England. We got to discussing jobs we would like to do, and he mentioned that ITN was looking for a political correspondent. I rang the next day to find out more, and before long I was walking up Wells Street in London for an interview with ITN's distinguished-looking editor, Nigel Ryan.

I heard nothing for weeks, and had indeed given up hope of joining ITN. I was on the verge of accepting a secondment to the BBC's radio newsroom in London when I received another letter inviting me to meet the then deputy editor, David Nicholas, 'to talk further about the possibility of an opening'. When in May 1973 I became an employee of ITN, it was with some trepidation, wondering how long I would last. I was to work for the company for twenty-one years.

CHAPTER 10

Sources at the highest level

THERE MUST HAVE been hundreds of people in the cavernous Labour Club on Merseyside. The noise was overwhelming, including, somewhere through the smoky atmosphere, a game of bingo being called. As we set up the cameras, the main question in my mind was how Harold Wilson was going to get the attention of this audience for what he had to say.

For the Prime Minister had chosen to make a controversial speech in the Labour Club in his own constituency of Huyton. It was early January 1975, and, although Wilson had settled the miners' strike and won the second general election the previous year, the economic omens were not good. Inflation was rising fast, and despite the new Labour government's so-called social contract with the trade unions, there was a worrying increase in industrial unrest. The main public focus was on the car industry, and in particular on British Leyland, which the government had recently rescued with a substantial amount of public money.

The Labour Club chairman did manage to silence the hubbub as the Prime Minister walked onto the stage. And the audience listened politely, if rather impatiently, as Wilson defended the public investment in British Leyland. But he then went on to say that the government could not justify 'the subsidising of large factories, involving thousands of jobs, which could pay their way but are failing to do so because of manifestly avoidable stoppages of production'.

It was that phrase, 'manifestly avoidable stoppages', which was constantly repeated in the media as first the Cowley engine tuners and then others went out on strike. I said in my report that Wilson 'was clearly expecting a greater degree of restraint from the workforce', but there was little evidence that the speech had any effect, except to anger the left.

Outside the Labour Club, ITN had set up an outside broadcast unit in order to send the pictures directly back to London. It was to be the main story on that night's *News at Ten*. The lights of the OB had attracted a large crowd, and there were a lot of children shouting and wheeling around on their bicycles. It was a difficult backdrop against which to do my 'piece to camera', and I could barely hear myself speak. But worse was to come. The OB had failed to establish a link with London, and it looked as if we would fail to get the story on air. We piled into two cars, and drove hell-for-leather to the Granada studios in Manchester. It was ten minutes to ten when the story was fed from Manchester, and the usual miracle was performed by the videotape editors in London to turn it round in time to go out as the lead item at ten o'clock.

In the following years, a group of academics from Glasgow University published a series of books criticising what they saw as the bias of television news against trade unions and working people more generally. They studied a lot of TV news output during the early part of 1975 and concluded that television 'laid the blame for society's industrial and economic problems at the door of the workforce'. And to my surprise, my report of the speech by Harold Wilson was a prime exhibit in the evidence for the prosecution. In *Really Bad News* (1982), they argued that bad management and under-investment were the real problems in British industry, especially in British Leyland, and that I, among others, had deliberately distorted Wilson's speech to make it an attack on the workforce.

This was wonderfully innocent, other-worldly stuff, but

in the mood of the times it was a critique which achieved considerable currency. Whatever the merits of their analysis of the British car industry, what I had to assess was Wilson's intention when he made the speech, and the context in which he was making it. Another academic, Martin Harrison, provided a more common-sense view after wading through ITN's archives. 'Whether or not Wilson's criticisms were well-founded, ITN seems to have read him correctly.'

Just a month later, I was given my first foreign assignment, to accompany the Prime Minister and his Foreign Secretary, James Callaghan, to Moscow. Although there was an increasing détente between the Soviet Union and the West, Anglo-Soviet relations had been made frostier by the expulsion in 1971 of 101 Soviet personnel from Britain on the grounds that they were spies. This was to be the first meeting between a British prime minister and the Communist leader, Leonid Brezhnev, since that event.

It was unbelievably cold in Red Square on that February morning, and the fur hat and wool-lined overcoat specially hired from Moss Bros provided little protection. I had flown out a couple of days early to do a report setting the scene for the visit, and we were using a local Russian crew, who were accompanied by an interpreter. I stood in front of the Kremlin to do a piece to camera which, referring to the background to the visit, mentioned the expulsion of the alleged Soviet spies in 1971. Nobody looks credible on camera wearing a large fur hat, so I took it off for the duration and quickly rammed it back on when I had finished. My main concern was that my chin was frozen and I worried that I was slurring my speech as if I was drunk.

The story was to be shipped back to London by the Russian news agency, Novosti. We handed the film into them and tried to find some lunch, never an easy prospect in Moscow in those days. I was lucky that Bob Southgate, an experienced ITN reporter who spoke some Russian, had been in Moscow reporting other events and was staying on for a couple of days to help me out. For when we got back to the Novosti office, we discovered that my report had not been shipped.

After quite a bit of shouting and banging on desks, we found out what had happened. The interpreter who had accompanied the crew had also been there as a minder to check on what we were up to. She had reported back to the agency that I had referred to the 'spies' thrown out of Britain four years previously. The director of Novosti shouted at us that they had not been spies and we should not say that they were. No amount of remonstration would persuade him to lift his block on the shipment. We later learned that he himself had been one of the 101 people Britain had accused of spying and had been thrown out of the country.

We had been censored. ITN had been censored. But it was not just an embarrassment for us, it was a potential embarrassment for Harold Wilson. If ITN was to say on air that its report from Moscow had been censored, it could serve to sour the atmosphere for his visit. Telephone calls to London took a long time to get through and telex messages were the usual form of communication. Eventually it was decided not to go public: apart from anything else, it would also hamper ITN's attempts to establish a reporting base in Moscow. No mention would be made of what had happened.

My assignment was not going well, and it did not improve. The next day I received a telex from the foreign desk of the kind which every reporter dreads: WHY NO STORY QUEEN TO VISIT RUSSIA?

My heart sank. What was this about? Where had this come from? The *Daily Mail* and the *Daily Mirror* had run a front-page piece predicting that one outcome of the visit would be a royal visit to Moscow. I could not check this out with the Prime Minister's press secretary Joe Haines because he was still en route with Harold Wilson. So I went on the hunt for the *Mail* and *Mirror* correspondents to see if I could pump them.

Gordon Greig of the *Daily Mail* was a shrewd operator, already well-established as a correspondent at Westminster. I found him having a very late breakfast in the massive Rossiya hotel where we were all staying. I explained that I was being chased on the story he had sent – where had it come from? Tapping the side of his nose, he said:

'Sources at the highest level, old boy, the highest level.'

Eventually, the tale unravelled. They had been having dinner the previous night in the Rossiya hotel with the Moscow correspondent of the BBC World Service, Anatoly Goldberg, in order to collect some background colour and analysis. During that conversation, the possibility of the Queen visiting the Soviet Union had come up, and the *Mail* and *Mirror* guys had decided to go with it. Anatoly Goldberg was a highly respected commentator on the Soviet Union, but he was hardly a source at the highest level. Then it dawned on me: the restaurant in the Rossiya hotel was on the twenty-third floor.

Of course, if you were prepared to wait for two decades, the story ended up being true.

The main outcome of the visit was a trade agreement, which Wilson signed with the Soviet Premier, Kosygin. I interviewed him in the British Embassy, in the part of the building which it was claimed the Russians could not bug. He was curiously uncertain in his manner, ostentatiously lighting his pipe in the middle of speaking. At one point, I had to prompt him with the name of an organisation he was trying to remember. Much later, I wondered if this was an early symptom of the mental deterioration, thought to have been caused by the onset of Alzheimer's disease, which was one of the factors in his resignation from office the following year.

On the last day of his stay in Moscow, Harold Wilson was to make a television address to the Russian people, the first time a British prime minister had been accorded such an honour. The British press corps had been banned from attending this event, although banned by whom was never clear. But we suddenly got a call from the front door of the hotel to say that our car was waiting for us. Someone had failed to tell Intourist, the agency looking after out travel arrangements, that we were off the list. So the ITN and BBC teams, together with a couple of photographers, scrambled into action and climbed into the Zil saloons that were parked outside. In no time, we were an official motorcade, using studded tyres to speed down the middle of the snow-covered road. But the impression of official status was abruptly broken. When we arrived at the Russian television station, the doors were locked and we were left standing outside in the falling snow.

Gradually, it dawned on the officials in the television station that it was going to be more embarrassing to leave us out in the snow than it would be to let us in. The next line of defence for them was to insist that our film cameras would be so noisy they would interfere with Wilson's broadcast. But when it became clear that the studio was already full of Russian cameramen with equipment that sounded like dentist's drills, they gave in. We were there in time to see Wilson enter the studio, followed two paces behind by Joe Haines carrying the Prime Minister's pipe reverentially in front of him, and make his appeal for greater understanding between the peoples of the two countries.

Wilson's greatest achievement in this period was undoubtedly the way he kept his government and the Labour Party in one piece over the issue of Britain's membership of the Common Market. Labour's election manifesto had promised a referendum after what was described as a renegotiation of the terms agreed by the Heath government when Britain had joined the European Community two years previously. This was something which could have split the Labour movement. The bulk of the membership, especially the left, was against British entry, backing the referendum because they thought that would lead to pulling out. Wilson managed to use the referendum to confirm and legitimise the decision to go in.

It was a masterpiece of party management, but the Wilsonian techniques were difficult for a television reporter to convey. He made speeches full of obscurities and equivocation, leaving the media, with the help of some briefing, to interpret what he meant. And it was the first occasion I can remember when a cabinet was absolved from the usual principle of collective responsibility. There was an agreement to differ on the issue of the Common Market, but I do not think even Wilson anticipated the vigour, even hostility, with which the likes of Tony Benn and Barbara Castle contended with Roy Jenkins and Shirley Williams.

For the live results programme in June 1975, I was detailed to interview Roy Jenkins, who had led the Yes campaign from the Labour side. In retrospect, it was slightly odd that it was he rather than Wilson or Callaghan, the Foreign Secretary, who gave the 'victory' interview as news came in of the defeat of the No campaign by a margin of two-to-one. I was given three minutes for the interview, and Jenkins timed his peroration to the second. But his eloquence prompted an instruction from the programme director, Diana Edwards Jones, to add another minute. Afterwards, Roy Jenkins could not hide his irritation that his peroration had been spoilt.

The day that Wilson resigned caught me, like everybody else, on the hop. For some reason, I was at ITN's office in Wells Street that morning when I had a call from Anne Lingley, who ran our Westminster desk. I could not believe what she was telling me, and she had to tell me several times. An announcement was due imminently from Downing Street that the Prime Minister was resigning that day. Prime ministers did not resign out of the blue like that. It was unheard of. I went to find Barry Sales, the producer of the lunchtime programme, then called *First Report*. He afterwards described me as running around like a headless chicken. I thought he was going to have a heart attack.

It was a resignation which prompted all sorts of conspiracy theories, but in fact Wilson had been planning it for some time, and was probably worried about his health. He was, by all accounts, tired of the problems of office and the economic problems in particular were mounting. He had just suffered a defeat in the Commons, when dozens of members of the left-wing Tribune group had abstained over planned cuts in public expenditure. I remember watching the Chancellor Denis Healey standing in front of the benches where the left-wingers were ostentatiously sitting out the vote. He was shouting obscenities at them, a fact which did not help him in his subsequent bid for the leadership.

Wilson gave a press conference in the afternoon, and I was detailed to shadow him for the rest of the day. He had arranged to stay at a friend's house in north London. He was a surprisingly considerate man and he could see the handful of journalists standing around in the gathering dark. It was arranged that he would come to the door and make a brief statement. He was pale, and looked unshaven, which I had failed to notice earlier in the day. As he uttered his last words before disappearing from public view, all I could remember was the white stubble on his chin.

CHAPTER 11

A swell job

THE PRESS GALLERY in the House of Commons does not just consist of the press seats overlooking the Commons chamber. It also comprises a warren of rooms where the journalists work, which you reach by a lift from New Palace Yard. Access to our room was via the Press Bar, which, in those more leisurely days, was already open by the middle of the morning and filling up with the evening newspaper correspondents who by then had done much of their work. The ITN desk was located in a room shared with a number of other newspaper organisations, not least the *Sunday Times*.

The man from the *Sunday Times* was Jimmy Margach, doyen of the Westminster correspondents, who correctly predicted the date of the election in February 1974. James Margach had arrived at Westminster when Ramsay MacDonald was Prime Minister. Margach had met MacDonald as a cub reporter working in the north-east of Scotland, and, so the story went, on Margach's first day in the gallery MacDonald looked up from the government benches and winked at him. Other reporters demanded to know how a young journalist on his first day in the Commons could know the Prime Minister so well.

Jimmy Margach was rarely seen at his desk. He would pass by occasionally, pause to say, 'You're doing a swell job', and genially wave his arm before disappearing once again.

But there were other journalists of lesser distinction. One of them was notorious for winning a journalism prize after correctly forecasting that there would be a tax on children's sweets in Selwyn Lloyd's budget of 1962. He had allegedly been rummaging through the wastepaper bins of journalistic rivals and rewritten somebody else's discarded 'copy'.

There was a distinction between gallery reporters and members of the Parliamentary Lobby, although it was a distinction which became increasingly blurred. The prime job of a gallery reporter, usually equipped with shorthand of 200 words a minute, was to record the proceedings in the chamber. Membership of the lobby gave you access to briefings, not least by the prime minister's press secretary, and, rather more importantly, access to the Members' Lobby directly outside the door to the Commons chamber. Here you could talk to MPs, and ministers if you were lucky, and I would spend whatever spare time I had loitering there in the hope of picking up a story. There were a lot of rules about what you could and could not do, such as not taking notes in the Members' Lobby and never, never running. But the most important rule of all was that every conversation was automatically off the record. In other words, you could not admit to the source of the information you were about to report.

Many, many years later, I was in conversation with Lord Dafydd Elis-Thomas, who had arrived in the Commons as a new MP in the February election of 1974. I had done him a kindness, he said, when he was learning the ropes, by explaining to him the mysteries of the Parliamentary Lobby.

I began my time at ITN working as regional correspondent, serving those ITV companies which were not represented at Westminster. It was a mind-fracturing job trying to balance the demands of so many different regional programmes and remember what might be newsworthy in so many different parts of the country. I did learn some early lessons. I was lining up to do a live piece into Ulster TV from ITN's studio in the Norman Shaw building across the road from the Commons. I rehearsed what I was going to say, doing it at double speed to save time, while combing my hair. The director in Belfast came back to me, complaining that I had done my piece too quickly.

He had apparently panicked when he saw me talking on screen and cut to me prematurely. The rehearsal had become the performance. I never did that again.

One of the biggest strokes of luck in my career gave me early release from the regional job. One of the ITN political correspondents, Richard Wakely, decided to leave to join the civil service. I could not imagine what had induced him to abandon the job which I most coveted, but I was exceedingly grateful to him. By early 1974, I was working for the ITN bulletins, including *News at Ten*. I was a part of the team at Westminster, run by the political editor, Julian Haviland, a gentlemanly character who could charm information out of the most recalcitrant backbencher. The other correspondent was a tough and experienced Scottish reporter, David Rose. Backbone of the team was Anne Lingley, who ran the ITN desk in the Commons for more than three decades. I had helped to appoint her, and it was the best appointment I was ever to make.

The family moved from Southampton to Ashtead in Surrey, but only after a major hiccup. One feature of the 'Barber boom', the Heath government's dash for growth, was a property boom which caused soaring house prices. Then, suddenly, 1973 saw one of the fastest-ever collapses in the property market. One day you were being asked to put up 100 per cent of the purchase price for a new house in order to secure it – in other words, to buy before you sold. The next day, you could not sell a house for love or money. I was caught in the middle, owning two houses for more than six months and having to pay out for a bridging loan. It made my start at ITN immensely uncomfortable financially, and I was grateful to my sister Mary for helping me out.

That was not the only challenge at that time. The new job at Westminster meant I had to learn a whole new independent way of working very quickly and, while Sian was undergoing treatment, Mathew was being looked after by my parents in Brecon, and I for a while was still commuting from

Southampton. It was inevitably a strain, and that is when I first began to suffer from a skin disease called psoriasis, which, in varying degrees and at varying times, has spread around my body. It was rarely visible on my face, and so few people knew about it. It could at times be little more than a minor irritation. At other times, it could cause considerable discomfort, bleeding and infection. The white skin flakes would sometimes fall from my scalp on to my shoulders, and considerate colleagues would brush them away in the belief that it was dandruff.

When the disease was first diagnosed in those early years at ITN, the consultant asked if I wanted the good news or the bad news. 'The good news is that it won't kill you,' he said. 'The bad news is that there is no cure.'

Ashtead was a comfortable suburban environment in which to bring up a family, close to the Surrey countryside. After the twelve-hour working days during the week, it took half a day to recover and there was plenty of time for walks around Headley Heath or Boxhill, or visits to the south coast at the weekend. We had friendly neighbours in Ken and Ann Donlan, our family life appeared much more stable, and our daughter Megan was born the following year in Epsom hospital.

Megan was to prove a surprisingly different character from her brother. Four years behind him, she was nevertheless determined to catch up with him as fast as she could. This degree of competitiveness led to some considerable argument at times, which it took the judgement of Solomon to adjudicate upon. Megan turned out to be intellectually competitive as well, doing well at school and she acquired a ready understanding of the world around her.

*

The first day I sat in the gallery for Prime Minister's Questions, I was struck by how small and crowded the chamber below me seemed to be. Small, and very noisy. It was the occasion when Ted Heath attacked Tiny Rowland and Lonrho as the 'unpleasant and unacceptable face of capitalism'. As the new boy, I was not in a good seat and struggled to hear what the Prime Minister was saying. It was comforting afterwards to see more experienced reporters checking the accuracy of their notes with each other.

Ted Heath was, in my view, a notably unsuccessful prime minister. His achievements, mainly securing Britain's admission to the Common Market, were outweighed by what everyone remembers him for: the collapse of his statutory incomes policy, the battle with the miners, rota power cuts and the three-day week. As an interviewee on television, Heath was wooden, giving long, stilted answers. I was lucky to get in more than two or three questions in a four-minute interview. His decision to call the election in February 1974 on the issue of 'Who governs Britain?' was a serious error of judgement. The people's answer was straightforward: 'Not you, Mr Heath.'

By the time he had lost the second general election in 1974, Heath had won only one of the four elections he had fought as party leader. Despite his grim determination to hang on, the majority of his Conservative MPs were fed up with him. The focal point of the attempts to get him out was Edward du Cann, chairman of the backbench 1922 Committee. Du Cann was an urbane, even oleaginous, character typified by the apochryphal story of the man who, when asked the time, would reply: 'What time would you like it to be?' A group of correspondents were invited to lunch at du Cann's Keyser Ullman bank at Milk Street in the City (hence the nickname 'Milk Street Mafia' for those alleged to be plotting against Heath).

I do not suppose I would be surprised now, but I was staggered then at the opulence of the executive dining room at Keyser Ullman – the number of flunkeys in attendance, the silver cutlery and the elaborate glass table. It was another world, not the world of work as I had always understood it to be. In retrospect, I think du Cann was softening us up for his own bid for the leadership. Although he never declared himself as a candidate, it was agreed that ITN could film a profile of him, including some 'at home' scenes in his country house in Somerset. There was one caveat: we were not to give any information which would reveal its location. When we got there, the caveat was understandable. It was an exquisite fifteenth-century manor house, complete with original frescoes in the hall, its own chapel and a moat around it. Perhaps advisedly, du Cann pulled out of the leadership contest, although I doubt whether he had any inkling of the big financial losses he was later to suffer at Keyser Ullman and his subsequent bankruptcy.

When the contest took place, there were only two candidates bidding to wrest the leadership from Heath. Hugh Fraser, the former husband of Antonia Fraser, was expected to pick up only a handful of votes from the right of the party. Margaret Thatcher, who had been a relatively junior member of Heath's cabinet, was regarded as too inexperienced to be a credible challenger. Nobody expected Heath to lose. The most that was expected was that Mrs Thatcher would pick up enough votes to force a second ballot. Her campaign manager, Airey Neave (later killed by an IRA bomb), was deliberately enigmatic whenever I asked for an indication of how it was going.

When the result of the first ballot was read out to political correspondents, there was a collective intake of breath and gasps of surprise. Thatcher had come top of the poll with 130 votes to Heath's 119, and Heath had no option but to resign. Many Conservative MPs had not wanted Thatcher as leader, they just wanted to get rid of Heath, and Airey Neave had skilfully underplayed the amount of support she was getting. But now that she had beaten Heath in the first round, she was unstoppable. Willie Whitelaw, who many had seen as Heath's natural successor but had felt bound by loyalty to his leader, now put his hat in the ring, but it was too late. Something totally unexpected had happened. The Conservatives had a woman as their leader.

For a brief period, there was relative harmony between

Heath and his successor, as Mrs Thatcher was obliged to follow party policy and support the Yes campaign in the referendum on the Common Market. I still relish the memory of the film footage showing Mrs Thatcher wearing a T-shirt saying 'Yes to Europe' with a smile on her face. But Heath remained unreconciled to losing the leadership and became increasingly bitter towards the woman whom he saw as having usurped his position. My own experience of this came at the occasional dinner which he held at party conference time for lobby correspondents. He would sit quietly at one end of the table and listen while we told stories which put Mrs Thatcher in a bad light. The ruder we were about her, the more he would laugh, his shoulders heaving up and down.

The Liberals, meanwhile, were suffering from the effects of one of the biggest political scandals of the century. Rumours and allegations were circulating about an alleged homosexual affair between the party leader, Jeremy Thorpe, and a younger man called Norman Scott. By 1975, Scott was repeating his claims about an affair with Thorpe in the early 1960s to anyone who would listen, and was soon to make them in a court hearing, which meant the press could report them. But worse was to come: accusations of a conspiracy by friends of Thorpe to silence Scott by hiring an assassin to kill him. The would-be assassin was paid £5,000, but, deliberately or not, only succeeded in shooting Scott's dog, Rinka. Thorpe emphatically denied the claims, even though more and more evidence was coming out. ITN managed to get its hands on some tape recordings of conversations between some of the conspirators and track how some of the payments were made. But, to the increasing discomfort of his MPs, Thorpe was refusing to resign the leadership.

One man who made the most of this situation was Cyril Smith, who at that time was chief whip. 'Big Cyril' was a popular character and a well-known public face, if only because of his sheer size and weight, which rose at one point to twenty-nine stone. Cyril loved dropping hints about how they were going to get Thorpe out, and I had at least one long, live interview with him on *News at Ten*, where we fenced over what was going to happen. At one Liberal conference, I was so keen to get an interview with Cyril that I agreed to meet him in his hotel bedroom – it *was* nine o'clock in the morning. Big Cyril was sitting on the side of the bed, struggling in vain to reach over his stomach to put his socks on. He must have succeeded eventually, because I made a particular note of his socks later in the day.

In May 1976, the *Sunday Times* published letters which Thorpe had written to Scott, one of which ended with the line 'Bunnies can and will go to France'. Thorpe still denied everything, including having any sexual relationship with Scott. But it had all gone too far, even for Thorpe's friends. He resigned the following day. The scandal, however, had several rounds to go. When the would-be assassin, Andrew Newton, was released from prison eighteen months later, he sold his story to the *Evening Standard*, which ran the headline: 'I was paid £5,000 to kill Norman Scott.' Thorpe decided to respond by holding a press conference.

The press conference was completely surreal. It was to be staged in the library of the National Liberal Club. Unfortunately, the club had been having its own problems: the club treasurer had sold off most of the books (and, allegedly, most of the contents of its cellars) before himself disappearing. So this large and gloomy room, lit only by a couple of feeble light bulbs, was lined with empty bookcases. All the seats were taken, the suppressed excitement almost tangible as we waited to hear how Thorpe was going to get out it of this time. Eventually, Thorpe arrived in front of us, accompanied by his close friend Clement Freud and a man none of us recognised. Thorpe read out a statement, again denying all knowledge of any murder plot or having any sexual relationship with Scott.

The BBC had sent one of the hard men of TV reporting, Keith Graves, to put a question. I was wondering what he was doing in the front row and I was about to find out.

'The whole of this hinges on your private life. It is necessary to ask you if you have ever had a homosexual relationship?'

The man we did not recognise leapt to his feet.

'My client will not answer that question,' he said.

Homosexual liaisons were no longer a criminal offence, but the press conference had opened up more questions than it had closed down. It was downhill all the way for Thorpe thereafter and he was soon to be charged with conspiracy and incitement to murder. The trial was delayed until after the 1979 election and I was on holiday in Wales when news came through of the verdict. After the long, slow unwinding of the scandal, Thorpe was acquitted.

There were those who longed for the headier days of Liberalism, when the party was actually in power. The contrast between then and now was shown in stark relief for me when I covered the election battle in the Caernarfon constituency in February 1974. I was in the Liberal club in the town trying to arrange coverage of the party's campaign. The agent asked me if I would like to go into the inner office to meet Lady Olwen. The tone of voice implied it was not a suggestion I was expected to refuse.

Lady Olwen Carey Evans was an imposing woman, the last surviving daughter of Lloyd George, who had, of course, represented Caernarfon for fifty years. What she was most concerned to do was impress on me the merits of the Liberal candidate, a Welsh-speaking barrister from London.

'Oh, he does so remind me of L.G.,' she said.

Unfortunately, his electoral performance did not remind anyone of Lloyd George. He came in a distant fourth, even behind a young Conservative candidate called Tristan Garel Jones – later a minister in Mrs Thatcher's government. It turned out to be difficult arranging the filming of Garel Jones' campaign, as he did not seem to have one. He spoke fluent Welsh, but that was not the problem. He had no campaign events lined up which we could cover. Because I had bought a picture by Kyffin Williams of a chapel which at the time I thought was in the quarry workers' village of Caesarea in Snowdonia, I suggested we went there.

'I'm not going to that *twll* (hole)', he said.

Eventually, in desperation, I filmed him speaking through a megaphone somewhere near Llanberis, warning a hillside of sheep, bilingually, of the dangers of a Labour government.

The victor in that election was Plaid Cymru, whose candidate, Dafydd Wigley, ousted Labour. With Dafydd Elis-Thomas and Gwynfor Evans (when he won back Carmarthen in the October election), Plaid now had three representatives at Westminster. The Scottish Nationalists had done even better, winning eleven seats in the October, and they soon made their presence felt. There was suddenly a greater demand for news coverage of Scotland, and I found myself at a Scottish National Party conference in Elgin. The debates resonated with assertions that the oil in the North Sea was Scotland's oil, and if that was recognised it would be a wealthy country. It was heady stuff, but what I also remember was a journey in a car that was so full that Margo Macdonald ended up sitting on my lap.

The Labour government under James Callaghan was now committed to bringing in devolution for both Scotland and Wales, and although the plans for a Scottish Parliament were very different from the proposed Assembly for Wales, the government had decided on a combined Scotland and Wales bill. Despite the best efforts of the Leader of the House, Michael Foot, the bill's progress was slow. An attempt to speed it up led to disaster. In February 1977, the government tried to guillotine the bill. From the soundings I had taken, it looked as if the vote was going to be close – a vote which was going to happen while *News at Ten* was live on air.

I nervously prepared three alternative scripts: a narrow win for the government, a narrow defeat and a tie, which would mean the Speaker giving the casting vote. The result, however, was a resounding defeat for the government by twenty-nine votes. I raced downstairs to the outside broadcast unit on College Green, throwing the scripts away, and ad-libbed my report into the programme. This was before the Commons proceedings were broadcast, and I had not had time to ring the news desk. The scale of the defeat was unexpected, and I was told there was a collective holding of breath until the result was confirmed in a wire report from the Press Association.

Separate Scotland and Wales bills were now introduced, but devolution was to continue to dog the Callaghan government and contribute significantly to its demise.

Chapter 12

The black underwear of power

A FEW WEEKS before Harold Wilson left office, George Brown resigned. He had resigned, or attempted to resign, many times before, but this time he was resigning from the Labour Party. In Wilson's previous administration, he had been a colourful and turbulent figure, eventually quitting as Foreign Secretary in a blazing row with Wilson in the middle of a financial crisis. He was now quitting Labour altogether, citing as his reason some trade union legislation the government was putting through Parliament.

All the media wanted an interview, because George Brown was still prominent in the public mind, and there would be the opportunity to extract a few choice quotes about the government. The problem was that he had gone to ground and nobody could find him. ITN optimistically set up the outside broadcast unit as close to St Stephen's entrance as they could manage, and my colleague Julian Haviland went to search for him. My job was to wait by the OB in the unlikely eventuality that Brown would appear of his own accord. It was a long wait, and by this time it was the middle of the evening. It was cold and dark. But eventually we saw Julian emerging and, yes, he had George Brown in tow. He had apparently found him hiding in one of the several bars in the House of Lords. As we half-expected, given his reputation, he did not look exactly sober.

The OB sprung into action, the lights went on, and Julian duly carried out the interview. Job done, we thought.

But just as Julian was escorting him back across the road, George Brown tripped on the edge of the pavement and collapsed into the gutter. Suddenly, the darkness exploded with flashlights. I had not realised that so many press photographers were there, but they had leapt into action with amazing speed. Julian and I sprang forward to pick Brown up, and he made a rapid return to the sanctuary of Parliament. He issued a statement blaming his fall on a new pair of spectacles he was wearing.

ITN decided not to use any of the interview with Brown on that night's *News at Ten*. He was too demonstrably drunk for it to be acceptable for transmission. But the ignominious end to Brown's career in the Labour Party was headline news the next morning. The *Daily Mail* carried a series of photographs on its front page, from the moment of his fall to the point where he was being picked up. My right forearm made it to the front page of a national newspaper.

George Brown was a problem from the past. The Labour government had enough problems in the present. Wilson's departure from office led to a leadership contest where the favourite, Jim Callaghan, found himself in a six-way fight. It was vigorously contested by what now reads like a cast-list of great Labour names: Roy Jenkins, Michael Foot, Denis Healey, Tony Crosland and Tony Benn. It was the last Labour leadership contest where only the party's MPs had the vote, and Callaghan could afford to go through all three ballots without once making himself available for a media interview. It was the last time that would be an acceptable strategy.

I had first interviewed Jim Callaghan when I was a reporter on the *South Wales Echo*, finding myself tagged on to the end of his constituency surgery in Cardiff one Friday afternoon. He could be genial and avuncular if he wished, but he could also be irritable and sometimes just bad-tempered. I never quite understood how he earned the nickname 'Sunny Jim', particularly when seeing him dressing down an unfortunate radio reporter whose equipment failed to work. But he was by this time vastly experienced, having been Chancellor, Home Secretary and Foreign Secretary before reaching No. 10. It was going to take all that experience to steady the Labour ship.

Almost as soon as Callaghan took over, the government lost its majority in the House of Commons. Over the next three years, it suffered more than thirty defeats on the floor of the House. Since the main votes in the Commons came at ten o'clock in those days, that meant that they came when *News at Ten* was live on air. Clearly, the *News at Ten* producers needed to know in advance how likely it was the government would lose, and if so, the extent to which it mattered. It was often my job to sniff out what was likely to happen – not an easy task, even for the party whips. Apart from the three main parties, there were also the SNP, Plaid Cymru and the Northern Ireland MPs to take into account.

I sought to establish a working relationship with the Conservative and Labour whips whose task was to help collate the headcounts. Jack Dormand, an able but understated Labour MP from County Durham, was pairing whip for much of the time so knew which MPs were likely to be present and which absent. Jack Weatherill, a Croydon MP who had previously been employed in his family firm of Savile Row tailors, was the deputy chief whip for the Conservatives. On the basis that I was not going to make anything public before ten o'clock, I could usually glean from them which direction they thought that night's vote was likely to go.

Jack Weatherill was, of course, to go on to become Speaker of the Commons, a Speaker who increased his own reputation in the job and the reputation of the House. But he did not have a high opinion of all his parliamentary colleagues. As a whip, his job was to persuade potential rebels in his own party to toe the line, and he was surprised, he told me, how easily they sometimes succumbed to that persuasion.

'I would take them by the arm and tell them quietly that they were putting their careers at risk,' he said.

He did not really have much idea what path their careers were going to take, and he was always, he said, a bit taken aback when the pressure worked.

I enjoyed patrolling the corridors and lobbies, because these were volatile times. I became a sufficiently familiar face for one Labour whip to mistake me for an MP. The whips frequently had difficulty keeping debates in the Commons going when most MPs were at their dinner and John McWilliam, who might have been a bit short-sighted, called across the lobby and asked me to go and speak from the Labour benches. I used to wonder how long it would have taken them to stop me if I had tried.

For the big votes at ten o'clock, ITN would install the OB unit outside the Commons, as we did for the incident involving George Brown. The idea was to get the face of Big Ben behind the reporter, in order to emphasise that the report was live. With me that was not so easy, because I was not tall enough: the cameraman could not get low enough to get the right angle. So, more often than not, I had to stand on a box, a fact which became a long-running joke. It was never comfortable perched on a rather unstable box, usually in the dark, with a script I could barely see – and if I *could* see it, it was often smudged by the rain. I always regarded it as a minor miracle if I survived to report another day.

It was more usual for us to do our pieces into ITN programmes from a small parliamentary studio in the basement of the Norman Shaw building on the other side of Bridge Street from the Commons. This studio had one camera, controlled remotely from the ITN building in Wells Street, and was staffed by just a floor manager. The job of the floor manager, usually the indomitable Pat Harris, was to convey any last-minute instructions from the programme producer and, with a wave of a finger, tell you when you were on air. Otherwise, you were on your own. It required an effort of the imagination to appreciate that, on the other side of the single camera lens, there were millions of people watching you. For this was the heyday of ITV, when *News at Ten* was Britain's most popular news programme with audiences of ten million or more. In drafting my script, I tried to make my story feel relevant to the lives of ordinary people. Why should Mrs Jones of Upper Cwmtwrch feel she should bother with what was happening at Westminster? It might not always be possible to get Mrs Jones interested, but that, I felt, should be the aim.

There were always obstacles to getting on air, and on one occasion it hurt. I was reporting for *News at Ten* from Blackpool, which at that time involved appearing live from a makeshift studio in the basement of the Imperial Hotel. I had rehearsed my script, coordinating with the director in London over the packages and clips which would be played in at that end. I was sitting back just counting down the last minutes to 'on air' when something very heavy clouted me on the back of my head. The cardboard backdrop depicting Blackpool Tower had collapsed and I was temporarily stunned. But I could still hear on talk-back the voice of another reporter offering to take my place and do the piece for me. I recovered with remarkable rapidity.

The government's problems with securing a majority in the Commons were eased for a while by the signing of the Lib-Lab pact. The new Liberal leader, David Steel, had taken his party into a deal with the Labour government, partly because, after the Thorpe affair, it was in no state to fight a general election. As part of the pact, there was supposed to be regular consultation over policy. Callaghan got on well enough with Steel, but Denis Healey's discussions with Steel's deputy, John Pardoe, often ended in bitter disagreement. Nevertheless, John Pardoe had an air of someone who was on an important mission. Frank Johnson, one of the funniest newspaper sketch writers at that time, described him as a man who had 'smelled the black underwear of power'. The morning that sketch was published in the *Daily Telegraph*, I met John Pardoe on the way into our office in the Commons. He demanded to know who this Frank Johnson was, what right had he to put that kind of comment into the paper, questions that rapidly escalated into a rant. He had disobeyed one of the first rules of politics – never let it show when the bastards have got to you.

The main issue facing the Callaghan government was, of course, the predicament of the British economy. When he arrived at No. 10, the rate of inflation had come down from a height of twenty-six per cent, but it was still well into double figures. There was huge pressure on sterling, with the Treasury constantly having to shore up the pound, either from the reserves or with the help of other central banks. I can recall on several days during that period being in the Members' Lobby and talking to Conservative MPs who had just come from their day jobs in the City. They would be white-faced, frantically worried about the economic precipice over which they thought the country was about to dive. There was an air of permanent crisis.

An agreement with the TUC on a pay limit of ten per cent (which today would seem an extraordinarily high figure), together with a squeeze on public spending, failed to ease the pressure for more than a short while. Sterling was almost in freefall in the early autumn of 1977, and the Chancellor, Denis Healey, decided he would have to go to the International Monetary Fund for a loan. This was a humiliation – having to go cap in hand to a bunch of international bankers to keep the country afloat. It was a humiliation matched only by John Major's forced exit from the Exchange Rate Mechanism in 1992. Healey was called back from Heathrow airport to make his case to a hostile Labour conference in Blackpool, where he put on a bravura performance which made the hairs on the back of my neck bristle. He clasped his hands above his head in a defiant salute to the boos of the left-wing delegates. But it was no way to run an economy.

Denis Healey was a tough and resilient character. It is difficult to think of any other politician who could have survived for five years as Chancellor during some of the most testing times for the British economy. He was something of an intellectual bully, happy to show off his knowledge of just about everything in order to put you in your place. But he was also amusing and fun, quite content to play up to the 'Silly Billy' catchphrase he had been stuck with. On one or two occasions I went to interview him at his home near the Sussex coast. He and his wife Edna loved gardening, and if it was the weekend I would find him in his wellies, a new shrub in his wheelbarrow waiting to be planted.

This period also tested Callaghan's mettle as Prime Minister. He had to steer a package of spending cuts through the cabinet to meet the terms of the IMF, which he did with consummate skill. Cabinet meetings at this time involved real debate, where the Prime Minister had to ensure he had the support of the majority of cabinet members. Consequently, meetings would frequently overrun. I know because, during this period, I used to run a lunch club where a small group of correspondents would meet with senior politicians, usually cabinet ministers. The minister would often be late because the cabinet meeting had gone on longer than scheduled. It was very different under Mrs Thatcher, who did her best to keep the cabinet meetings to formal business, so they usually lasted little more than an hour. She exercised her prime ministerial power through bilateral meetings with her ministers. It made it much harder for any of them to challenge what she wanted to do.

For a while the economy improved and the government's fortunes with it. Healey would always argue that the situation was never as bad as the Treasury and the markets made out. Apart from anything else, there was the growing revenue from North Sea oil coming on stream. But the government was facing increasing resistance from the trade unions to any form of pay controls. Despite warnings from union leaders that they would not be able to hold the line, Callaghan decided in the summer of 1978 to go for a five per cent pay norm.

For me, the day the government lost control came in

November, when Denis Healey called a press conference at the Treasury to announce TUC agreement to the renewed round of pay restraint. The press conference was scheduled for late afternoon (I think it was four o'clock) but there was no sign of the Chancellor. The early evening bulletin passed, and there was an overwhelming sense that something had gone wrong. And it had. The TUC General Council had failed to vote for the policy. When Denis Healey finally appeared, he tried to argue that, because the vote in the general council was tied, they had not rejected it. It was unconvincing stuff. Yet when I came to interview him a little later, he put on an amazing show of bravado. Every interview needs what are called in the trade 'cutaways' – shots of the reporter to be cut into the edited version of the interview. This involves trying to put on a serious and interested look, but Healey did his best to make me laugh, pulling extremely funny faces. Then, knowing the two-shots – the shots of the two of us together – were going to be mute, he whistled loudly through his teeth. At the point his economic policy was falling about his ears, he was prepared to play the fool.

Another misjudgement was Callaghan's surprise decision not to go for the general election that autumn which everybody was expecting. The TUC was completely misled, as was everybody else, by the little ditty Callaghan had sung at the end of his speech at their 1978 conference: 'There was I waiting at the church…' So when, on 7 September, Downing Street said that the Prime Minister would be making a TV broadcast at six o'clock that evening, it was generally assumed he would be announcing the election. An hour or so beforehand, I bumped into a Labour MP, Mike Thomas, who told me he that he had it on authority that Callaghan was going to call it off. I afterwards discovered that he had been involved in the party's polling which was predicting Labour would lose an autumn election, and he remained one of the small minority who thought Callaghan had made the right decision. It was enough to take the edge off the wrong assumptions in the early evening bulletin which preceded Callaghan's broadcast.

In early January, I flew from a snow-covered Heathrow airport to the West Indies to cover the four-power summit on the French island of Guadeloupe. We were so late taking off that, along with some of the Prime Minister's security detail, we had to stay overnight in Antigua where the customs officials insisted on impounding my typewriter. My initial task in Guadeloupe was to set the scene for the summit, and the scene was a world away from cold, snowy, strike-ridden Britain. The sun, the beaches, the plush hotels meant it was where wealthy Parisians came for their winter holiday. And French sunbathing meant topless sunbathing.

I wanted to convey some of this atmosphere by doing a piece to camera on a beach, but it would rather undermine the seriousness of the story if there were naked breasts in shot. I positioned myself carefully and gave strict instructions to the cameraman, an American from Miami, to ensure there were no topless sunbathers in view. When I got to see the takes, there was a topless sunbather over my right shoulder in every single one. It was too late to do anything about it, and I just hoped they were not too noticeable. I never really discovered the reaction back home, because all communications from the island went via Paris and it took hours for a telephone call to come through and telex messages were confined to more immediate and practical matters.

On this assignment, I was up against Martin Bell, the formidable BBC foreign correspondent, who later became an independent MP. There was an agreement between the BBC and ITN to share facilities at the TV station on the island. It turned out, however, that there was only one film-editing machine available. Despite the hair-raising thirty-mile drive back from the conference centre, Martin Bell always seemed to get there first and bag the edit machine. I was lucky that with me was an experienced film editor, Leo Rosenberg, and he stuck together a Heath Robinson device which involved winding the developed film by hand through a viewfinder clipped to the edge of a wooden table. He guessed the duration of the piece from the number of frames in each edit, and he was nearly always right. The contrast with the operation of the American networks could not have been greater. CBS, NBC and ABC had pooled together for a ground station right at the conference centre; the cameramen were equipped with electronic video cameras and there was a myriad of producers rushing around and yelling into walkie-talkies. I felt that I was in the equivalent of the Stone Age, and indeed, it was only a matter of months before ITN itself brought in electronic news gathering equipment.

The four-power talks between Callaghan, Jimmy Carter, Giscard d'Estaing and Helmut Schmidt, were primarily about disarmament and, for Callaghan, the future of Britain's independent deterrent. It was not surprising that such heady international issues, together with the relaxed tropical climate, made the problems at home seem far away. The sight of Schmidt using a machete to open a coconut seemed more immediate than news of the lorry drivers' strike back home. Callaghan's adviser, Tom McNally, and his chief press officer, Tom McCaffrey, were keeping in touch with Downing Street, and I can remember late one afternoon, sitting in the sun in a small group of correspondents chatting with them, and the news did not seem so bad. Some of that must have rubbed off on the Prime Minister when he chose, on arriving back at Heathrow, to give a press conference. He was far too dismissive of what one reporter had called 'the mounting industrial chaos', and the *Sun* created its famous headline: 'Crisis, what crisis?' It was in fact the crisis of the Winter of Discontent which was to ensure the downfall of his government.

In the face of spreading strikes, there seemed to be a sense of drift in the government. But it was the issue of devolution which was to deliver the final blow. The government had conceded that there would be referendums before the Scottish Parliament and Welsh Assembly could be established, and these were to take place on 1 March, St David's Day. I was not surprised to be dispatched to Wales to cover the referendum campaign. In a piece I had done for ITN a year or so previously, I had already discovered the antipathy towards devolution among Labour loyalists. In a workingmen's club in Mountain Ash, the view most commonly expressed was: 'I don't speak Welsh, I'm British,' a sentiment which the No campaign, led by Neil Kinnock and Leo Abse, were not averse to exploiting. Despite my own pro-devolution views (which I, of course, kept to myself) I enjoyed working with Neil Kinnock. He was accessible and relaxed, even when he crashed his car into a snowdrift on a mountainside above the Rhondda. The ITN crew had to help him dig it out.

The problem was that, with Labour debilitated by its open divisions on devolution, it was increasingly a battle between the No campaign and the nationalists. Gwynfor Evans, when we filmed him in Aberystwyth, was dignified and eloquent, but the tide was against him. Not long before the poll, the head of the Yes campaign, Elystan Morgan, gave me a lift in his Jaguar. He still insisted they could win, but he was very subdued. He must have known they were heading for defeat, but not the scale of it – by a margin of four to one.

In Scotland, there had actually been a majority in favour of devolution, but well short of the hurdle of forty per cent of the electorate which the legislation had specified. As a result, the SNP withdrew support from the Labour government, and Mrs Thatcher took advantage by tabling a motion of no confidence in the government. On 28 March, throughout the day, I tried to work out which way the vote would go at ten o'clock that night. We knew it was going to be close, and for hours I patrolled the lobbies and corridors trying to find out more. The Liberals were going to support the Conservatives because, it was widely believed, David Steel wanted an election before the Thorpe trial, which was due to take place in the summer. A deal had been done with the three Plaid Cymru MPs who, in exchange for voting for the government, would secure compensation for disabled quarry workers. So it was down to an assorted bunch of MPs from Northern Ireland.

There was a rumour that Roy Hattersley was trying to do a deal with some of the Unionists, and by good fortune I came across him. By pretending to know more than I actually did, I gleaned that he was fairly confident of securing some kind of deal (in fact, he brought over just two of them). The other variable was an Independent Republican, Frank Maguire, who rarely left his pub in Fermanagh. I searched for him, but failed to find him. But he was in the Westminster precincts somewhere, having famously decided to come and 'abstain in person'.

When the result of the vote was announced by a Conservative whip, the government had lost by just one vote. I watched as Callaghan stood up and, in just a few brief words which he had obviously prepared for, announced he would seek the dissolution of Parliament and a general election. It was the first time for half a century that a government had fallen on a vote in the House of Commons.

Chapter 13

No less a journalist

After the general election in 1979, I had a two-year spell away from Westminster as what was rather grandly called a 'home affairs correspondent'. This involved a portmanteau of subjects, including health, education, social security and criminal justice. Not surprisingly, it was difficult simultaneously to acquire sufficient expertise in such a wide spectrum of issues. So general was the brief that I was given that it was possible one day for the duty news editor, Mark Andrews, to stop me in the ITN newsroom and ask whether I was tied up that day. I told him I had nothing fixed, so he told me I was on the next plane to Rome. It was the assassination attempt on Pope John Paul II and my role was to back up Martyn Lewis in reporting developing events. Afterwards, I asked Mark why he had picked me.

'Oh, I thought you were the Rome affairs correspondent,' he joked.

In this job, I was based back at ITN in Wells Street, and it was for me a useful period, integrating me into the ITN news operation in a way that I could not experience from the ITN desk at Westminster. Not least, I learned vital lessons about working with the still relatively new electronic video equipment. At Westminster, the bulk of my reporting had involved reading scripts to camera, coupled with interviews where possible. Now I had to get to grips far more with reporter 'packages', involving pictures, clips of interview and voice-over. It was a central principle of ITN's modus operandi that a film or video editor was assigned to every story scheduled for transmission, and the reporter would work with them to get the best out of the piece. In particular, the reporter could select the best of the pictures and write the script to fit. Many years later, when I worked for the BBC, I found that far too often I had to lay down the soundtrack first, leaving it to somebody else to fit the pictures – a far inferior method.

I also learned how often the element of luck comes along – good luck and bad luck. On the sudden and unexpected trip to Rome, my luck was in. We had arrived late at night, and by seven the next morning we were in the Rome office of the TV news agency UPITN (United Press International Television News was then one of the big players across the world) trying to work out the coverage for the day following the attempted assassination. Staff at UPITN had heard a mention on Italian radio that the Vatican Secretary of State, Cardinal Casaroli, was flying back from America and was due to arrive that morning. In no time, I was in the back of an Alfasud being driven at breakneck speed through narrow cobbled streets, the Italian cameraman not even pretending to stop at red lights. At the airport, the cardinal's flight had already landed. There was nobody else around, not even the Italian media. In the excitement of the moment, I could not remember for the life of me how you addressed a cardinal, but whatever I said was enough. He was charming, and allowed me quite a lengthy interview. The crew, knowing that they had a scoop, drove even faster back into the city centre. By ten o'clock that morning, the interview had gone around the world.

Like plenty of other people who appear on television, I was frequently asked about my job. And there were two questions which most irritated me. They were: 'But what do you do when you are not appearing in the studio?', and 'Do you write your own scripts?' To help me respond to such questions, I noted down the details of one particular day in 1980. It was the day when the Conservative government finally gave in over the establishment of a separate Welsh-language TV channel. The Conservatives had reneged on a previous promise that such a channel would be set up, and now they were about to do another somersault. There was little doubt that foremost in their minds was the threat by the Plaid Cymru leader, Gwynfor Evans, to starve himself to death.

I myself had an intimation of the potential trouble ahead. At the wedding in south Wales of my younger sister Ceinwen not long before, I was tackled by two or three people, obviously Plaid supporters, who had warned me there would be 'blood on the streets' if Gwynfor died. Whether that was an exaggeration or not, there were others in Welsh-speaking Wales who were becoming alarmed. I filmed the Bishop of Bangor, my old headmaster G.O. Williams, leading a deputation to see the Home Secretary, Willie Whitelaw, who was in charge of broadcasting policy. But it was left to the Welsh Secretary, Nicholas Edwards, to make the capitulation at a press conference in Cardiff.

In the ITN newsroom, we did not hear about the press conference until after eleven o'clock in the morning, and having got a crew together we were on the road before noon. The press conference was to happen at three o'clock, and we made it with half an hour to spare. There was just enough time to set the camera up and negotiate an interview with the Welsh Secretary before everything kicked off. It was then straight to the HTV studios to prepare the report. The problem was that it was a busy day for HTV's own news programme and the facilities were hard-pressed. Getting studio time was a problem, and there seemed little chance of being able to edit the Nick Edwards interview. But the ITN early evening news, which then went out at 5.45 p.m., had made it their lead story. By about 5.20 p.m. I had written the bulk of my script, and was told I could have a few minutes on an editing machine. At about 5.25 p.m. I was lost in a backyard with a roll of film in my hand and desperately trying to find the film editor. By 5.40 p.m. I was back in the HTV newsroom ringing my producer with the final details, not least the expected timings. With ninety seconds to spare, I was sitting down in front of the studio camera ready for the live link with London, and there was barely time to catch my breath before the floor manager was counting me down to the start of my piece. It had only worked because of the help of the HTV staff, who had managed to fit me in. When I got back to London, the studio director, Diana Edwards Jones, said she had thought I was not going to show.

In the portmanteau portfolio I was supposed to be addressing, it was the subject of prisons and penal policy which caught my imagination. It was not just the filming inside Reading prison, before which I had re-read Oscar Wilde's 'Ballad of Reading Gaol'. In fact, the atmosphere inside was nothing like as dramatic as Wilde's poem. It was crowded and oppressive, but the mood was sullen rather than dangerous, and it was the smell I remembered most, a smell of human sweat and cabbage water.

There was then, as there still is now, a crisis in our prisons, too many prisoners being squeezed into too few places. The overcrowding was putting a strain on the system, with two or three prisoners to a cell. Britain was incarcerating a higher percentage of the population than just about every other European country, and since then the numbers have kept on climbing. Willie Whitelaw was a humane home secretary and wanted to encourage alternatives to prison, and in particular wanted to deter young offenders from a life of repeat prison sentences. I accompanied him to the junior detention centre at Send in Surrey, where he launched the policy of 'short, sharp shock', where teenagers were to be given a taste of army-style discipline. It did not seem to have much effect. I was more persuaded by what I saw at a prison in northern Holland, where those convicted of non-violent offences could, for instance, serve their sentences at weekends so that they could keep their jobs and still maintain their families. We filmed as they got off the bus and walked into prison of their own accord.

After working at ITN for more than seven years, I found I

was entitled to a sabbatical. It had to be related to my work, and I decided to look at the prison system in the United States. Since this was my first opportunity of a visit to America, I selected prisons as geographically diverse as I could sensibly arrange, and I was grateful to the deputy editor, Don Horobin, for helping with the costs. It was an eye-opener of a visit. The rate of incarceration was twice that of Britain and black males were ten times more likely to be in prison than their white equivalents. Time and again, tougher laws were being passed in response to public demand for longer sentences. The result was prisons with an astonishing level of violence. Set in the beautiful Massachusetts countryside, the Walpole 'Correctional Institution' had at one time an average of five killings every month – that is, prisoners killing prisoners. The many laudable efforts at rehabilitation which I witnessed paled into insignificance compared with that kind of statistic.

At Rahway in New Jersey, I found myself having lunch in the prison executives' canteen. One of the prisoners serving us, obviously a 'trusty', was a middle-aged white man with a gentle face and limpid eyes. One of the guards whispered to me that he had been a professional hit-man for the Mafia and others.

'Go on, ask him how many people he's killed,' he said.

So I asked him.

'Twenty-three,' he replied.

'But,' I blurted out, 'you've got such a kind face.'

'I know,' he said. 'That's why I'm so good.'

In the southern states, the reputation of the prisons was worse (indeed, there was a standing joke that if you were committing an offence you had best drive across the state line, because then it would be a federal offence and federal prisons were comparatively humane). At Columbia in South Carolina, the Central Correctional Institution was being compelled by legal action to reduce the overcrowding. Men were held in wire cages or in large dormitories where the guards just locked the door at night and left them to it. And then there was death row, twenty men with their sentence written above the doors to their cells. Here there was a lethargic quiet; the condemned men, most of them black, lay on their bunks reading or gazing through the bars. One had been there for four years, while the legal challenges wound their way through the courts.

The electric chair was housed in a small, brick building, with an ostentatiously large padlock on the door. I noticed the padlock was getting a little rusty: the building had not been used for a while. Inside, the wooden chair had been refurbished. It was well-polished and the straps and buckles had been tidied away to the sides. The guard invited me to sit in the chair. I shuddered. With ghoulish prison humour, he promised to keep away from the switches. I still declined.

In San Quentin in California, the death sentence was carried out by means of a gas chamber. It looked like something out of a fairground ride, except it was bolted to the wall with a sinuous tube emerging from the top. It was a two-seater, just in case business got too busy. I was told it could take up to eight minutes to die after the gas had started pumping in.

The death penalty was one of the few issues about which I found it difficult to retain any sense of journalistic impartiality. A few years earlier, there had been a debate in the Commons on bringing back the death penalty for the murder of policemen and prison officers. In trying to assess how the vote was likely to go, I found myself arguing with supporters of the death penalty like Keith Joseph, rather than asking questions. Fortunately the opponents, spurred on by the oratory of Brian Walden, comfortably won the day.

In the spring of 1981, I was suddenly back working in the House of Commons. ITN's political editor, Julian Haviland, had moved on to become political editor of *The Times*, and, much against my expectations, I took over from him. We were joined by David Walter, an Oxford classics graduate, who considerably raised the intellectual quotient of the ITN political team. The corridors of Westminster sometimes seem to have a strange, timeless quality – perhaps it was the influence of the architecture. I had been away for two years, but the general reaction was: 'Oh, I haven't seen you around for a few days.' I always felt it was a privilege to work there, giving me a front seat at the political theatre.

But one of the rituals of reporting politics at Westminster was increasingly being questioned. The system of non-attributable briefings which lobby journalists attended every day was getting a lot of public flak. Every morning there was a meeting in No. 10 with the Prime Minister's chief press secretary, and in the afternoon, the No. 10 spokesman would come to the lobby room in one of Westminster's towers, and there was some silly nonsense surrounding all this – the meetings were not acknowledged to be happening and the room in the tower was not supposed to exist. The central allegation was that the lobby system was a way for the government and senior politicians to spoon-feed journalists with information which would not be traced back to them, a kind of cosy collusion. I regarded that charge as being absurd – if anything, the private sessions could be more confrontational than the public ones. And I would not be doing my job properly if I relied solely on what I was told in such briefings. In an article in *Media Week*, I was quoted as saying, rather defensively: 'We are no less journalists for being in here rather than outside.'

Part of the problem was that Mrs Thatcher's press secretary, Bernard Ingham, was very good at his job. You knew that what you were getting from him was what the Prime Minister thought, and he knew well how to handle the media, despite occasionally overstepping the mark – such as when he described John Biffen to the lobby as a 'semi-detached' member of the cabinet. The other problem was that television reporting required politicians in front of the camera, not speaking unattributably. Briefings by ministers or opposition leaders were of far less use to broadcasters if they stayed off the record. So I stood for the chairmanship of the lobby on a reform ticket, even though they were to prove only modest reforms. After a round of consultation, I proposed that briefings with government ministers and party leaders could be on the record, provided briefers and briefed agreed in advance. The arguments were surprisingly acrimonious for what, in retrospect, appears to be such a minor change. But in a ballot of all lobby members, it was accepted by sixty-seven votes to fourteen.

I had failed, however, to get any change out of Bernard Ingham. The briefings by No. 10 were to remain unattributable at all times. Bernard argued that the Prime Minister was directly accountable to Parliament, and he, as a civil servant, could not usurp that role by making an announcement to the press. I said at the time that this pretence was becoming incredibly thin, since that in practice was exactly what he was doing. In the end, it was Tony Blair who blew that argument away by deciding to institute televised prime ministerial press conferences.

The lobby did have its lighter moments, not least the Christmas party for the families of correspondents. The Press Gallery would be transformed with balloons and children's party fare. Someone, usually the Press Association correspondent, Chris Moncrieff, would dress up as Father Christmas. One year, when she was still leader of the Opposition, Mrs Thatcher turned up. It was slightly odd seeing such a public figure going round the table and helping children with their meals. My daughter Megan still remembers Mrs Thatcher serving her Coca-Cola.

I had also secured the presence of one of ITN's newscasters, Gordon Honeycombe, whom we hoped the children would recognise. But my son Mathew rather spoiled the atmosphere when, perhaps overawed by Mrs Thatcher, he was sick over Gordon Honeycombe's shoes.

Chapter 14

As Queen Victoria once said

THE PHONE CALL was from Bernard Ingham, chief press secretary at 10 Downing Street.

'You recall the invitation ITN made to the Prime Minister for an interview?' he asked.

I was briefly stumped. I could not remember any such invitation. Before it was too late, I realised that there was a convention, if only a superficial one, that Downing Street did not offer the Prime Minister for interview but only responded to requests. And, since the BBC had conducted the previous interview, it was the turn of ITN.

'Yes, of course,' I replied.

'Well, the Prime Minister has agreed to do the interview, and we would like to do it next Monday.'

It was April 1982 and Mrs Thatcher was, according to the opinion polls, more unpopular than any previous prime minister. Unemployment had risen to three million; there had been street riots in Brixton and Toxteth. Some of her cabinet were openly disaffected. So the interview, which was to be eight minutes in duration – a long interview for a news programme – promised to be interesting. Little did I know.

That Friday, the news came in of the Argentine invasion of the Falkland Islands, and suddenly the whole political landscape had been turned upside down. On the Saturday, there was an emergency session of Parliament, the only weekend session

I can remember. The mood in the Commons was excitable, a mixture of anger at the effrontery of it and blame for the fact the government had been caught napping. The Foreign Secretary, Lord Carrington, took responsibility for the latter and resigned on the Sunday. On the Monday, the task force was assembling at Portsmouth ready to leave for the South Atlantic. And on the Monday afternoon, I was still due to have my interview with the Prime Minister.

From papers released by the Thatcher Foundation it is apparent that Bernard Ingham wrote a briefing note to Mrs Thatcher, pointing out that this would be her first broadcast outside the Commons since the crisis began: 'I have had a word with Glyn Mathias who is to interview you tomorrow at 4.30. He will wish to concentrate on the Falklands, the prospects for the next few weeks, the impact of the crisis on the political situation, and its effect on public spending and the economic situation.'

This was a list covering all options. 'He is thinking of eight to ten minutes and will record, as agreed, in my office. They propose to put part of the interview on the 5.45 p.m. news and run it in full at 10 p.m.'

Another Downing Street adviser, Hugh Colver, had suggested to Mrs Thatcher that she should not go ahead: 'You have a very full day, quite apart from the Falkland Islands situation. Do you still want to go ahead, bearing in mind that ITN are now all the more interested in the interview and have put the Falkland Islands issue at the top of their list?

Another factor is that ITN will be able to claim an exclusive interview with you on the subject although we would of course be able to say that this was arranged a long time ago.'

To which the Prime Minister replied in a hand-written note: 'It has already been announced. MT.'

To say that the atmosphere inside Downing Street on that afternoon was tense would be an understatement. After all, Mrs Thatcher was launching one of the biggest military operations since the Second World War, and from a standing start. The

First Sea Lord, Sir Henry Leach, was on his way out as I was ushered into the Prime Minister's room. Mrs Thatcher was understandably charged up by the gravity of the decisions she was having to make and I could feel the electricity bouncing off the walls. And now she had to present her case to the public. She wanted to know what sort of questions I was going to ask. This was not the easiest moment to stick to the rule that questions are not revealed in advance. Instead, I gave a broad indication of the ground to be covered.

'That's not going to last eight minutes,' she said.

'I think, Prime Minister, it probably will,' said Bernard Ingham.

The outside broadcast unit had been setting up in the chief press secretary's office, ready to feed the interview to ITN for recording as it was under way. But it was now well past five o'clock, and the early evening news was haring towards us. There was little more than ten minutes to go when Mrs Thatcher sat down in the chair opposite me and the interview began. I left to the end the key question: if Britain failed to regain the Falklands, would she resign as Prime Minister?

'Failure?' she replied. 'Do you remember what Queen Victoria once said? Failure? The possibilities do not exist. That is the way we must look at it... We must go out calmly, quietly to succeed.'

There was just time to turn round the last two minutes of the interview and play them into the early evening news. The producer, Derek Dowsett, had been on tenterhooks and said later he had thought I was never going to ask that last question. The full interview was transmitted on *News at Ten*.

There was a considerable period when it was not clear whether the crisis would end in military conflict. The Americans were keen to broker some kind of deal, and the Foreign Secretary, Francis Pym, was considerably less gung-ho than his boss. I was dispatched to Washington to report on a critical round of talks between Pym and Alexander Haig, the American Secretary of State. Haig was trying to juggle

American interests in their own 'backyard' of Latin America with support for Britain. In retrospect, it was always unlikely that he could persuade the Argentine dictator, General Galtieri, to agree to anything that Mrs Thatcher could accept, but that was not obvious at the time. I was lucky that I had with me as producer Alexandra Henderson, who happened to be the daughter of the British ambassador in Washington, Sir Nicholas Henderson. Thus I was the only reporter who, on one occasion, was able to walk into the State Department through the front door rather than the media entrance. The Haig/Pym press conferences there were unrevealing, but the vibes were clear. Alexandra was scrupulous in not revealing any improper information, but together with some surprisingly good briefing from the embassy, it was obvious that little progress was being made.

Back in London, the Ministry of Defence had become the main source of information about what was happening in the South Atlantic, with the famously robotic performances of their spokesman, Ian McDonald, at their televised press briefings. There were emergency statements in the Commons about the attacks on British ships, and ITN, like the BBC, ran extended news programmes during the conflict. But in reality information out of the conflict zone was heavily controlled – a control which was possible because of the remoteness of the location and because only the British military then had the ability to transmit material back to the UK. They could give priority, for instance, to more upbeat reports, such as Michael Nicholson's account of the attack on Bluff Cove or Brian Hanrahan's report on British Harrier jets which included the memorable phrase: 'I counted them all out and I counted them all back.' This led to considerable debate about the role of the media in wartime, which was to raise its head again during the Gulf War.

The Falklands War transformed the politics of the 1980s. From being a prime minister likely to be swept from office at the next election, Mrs Thatcher now became the powerful figure we all remember. To the victor, the spoils – in a kind of a way. There was an inquiry into the extent of the government's culpability in failing to foresee what the Argentine junta were up to. The body of the report by Lord Franks's committee was pretty damning, and I underlined several passages which were highly critical of the government, not least the decision to withdraw the patrol vessel *HMS Endurance* from the South Atlantic. Ted Rowlands had been the Foreign Office minister in the Callaghan government responsible for this area of policy, and they had seen off a threatened move against the Falklands by letting it be known that a nuclear-powered submarine was being deployed to the area.

This time, no precautions had been taken, despite concerns about Argentina adopting a more aggressive posture. And yet the Franks Committee, in its conclusion, absolved Mrs Thatcher's government from any criticism or blame for the invasion of the Falklands. I was surprised that even Labour's Merlyn Rees signed up to this form of absolution. But I should not have been surprised. It is politically difficult to criticise a victorious government over the causes of a war it has just won, and would have gone against the public mood.

Over Hong Kong, Mrs Thatcher was up against a different kind of opponent from the Argentine junta. Britain could not send a task force to defend Hong Kong against the Chinese, the most populous nation on earth. So when she arrived in Beijing later that year, she did not hold a lot of cards in her hand. She insisted that Britain had sovereignty over the island of Hong Kong, but Britain's lease over the New Territories was due up in 1997, and the Communist government in Beijing was determined to recover the lot. Just before his meeting with Mrs Thatcher, the Chinese Premier, Zhao Ziyang, came out beaming and smiling.

'Oh yes,' he said, 'we will recover our sovereignty over Hong Kong, but there is no need to worry about it.'

It sounded threatening or encouraging, depending on who translated it for you. What Mrs Thatcher was hoping was that the Chinese would agree that the British could continue to administer Hong Kong even if sovereignty was handed over. But when she met the Chinese leader, Deng Xiaoping, he would not budge an inch. All she got was a joint communiqué accepting a common interest in the stability and prosperity of Hong Kong.

Reporting from Beijing was, for me, slightly surreal. The country was then so different from anything I had seen before, right from the point of flying in over the rice fields into the tiny little airport. The streets were teeming with bicycles, with barely any cars to be seen. It was like stepping back in time some sixty years, with little sign of the industry and technology which was to transform the country over subsequent years. Visiting the Forbidden City, we would be stared at endlessly, as if we had arrived from outer space.

This was some years before the demonstrations in Tiananmen Square, and it was striking how secure the regime felt itself to be. There was little or no security around the public buildings or the main public figures. For the public session of Mrs Thatcher's talks with Deng Xiaoping in the Great Hall of the People, all that separated the leaders from the press was a small rope about a foot off the ground. But they had not reckoned with the Hong Kong media, a substantial contingent of whom had unusually been allowed to travel to Beijing for the visit. They had the capacity to reduce every event to a seething scrum, and no sooner had the leaders exchanged some initial banalities than a Hong Kong cameraman decided he could not see enough and tried to climb on somebody else's back. The ensuing fisticuffs came within a few feet of bowling the diminutive Deng into the Prime Minister's lap.

When you are reporting from abroad, it is vital to know how you are going to get your story back to base. In this case, our instructions were vague. We had been told to go to a certain bedroom on the top floor of our hotel, and that was it. At the appointed time, with the edited report in our hands, we found a small bedroom with about half-a-dozen Chinese men sitting around and some brand-new equipment stacked up against the window. No-one spoke any English, but we gathered that the tape would be played out to a ground station somewhere outside the city and thence around the world to London. We could not speak to anybody in London, so played it several times and decided to trust it to luck. It seemed so incongruous to find what was then such technically advanced equipment in such surroundings, but it all worked.

By this time, I was late for the banquet being held for the visiting Prime Minister in the Great Hall of the People. The main party had long since left, and I had given no thought as to how I was going to get there. By chance, I managed to hitch a lift with a Canadian correspondent who seemed, as we drove there, to have the only car on the road. Nobody challenged me as I climbed the steps of the Great Hall on my own. The two sentries seemed to be there more for decoration than anything else. I was guided only by the sound of the distant banquet in the depths of the building, and I slid into my place just as the toasts of mutual friendship were being exchanged.

Among the press corps accompanying Mrs Thatcher, there were a number of big names such as Anne Robinson, then working for the *Daily Mirror*, and Clive James, who was writing, I think, for the *Observer* at the time. It was Clive James who decided to enliven the long plane journey home by scripting a short play for the press corps to perform to the Prime Minister and her entourage. It was something of a skit on her visit to the Far East, and my role was minor. It was a mock piece to camera, and the punch line was in the sign-off: 'Glyn Mathias, *News at Ten*, with Mrs Thatcher – but in a worse hotel.' I saw that the Prime Minister, not noted for her sense of humour, was laughing.

Waiting to interview Mrs Thatcher was a bit like waiting at the dentist's. It was not going to be a relaxing occasion. Her personality in private was exactly the same as her personality in public – brisk, dismissive of opponents, and, particularly later on, sometimes hectoring. She did not bother much with small talk with journalists, but on the other hand she did not try and condescend towards us. It was quite easy to see how ministers who got on the wrong side of her could feel bruised and even humiliated. Geoffrey Howe was to get his revenge in the end. One politician who always seemed to be on the right side of her, however, was Cecil Parkinson, but he was set to cause her a deal of trouble. After her victory in the 1983 general election, she wanted to make him Foreign Secretary until he confessed to her about his affair with his former secretary, Sara Keays. Despite this knowledge, Mrs Thatcher made him Secretary of State for Trade and Industry.

At the Conservative Party conference that autumn, Cecil Parkinson was determined to use his speech from the platform to re-establish his political reputation. Coupled with that, ITN's Sue Tinson had secured an exclusive interview for that night's *News at Ten,* which I was to do. The speech fell rather flat, and during the interview in his hotel suite, he seemed preoccupied. As well he might. Later that night, I was attending a late-night function when I saw Parkinson and his wife Anne come in and tour the room. Within half an hour they were leaving again, Parkinson looking ashen. They had just been told that Sara Keays had given a statement to *The Times* which was splashing it on the front page the next morning.

After an early breakfast, I was at the hotel reception desk trying to check out of my room so that I could leave for London later in the day. There was a tap on my shoulder. It was Edward du Cann.

'I wouldn't go anywhere, if I were you, old boy,' he said.

As du Cann presumably knew, Cecil Parkinson had already resigned after an early morning meeting with the Prime Minister in her hotel room. Sara Keays had done for him with her attack on his conduct in *The Times*. According to her, he had twice proposed to her and each time changed his mind. And she confirmed that she was pregnant with his child.

Two years later, I drove to a village near Bath for an exclusive interview with Sara Keays at her parental home. We were allowed to film her daughter Flora, the child she had with Cecil Parkinson. The interview was planned by Sara Keays to publicise a book, a detailed account of the whole affair. The central accusation I put to her was that her actions, two years ago and now, were vindictive, born of a spirit of revenge. She maintained throughout that all she was trying to do was to defend her reputation, and if Parkinson had not taken office after the 1983 general election, 'none of this would have happened'.

A couple of days later, I was back in the Members' Lobby of the House of Commons when Cecil Parkinson hove into view. I looked around for an escape before he could spot me, but it was too late. To my surprise, he did not upbraid me for the interview. He seemed solely concerned about his daughter, who had some health problems. This was the only time he had seen his daughter – on the television screen, and he certainly gave me the impression that was not his fault. Whatever the truth of it, it taught me not to forget the personal tragedies behind the headlines.

In terms of tragedies, the IRA bombing of the Grand Hotel at Brighton, was one of the worst, but I was somewhere else. I had gone down with one of the worst bouts of flu I had ever suffered, and was shipped home from the party conference by my wife Sian. So I was lying on my sickbed when my opposite number, John Cole of the BBC, secured the emotional interview with Mrs Thatcher in the early hours of the morning when she expressed her determination, in spite of so many deaths and the destruction of the hotel, that the conference should go on. It was one of the least glorious passages of my career.

The most bizarre crisis of the Thatcher period was the one involving helicopters. It was incomprehensible then, as it is incomprehensible now, that a government could lose two cabinet ministers and almost lose a prime minister over such a minor issue of procurement. It was almost impossible to explain to viewers the ins and outs of the Westland affair, but suffice it to say that Michael Heseltine was determined that the Westland helicopter firm should link up with European partners, while Mrs Thatcher seemed equally determined that the link should be with American partners. Heseltine became obsessed with the issue, ringing up journalists like myself with his version of the latest twist or turn of events. When he failed to get his way, he stormed out of a cabinet meeting, catching the camera crews in Downing Street by surprise. The BBC managed to switch on just in time to record him announcing his resignation. The ITN crew had unfortunately gone for a coffee.

But the crisis was not over. It just got more complicated, and this time it was Leon Brittan, the Trade and Industry Secretary, who was in the firing line. The Solicitor General, Sir Patrick Mayhew, had written a letter criticising 'material inaccuracies' in a statement Heseltine had made, and this was leaked by someone in Leon Brittan's department to the Press Association. Brittan's press secretary at the time was Colette Bowe (who subsequently left the civil service and went on to become chair of the telecommunications regulator, Ofcom). It was widely assumed that she was involved in leaking the information, and the spotlight now shone fiercely on Leon Brittan, never a popular figure in the Conservative Party. It all showed how bitter the internal battle inside the cabinet had become, and Brittan was to be the fall guy.

It was early Friday afternoon and there was hardly anybody around in the Commons. But it did not feel right, and I was tense. The political correspondents for the Sunday newspapers had all gone to a briefing with Bernard Ingham, which the rest of us were not permitted to attend. Even the Press Gallery seemed denuded. So I went for a walk to the Members' Lobby. The proceedings in the chamber had finished and there was absolutely nobody there either. I was about to leave when a Conservative MP walked in. It was Gerry Malone, who was Parliamentary Private Secretary to Leon Brittan. I asked as casually as I could if anything was happening, and he said, yes, that his boss had just gone in to see the Prime Minister in her room in the Commons. He was taking responsibility for what had happened and was determined to resign.

I looked around me. There was still nobody else around. I asked whether anyone else was aware of this yet. Nobody was, he said, because the meeting had only just begun. I thanked him, and trying desperately not to run, got back to my desk and rang the news desk at Wells Street. They were really on the ball, and within minutes, ITN broke into ITV's afternoon transmission with a newsflash. The wording we decided on was that Leon Brittan had offered his resignation, to cover the possibility that Mrs Thatcher might persuade him out of it. A selection from the wire stories that afternoon gives a taste of how it went.

> Reuter Fri Jan 24, 15.48
> British Trade Secretary Leon Brittan today offered his resignation to Prime Minister, independent television said.
>
> Reuter Fri Jan 24, 15.58
> Officials at the British Trade and Industry Department today denied reports that the Trade Secretary Leon Brittan had resigned. A spokesman said the report on British Independent Television was untrue.
>
> PA Fri Jan 24, 16.00
> Downing Street and Department of Trade refused to confirm independent television report that Mr Leon Brittan had offered to resign as Trade and Industry Secretary.
>
> Reuter Fri Jan 24, 16.21
> British Prime Minister Margaret Thatcher, grappling with her worst domestic political crisis, summoned Trade and Industry Minister Leon Brittan for a meeting today amid mounting speculation that he had offered to resign.
>
> Brittan, at the centre of a row over a government leak, emerged from the meeting refusing to comment on reports that he had bowed to pressure inside his own party to quit.
>
> The report of the resignation was first carried by British Independent Television. Officials at Brittan's ministry at first said it was untrue but later said they did not know.

> PA Fri Jan 24, 17.43
> Leon Brittan boarded 17.30 train for York from King's Cross but refused to comment about his reported resignation.
>
> PA Fri Jan 24, 18.09
> Trade and Industry Secretary Leon Brittan has resigned – Official. Official statement from Downing Street said Mr Brittan had tendered his resignation and Prime Minister accepted it with regret.

Afterwards, the news editor that day, Nigel Hancock, said with the elegant phraseology for which news editors are renowned: 'I bet you had your arse open for a while there, Mathias.'

Chapter 15

The transitional stage

It was the day of the election of a new leader of the Labour Party. Michael Foot had taken Labour to its worst defeat since the 1930s, and at the party conference at Brighton in October 1983 Neil Kinnock was to succeed him. Indeed, so predictable was the result of the leadership election that on the morning of the election, Neil and his wife Glenys agreed to do a photo-call for the media. The ITN and BBC cameras set up on one of the piers overlooking the beach, with Neil and Glenys walking hand-in-hand towards us. But they were not watching the tide. A wave came in unexpectedly quickly, and Neil – in attempting to pull Glenys clear – fell over. A gesture of defiance from Neil only made the incident even funnier. I knew they were going to be great pictures, even more so because I was convinced that the BBC camera had, at that precise moment, been switched off. I was therefore somewhat surprised to see the sequence on the next BBC bulletin. A little bit of piracy perhaps, but it was a mystery I never solved.

Neil Kinnock inherited a Labour Party which at the previous election was committed to pulling out of the European Economic Community, unilateral nuclear disarmament and a return to nationalisation. Above all, it was a party in which the left appeared to be in control. And if one man symbolised this, it was Tony Benn. He had lost his Commons seat in the 1983 general election, but was soon in the running for a vacant seat at Chesterfield. There was fierce media interest in whether Benn would soon be back at Westminster to make life difficult for the new leader, and I spent several weeks that winter in Derbyshire. The hotel where the ITN team was staying was called, unoriginally, the Chesterfield Hotel, but some of the letters were missing on the front of the building. So every night we went back to the Sterfield Ho.

What was going to be particularly interesting was the extent to which leading Labour figures were going to bring themselves to back the candidature of Tony Benn. Neil Kinnock arrived in Chesterfield to be greeted by one of the biggest media scrums I have ever seen. From a rooftop position, we could see the whole of the market square packed with TV crews trying to get close to Kinnock and Benn doing what, in our jargon, was called a 'walkabout'. No genuine members of the public had a chance of getting near them as they sat down in a café for Tony Benn's favourite mug of tea. We did manage to catch the party leader calling Benn 'a first-class candidate'.

A visit by Denis Healey to the by-election campaign was awaited with even greater anticipation. He was due to speak at a campaign meeting in a village hall one evening where the organisers, in honour of the event, had placed a miners' banner at the back of the stage. The hall was packed, with Healey in typically rumbustious form, but he was well-known to view Benn with a dislike bordering on contempt. How was be going to bring himself to endorse the candidate? With Tony Benn on the platform beside him, he got to the point.

'Me and Tony,' he said, 'we're like Torvill and Dean.'

The laughter was thunderous, and, as if in shock at so monstrous a fib, the miners' banner fell slowly to the floor. Healey looked behind him, and quickly responded.

'I blame the meeja,' he said.

It was common at this time for the left of the Labour Party to believe that all the media were biased against them, the trade unions and what they saw as the working class. We may not exactly have been the running dogs of capitalism, but, whether we were a broadcaster or a Conservative newspaper, we were regarded as part of the establishment they were trying to overthrow. So I occasionally encountered some hostility, not least when I spoke at the Labour conference that autumn. There was then a tradition that each party conference would end with a speech of thanks from the press, and that October it fell to me as chair of the Westminster lobby. When I reached the podium, I was greeted with boos from some of the delegates in the Winter Gardens at Blackpool. The conference chairman was Eric Heffer, whom I knew reasonably well and who intervened to try and protect me. But the best protection was humour. I had spent the previous twenty-four hours writing and rehearsing what I was going to say, and it was mostly a series of jokes. The one that got the biggest laugh began with a line referring to 'the reluctance of Neil Kinnock to walk on the beach this year'. I had got away with it, but I thought I would not want to do that for a living.

The Labour conference that year reaffirmed the party's policy of unilateral nuclear disarmament, and I was quickly aware of the sensitivities of the moderate old guard of the party on the issue. Denzil Davies, who spoke from the front bench on defence, became upset when he thought that my report of the debate had made the party seem even more left-wing than it was. Neil Kinnock took the policy with him to Moscow to discuss with the Soviet leaders in the Kremlin. The General Secretary of the Soviet Communist Party at this time was Konstantin Chernenko, the embodiment of the moribund gerontocracy that was in charge of the country. At a very brief photo-call, we were not allowed to get too close to Chernenko. He had make-up on, and appeared hardly able to stand, with a colleague propping him up. And I got the impression that Kinnock's meetings in the Kremlin were not productive. The Labour leader was advocating a policy of mutual restraint – if Britain got rid of its nuclear weapons, would the Russians agree not to target *their* missiles at Britain? When I interviewed him afterwards overlooking the

Moscow River, Neil Kinnock looked unusually nervous and uncertain.

But he was on good form on the train from Moscow to Leningrad, where he was travelling for a weekend stay. Kinnock's chief of staff, Charles Clarke (later to become a cabinet minister), invited the accompanying journalists to the leader's compartment for what turned out to be a chat and a sing-song. The compartment was so crowded that Simon Hoggart, a long-serving Westminster correspondent, was sitting on the luggage rack above my head. As we launched into a few Welsh hymns, the sliding door was opened and a Russian in a large fur hat, who seemed very drunk, asked in broken English whether he could join the party.

'Hey, somebody wants to join the Labour Party,' said Simon.

At which point, Neil came out with an ingenious aphorism.

'Alcoholism,' he said, 'is the transitional stage between capitalism and communism.'

(For many Marxists, socialism was the transitional stage between capitalism and communism. Alcoholism was endemic in the Soviet Union.)

It was unfortunate that this period of Kinnock's leadership was bedevilled by the miners' strike. Given his background, he was trammelled by his sympathy for the miners themselves and, as the strike dragged on, the hardships they and their families were suffering. It is always harder to argue against an extremist on your own side, and Arthur Scargill employed the rhetoric of the left to good effect. I found Scargill's speeches at this time unpleasant; his principal weapon was sarcasm, and he had turned an industrial dispute into a political confrontation which the Thatcher government could not afford to lose. The battles between police and flying pickets only served to entrench the political divide and made it harder for Kinnock to take a stand soon enough and strongly enough against Scargill's disastrous leadership of the strike.

It almost certainly helped him decide to be much tougher

when it came to the Militant Tendency, the Trotskyite faction which was infiltrating the Labour Party, and had indeed taken it over in Liverpool. The speech he made at the Bournemouth conference in 1985 was one of the most dramatic I have witnessed. The advance copy of that speech which I had in my hands did not include the impassioned attack on the 'rigid dogma' of Militant and the 'grotesque chaos of a Labour council hiring taxis to scuttle round the city handing out redundancy notices to its own workers'. The surprise was total, not least for Derek Hatton who, as well as Eric Heffer, walked out of the conference hall.

In the last few weeks of my time as ITN's political editor, I accompanied the Labour leader on a visit to India. I was immediately captured by this technicolour country that, against all the odds, had remained a democracy. The photo opportunities were plentiful – Neil and Glenys in front of the Taj Mahal or a garlanded Neil at the ashram of Mahatma Gandhi in Ahmedabad. Then, to my puzzlement, I found a note in my hotel room inviting me to interview the Indian Prime Minister. It turned out to be a courtesy to the visiting party from abroad – we were deemed to be part of the Kinnock delegation. Thus it was that I found myself in the Prime Minister's office, built by Edwin Lutyens, in New Delhi, waiting to speak to Rajiv Gandhi. The controversial issue in the Commonwealth at this time was how to handle the apartheid regime in South Africa. Despite the wish of the majority of Commonwealth countries to impose sanctions against South Africa, Mrs Thatcher was opposed and fighting a rearguard action in the run-up to a forthcoming Commonwealth conference. I was hoping I could get the Indian Prime Minister to say what he thought about that.

We were waiting a long time. The local cameraman I was working with, Sanjiv Talreja, was clearly in awe of Gandhi and could not believe this was really happening. He nervously moved the furniture around several times before he was satisfied with the position of the seats for the interview. And still we waited. According to Rajiv Gandhi's secretary, a meeting with an American senator was badly over-running. And a while later he, ever so politely, suggested that, because the Prime Minister had no time left, the interview would have to be cancelled. I reacted with horror and, not quite so politely, said that ITN had paid a large sum of money for the satellite time to transmit the interview back to London. Besides that, I knew that the BBC's India correspondent, Mark Tully, was out in the corridor furious that I was getting an interview and he was not. The chance of a scoop over the BBC would be lost.

Within minutes, Rajiv Gandhi walked into the room. I was immediately struck by the way in which he radiated calmness and an inner quiet. He was little more than forty years old and it was only about two years since he had taken office after the assassination of his mother. Whatever his secretary had said, he gave no appearance of being in a rush. He allowed me to take him through the dispute over sanctions against South Africa, and it was his softly-spoken style that gave extra force to his dismissal of Mrs Thatcher's arguments against sanctions. By this time, we were perilously close to the deadline for the satellite, but we made it and the interview was reported around the world. Five years later, Rajiv Gandhi was, in his turn, assassinated.

In December 1984, Mikhail Gorbachev paid a visit to Britain, an event which gave the first sign, perhaps, that things were about to change in the Soviet Union. Gorbachev, then the Deputy General Secretary of the Communist Party, was already being tipped as the next Soviet leader. His meeting with Mrs Thatcher lasted five hours and was described by No. 10 as very friendly. But, as I followed him around, it was the manner of his visit which signified a different approach. For a start, he was accompanied by his wife Raisa; the wives of Soviet leaders had hitherto rarely been seen in public. The visit to the tomb of Karl Marx at Highgate cemetery was an expected ritual, but Gorbachev seemed far more at ease than many of his minders.

The visit was to end with a stay in Edinburgh, hosted by the Scottish Secretary, George Younger. But before anything much got going, I received word that Gorbachev was leaving early and the press should turn up at a hastily-arranged event where he was going to give a formal farewell. Gorbachev and George Younger duly appeared and both made polite little speeches which gave no reason for the sudden departure. They shook hands and turned to leave. This was too frustrating, so I shouted a question to Gorbachev, asking him why he was going. He turned back to answer in perfectly good English, and it was the first official news of the death of the Soviet Defence Minister, Marshal Ustinov. Within a few months, Gorbachev had become the Soviet leader, and the death of Ustinov was a key factor in that happening. He could not afford to be out of Moscow at a critical time.

The big question mark for me over British politics in the early 1980s was over what happened to the Social Democratic Party. It was a party that was going to 'break the mould' of British politics, and yet it fizzled out within just a few years. Before the Falklands War, the SDP – in alliance with the Liberals – was running ahead of the two main parties in the opinion polls. As Labour MPs like Bob Mitchell, in whose Southampton constituency I had lived, joined the SDP, there seemed to be a surge of public support for a third, or centre, party. At a press conference in the run-up to the 1983 general election, the SDP leader, Roy Jenkins, was still optimistic about what he called a 'big breakthrough'. Jenkins was famously unable to pronounce his 'Rs', so it sounded more like a big 'bweakfwew', and a foreign journalist had difficulty understanding him:

'What's that about a big grapefruit?' she asked.

Roy Jenkins was a politician for whom I had a great deal of admiration. There was much to admire about his track record as Chancellor of the Exchequer and Home Secretary. But he struggled to make his mark as a party leader, either in the Commons or with the public at large. He was increasingly under challenge from his Liberal allies during the 1983 election campaign, yet the Alliance still won nearly as large a share of the popular vote as the Labour Party. But thanks to the first-past-the-post voting system, they won only a tiny fraction of Labour's total of seats in the House of Commons. I think it was at this time that I began to consider the advantages of proportional representation, preferably the single transferable vote, although I would never have put it at the top of my political agenda.

Given the lessons from that election, I found the behaviour of David Owen over the following years increasingly absurd. He was one of the best performers on a political stage that I have heard, with a real ability to connect with his audience on the issues about which they were concerned. He was listened to with respect in the Commons. And, although this produced tensions with the Liberals, he took the SDP to a tougher position on the economy which broadly presaged Tony Blair's New Labour. But without a change to the voting system, the SDP was always unlikely to make progress on its own. David Owen, however, refused to accept the blindingly obvious, and I was constantly bemused by his claim that there was room for a fourth party in British politics. By opposing the merger with the Liberals after the 1987 election, he effectively marginalised himself and those supporters he took with him. I still think that was a huge loss to British politics.

But now came one of the most difficult decisions of my career. In 1986, I was persuaded by the editor, David Nicholas, to join the company's management, with particular responsibility for the televising of Parliament. It is a decision about which I still feel ambivalent. After more than a decade reporting Parliament, I was going to miss the drama and the adrenalin flow of meeting deadlines, but my career now took me in a new direction and allowed me a role, if a minor one, in shaping events rather than just reporting them.

CHAPTER 16

A quartering sea

MY FATHER AND mother, in the meantime, had moved to Brecon in 1969 where my grandmother still lived. That was not surprising, perhaps, given the family connections there. What was surprising was that my father had decided to retire at the early age of fifty-four, after serving as headmaster of secondary schools at Belper in Derbyshire and King Edward VI Five Ways in Birmingham. He wanted to concentrate on his literary work, and perhaps against his expectations, his retirement was to last for nearly forty years.

There was a pattern of behaviour here, which I was to repeat. My father had been born near Talybont-on-Usk, but had been moved to Germany at the age of five, and had not lived in the area since. My grandfather had never lived there either, except briefly as a student at the Memorial College. But both, for slightly different reasons, chose to retire to the town. It was certainly an attractive place to do so, nestling at the confluence of the Usk and the Honddu and looking up to the Brecon Beacons. At the end of the 1960s, the centre of the town had not changed a great deal since my grandparents had arrived in 1940. The railway line had been closed by Dr Beeching and the viaduct over the Struet taken down. The planners had brutally widened the bridge over the Usk, because it had barely space for one line of traffic. The street leading up from the bridge had been similarly widened, with some centuries-old buildings demolished and replaced by a library of a 1960s design desperately out of keeping with its surroundings.

But the streets of Georgian buildings remained, even if some were in need of refurbishment. The cattle market was still there in the centre of the town, which brought in the farmers on Tuesdays and Fridays. Many of the shops which I remembered from childhood were still going, not least F.H. Jones with its wonderful smells of paper, ink and the other accoutrements of office and study. And, of course, there were the mountains; you could just walk out of the town and up the nearest hill to secure spectacular views.

My parents bought a bungalow, only recently built, with a view south to the Beacons, from which they could walk into town. The garden, much larger than you would normally get these days, became my mother's pride and joy. Over the next decades, she developed it using her specialist knowledge of plants, to the extent that by the 1990s it was being opened to the public on certain weekends. I was never sure whether the visitors were genuinely interested in the horticulture, or just wanted a nose around someone else's property.

There were a few penurious years at the outset of their retirement to Brecon. My parents were not very communicative about what they regarded as private matters, but, as I understood it, my father's pension was not due to be paid out until he was sixty, so that they had to live on their savings for the intervening years. He did receive a bursary from the Welsh Arts Council, but otherwise tried to make ends meet with his lecturing and writing. His fifth book of poems, *Absalom in the Tree*, was to earn him a poetry prize in 1972, and he was still for a few years yet the editor of *The Anglo-Welsh Review*, one of the longest-lived English-language literary journals in Britain.

I did not really measure up to the range of my father's literary interests. He inhabited a world which I did not. He might be disappointed that I did not appreciate the work of John Cowper Powys; I could be equally disappointed that he did not seem very interested in my work at Westminster. But I admired his achievements and enjoyed in particular those of his poems which celebrated the bleak landscape in which our forefathers had survived.

For me, visiting from my hectic life in London, it seemed a peaceful existence. As I drove along the A40 and caught my first glimpse of the Usk valley and the mountains beyond, I felt a weight lifting from my shoulders, and a sense of anticipation at the prospect of a few days away from the demands of journalistic deadlines.

But my parents still had a soft spot for Pembrokeshire, where my father had first become a headmaster in the immediate post-war years. In the early 1970s, they bought a cottage just outside the village of St Twynnells, a few miles south of Pembroke and within sight of the sea. For them, it was a bold decision. The building had been abandoned for a few years by the time they acquired it, and the land around it was overgrown. But the structure was reasonably sound, apart from some persistent damp at the rear, and I loved the thick walls and the small upstairs windows with ledges on which you could sit and gaze down to the coast.

The house was at the bottom of a long lane off a very minor road leading along the line of the hill which stretches from St Petrox in the east to the Castlemartin tank range to the west. The battlemented church at St Twynnells was one of four which marked this line and which, in an earlier age, were used as a last form of defence against raiders from the sea. I used to climb the tower at St Twynnells with the children, past the ancient bell and the corpses of pigeons, to achieve the panoramic sweep along the coast. Mathew and Megan were usually more interested in jumping over the slugs and snails along the walk to the village, of which there always seemed to be hundreds out in the open after the overnight rain.

For me, it was a chance to show my family the beaches and coastline of my childhood. It was the shortest of distances to Broadhaven and Barafundle, to Stack Rocks and St Govan's Head. The children might grumble a little at the forced exercise, but we used to park the car at Bosherston and walk down past the Lily Pools to the expanse of sand at Broadhaven – surely one of the loveliest walks in Wales. The weather was, as usual in Pembrokeshire, always changing, but every summer there was at least part of the day you could go to the beach. The only exception was the heat wave of 1976, when we seemed to pick the only cloudy weather of that summer.

The problem was the amount of work required to maintain the property, even after the house had been brought to a liveable condition. There was about half-an-acre of land, which always seemed on the verge of being overrun by the surrounding undergrowth. It was my job to mow what passed for a lawn at the rear, a patch of grass which was riddled with giant weeds. It was while attempting to start the recalcitrant mower that I ruptured my hernia, an injury which led to a series of hospital operations. In fact, both my hernias had gone, but the two separate operations to repair them at my local hospital in Surrey both failed. It was then that Don Horobin, the deputy editor at ITN, stepped in to help. He got me an appointment with a Harley Street consultant, who immediately referred me to a specialist at the Middlesex Hospital. Within a matter of weeks, I was back in a hospital bed (I think there were at that time too many teaching hospitals in central London, and so not much of a waiting list). The key to success was apparently a form of catgut, and thereafter I had no further hernia trouble.

What was special about the cottage at St Twynnells was the well in the grounds. It had an old iron grille over the front of the little hump-backed stone cover, and we gradually stopped having nightmares about the children falling in. Every day, especially if anyone wanted to use the massive old bath, water had to be pumped up from the well into the tank in the house. But one day, the pump quickly started spitting air, and after much head-scratching it appeared that the well had run dry. There appeared to be no climatic reason why this had happened, so we had to ask around the neighbouring farms. It transpired that one outlet for the well was a cattle trough in a field below us. A cow had apparently licked the tap open, and the water from our well had drained away into the field. It was days before we had an adequate water supply again.

I still have an original painting of the well at St Twynnells, which was given to my parents. It is by an artist well-known in her time and whose reputation has survived. Ray Howard Jones was by this time living for long periods in a wooden hut on the side of a Pembrokeshire cliff not far from Martin's Haven. I could tell that my mother wordlessly disapproved of her lifestyle. It was said that in her eighties she swam naked with the seals in the sea at the foot of the cliffs. I remember an energetic, dishevelled and talkative lady, and I only wish I had been there when she was painting the well. She created a rather brooding atmosphere around the garden of the cottage as if a storm was coming in from the sea.

There is something about Pembrokeshire which attracts artists, and just down the road from St Twynnells lived Arthur Giardelli. He was a pacifist and conscientious objector like my father, and they got on well. He lived in a converted schoolhouse with his wife Bim, an artist in her own right, just next to the army range, and the crump of the guns could clearly be heard. He was a musician, a linguist, and had spent much of the 1930s in Paris where he collected the works of artists like Picasso and Braque. I often wondered what such an extraordinarily cultured man was doing in such a distant place.

One day, when he was well into his nineties, he told me the story. Almost half-a-century earlier, he had 'run away', as he put it, with Bim – both leaving their families behind. They had found the run-down schoolhouse, and initially were more or less just camping out in it. One day, they looked up from eating their lunchtime sandwiches to see the heads of local people peering in at them to see what it looked like to live in sin.

But time is a great healer, and fifty years of devotion to each other changed that perspective irrevocably. We have one painting by Arthur of the beach at Amroth, probably his favourite place on the coast, and one picture by Bim of the beach at Freshwater West, which I bought in the 1970s. In their house, they themselves had the most extraordinary collection of works by other artists. I said to his son Lawrence: 'You do realise, don't you, that there is an original Picasso hanging just above the stove?'

'Oh yes,' he said, 'it's been there for fifteen years. It hasn't come to any harm.'

Working for ITN at Westminster in the 1970s and '80s meant long hours and late nights, and I often did not get home until eleven o'clock or later. The votes in the House of Commons at ten o'clock and the demands of *News at Ten* made that inevitable. So I did not see my children most weekdays before they went to bed. My life was being hustled along at breakneck speed, and I sometimes wondered what they made of me.

One evening, I had recorded a piece for *News at Ten*, and arrived home just in time for its transmission at ten o'clock. Mathew, who was about five years old and usually a good sleeper, was untypically still up and sitting on the sofa with his mother. I told him that I was about to appear on the television, and watched for his reaction. When the piece began, he took one look at me and one look at the TV set, and clearly could not understand how there were two of me in the room at the same time. He got off the sofa and walked behind the TV set to look for the other version of his father.

I rarely tried to analyse my role as a parent. I did not want to be as stern as my father had been to my sisters and myself. And there was always ground to be made up because of the long hours I spent away from home. It did not help that Sian's health seemed increasingly fragile and, although a slight figure, she was losing weight. There were several admissions to hospital which produced indeterminate outcomes. Her previous addiction had taken its toll, and it now often happened that I would take Mathew and Megan out for long walks at Boxhill or Headley Heath, just the three of us. I think that, perhaps in spite of everything, the children had a reasonably contented childhood at that time.

As Mathew grew into his early teens, I thought I should

try and find something we could enjoy together. When he was about fifteen, we learned to sail off the Pembrokeshire coast. It was a small flotilla, just a handful of yachts following the skipper's lead vessel along Milford Haven, and, if the weather permitted, out through the 'Heads' to the Irish Sea beyond. It was quickly established that my skills were limited to steering the boat, and I soon became notorious for my inability to master the most basic of rope knots. For Mathew, however, it was to provide not just a pastime but a career. He earned his Yachtmaster's certificate and skippered flotillas around the Aegean and Adriatic.

Even if I was really only a passenger, I still loved being on the water. As soon as the coast began to slip away, you could leave all your weekday cares and worries behind – if only because you were now concentrating on survival. One day in particular sticks in the mind. The wind was fresh, but not too strong, and we bounced past St Ann's Head over the incoming waves and set course for the island of Grassholm, about fifteen miles out to sea. It was a clear, bright day with scudding clouds, and we could smell Grassholm as soon as we came downwind of it. The rocky outcrop was covered with guano, and from a distance it looked like snow. We rounded Grassholm, and with the wind on the beam, we headed, under full sail, for the island of Skomer.

The ageing 28-foot Westerly was now almost surfing the waves, being pushed along by a quartering sea. Nobody afterwards believed the speed of nine-and-a-half knots we recorded. In the afternoon sun, Mathew put a line out over the stern and was soon reeling in several mackerel. We moored up in North Haven on Skomer, a bird sanctuary, and watched the puffins flying like bullets through the rigging. When night fell, we rowed over in the moonlight to one of the other boats for a curry dinner, the splashing of the oars on the water creating a magical phosphorescent light.

Mathew and I continued to sail with a friend of mine, Don Moreton, who owned a series of progressively larger yachts.

We sailed mainly out of Chichester harbour at first and then out of Gosport. I was quickly out of my league, as Don competed in a variety of races, building up to the race around the Isle of Wight. On one such day, the Solent was so rough that it was difficult to maintain a position near the starting line, and the jostling for advantage going around The Needles was terrifying. With their expensive yachts just inches apart at times in a tossing sea, the skippers would be screaming at each other across the wind to get out of the way. My job was to hang on to a rope and pull it or let go when the order was given. I invariably got it wrong.

I was not the only one to get it wrong. After an interval of some years, Don invited me to join an outing on a 50-footer on what he suggested would be a gentle sail from Portsmouth to Cowes and back. There were several experienced yachtsmen on board, and, as it turned out, some professional caterers. This was going to be a pleasant little jolly. It was cold for April, but the wind seemed relatively gentle, and the trip to Cowes was uneventful. We moored off Cowes and the lunch was excellent, helped down by a few bottles of wine.

As we set off on the return leg, the wind was sufficiently quiet for the crew to decide to take the reef out of the mainsail and hoist the spinnaker as well. As we rounded the headland, we were hit by a squall, and in no time the yacht, despite its size, had capsized. The boat was on its side, the deck now almost vertical, and the sails were in the water. I let go of whatever rope I was supposed to be holding and hung on to the guardrail instead. The incident seemed to last forever until one of the younger yachtsmen ran around the gunwale and managed to haul the sails out of the sea. I decided that was probably the end of my sailing career.

In 1986, when little more than seventy, my father suffered a massive stroke. Nature was being especially unkind, for the stroke not only paralysed his right arm but also blew away his power of speech. The writer and poet could now no longer speak, write or even make himself understood. The prognosis was bleak, but not only did he regain the use of his arm, but he taught himself to read and write again. Or rather, it was my mother who taught him, starting from the very basics of language. For my father literally had to learn again from scratch. My mother would pin labels on the everyday objects around him and make him repeat the words at regular intervals. She made him do the regular exercises to recover the use of his arm. She wrote out sentences, which he then had to copy.

But he was never quite restored to his old self. He did publish a new volume of poetry, *A Field at Vallorcines*, in the mid-1990s. But he could not always articulate what he wanted to say, even though his memory, especially for things literary and historical, remained remarkably accurate. As he got older we would often have fun trying to guess the right words for him, and he was always remarkably good-humoured about it. It was my mother who took the strain of looking after him, worrying as she did about what he ate, what exercise he took, how he would manage if they went on holiday.

As is often the case, it is the carer, rather than the cared-for, who suffers most in this kind of situation. And so it was my mother who, in 1996, suddenly died. She had appeared to be in good health when I was telephoned by one of their neighbours to say she had been found on the floor of the bathroom and had been taken to hospital. It took me a while to grasp what I was being told. It was not until I got there that I understood. She had suffered a cerebral haemorrhage and died after a few days in hospital.

I was surprised by my reaction to her death. Since I had reached adulthood, I had been entirely independent from my parents. Yes, we visited and spoke on the phone at regular intervals, but to say that I was close to my mother would be an exaggeration. And she had almost reached her eightieth birthday, a good age. And yet her sudden death just took me apart for a while. On a cold November day, her ashes were buried at Aber Chapel in the Glyn, where my father's family also lie.

It was not as if, by this time, I was unacquainted with death. My wife Sian had also suddenly died seven years previously. Her death came just a short time after the deaths of her mother and then her father. In just a handful of years, the whole family had disappeared from my life.

It was the death of her mother which triggered Sian's return to drinking, and now her father was living with us. Gwynfi was a good and kindly man, but had never seemed to comprehend his daughter's problem. She in turn found it hard to watch her father live out the last months of his life.

For me, it was an overwhelming sense of déjà vu. As the drinking intensified after Gwynfi's death, I could not find in myself the same level of forbearance the second time around. Besides, there were the children to worry about. They were only at this stage aware of their mother's frequent 'illnesses', but it was only going to get worse. As the cycle of waking, drinking and sleeping became shorter and shorter, I knew she would not be able to look after the children for much longer.

Sian herself suddenly announced that she wanted to go and live on her own. In her own words, she wanted to be 'free'. Her family were a restraint on her freedom to drink. I decided – and for this I continue to feel a strong sense of guilt – to encourage her and she moved out to a small, damp terraced house in Balham. If I had then had any inkling that within six months she would be dead, I would not have agreed to it.

I still do not like to think too much about the life she must then have led. She did work for a short while, but any tolerance of her drinking soon disappeared. I took the children to see her on a number of occasions, most notably on the Christmas Day before she died. It was an odd kind of day, with an unseasonably bright blue sky and the streets of Balham were deserted. It was like walking onto a film set after the actors had all left. Sian cooked the lunch for the four of us, but then, sensing her condition, I took the children for a walk. When we returned, we could not get Sian to answer the door. She had passed out and was impervious to any noise. We walked around the streets, eerie with their emptiness, for another couple of hours before finally succeeding in gaining admittance.

She was in hospital in central London when I was called by the nurse in charge of her ward. Would I come to see her straightaway? I had already been to see her that day, but as I drove in I realised the worst. By the time I got there, she had already died.

Despite everything, it seemed very sudden. As far as Sian was concerned, she was just going to have some tests done. But at the age of forty-five, she had died from acute liver failure. The emotion which overpowered me then was that it was such a terrible waste of a life. She had so much more to live for, but had just thrown it away.

I was now a single parent, with two children in my charge. They had taken the events of the past six months in different ways. Neither had noticed there was anything especially wrong with their mother before she left home – her acting skills proved good to the last. Mathew, now seventeen, was immensely upset at what he saw as his mother's rejection of him when she moved out, but after her death he seemed to lock it away and put it behind him. Megan, at just thirteen, was at a particularly vulnerable age to lose her mother. Even if I had been a full-time house parent, which I was singularly ill-equipped to be, it could not make up for that loss. In addition, Megan felt a sense of guilt – that her mother's departure and death was something to do with her. I do not think I had the emotional equipment to assure her it was not her fault.

As for myself, Sian's death was a shock, but the shock was mixed up with a sense of relief. In that numbing period preparing for the funeral, I was consoled by the thought that her self-destructive life would only have deteriorated had she lived longer. And now I had to go back to work while looking after the children at the same time.

It helped that I had switched jobs within ITN, no longer working as a reporter and so no longer liable to work such late hours. I had previously made arrangements for someone to be at home when they got back from school. It was difficult finding anyone to do this on a long-term basis, and I tried to get back from central London as soon as I could in the evening. This did, however, mean there were periods when the children were on their own, and although Mathew was now approaching eighteen, I was still anxious about it.

My anxieties were realised one day when the house was burgled. It was a bunch of teenagers who were looking for jewellery and cameras, and – as it happened – I turned up at the front of the house as they were escaping out the back. It was lucky that the children, and particularly Megan, were not there at the time. I decided enough was enough, and that Megan would have to board for a while at her school, the City of London Freemen's School in Ashtead. It was not something I wanted for her and Megan certainly did not want it for herself. Perhaps in retrospect she saw it as another form of rejection, of separation from her family. I was not being very successful as a father.

Chapter 17

Head and shoulders

I COULD TELL from the reaction of many of my former colleagues at Westminster that they thought I had made a big mistake. The goal I had been given on behalf of ITN was the televising of the House of Commons, and everyone knew the odds were stacked against me. After all, the Prime Minister had made it clear she was opposed to the television cameras being allowed in, and if Mrs Thatcher was against it, that was that.

Maybe it was because I was in the broadcasting trade, but to me this attitude seemed a complete anachronism. Millions of people in Britain watched television and it was the main means by which the majority learned what was going on in the world. It seemed bizarre, therefore, that the central forum of our democracy should continue to exclude what was far and away the most popular form of communication. And it was not as if this was a brand-new idea which nobody else had thought of. The vast majority of democracies around the world televised their parliaments, and I had been to inspect the systems in place at the US Congress and in Ottawa, where televising was taken for granted. What is more, just up the corridor, the House of Lords had been televised for the past couple of years and the sky had not fallen in. Yet there was apparently something so unique about the Commons that the intrusion of the cameras would destroy it.

The Commons had permitted sound broadcasting since 1978, and indeed it had helped to make George Thomas famous as Speaker, with his cry of 'Order, order'. But this meant that on television bulletins, like *News at Ten*, we could only use the sound of an MP speaking in the chamber against a still photograph – which created a curiously remote and disembodied effect compared with the immediacy of other television footage. Yet in November 1985 the Commons had again voted down a motion to let the cameras in.

Their Lordships had been far more progressive. On 23 January 1985, the Upper House had gone live on television for the first time. That date was chosen in part because there was a big debate scheduled in which the Earl of Stockton, the former Prime Minister Harold Macmillan, was due to speak. I was to be the commentator for ITN and David Dimbleby for the BBC. The problem was that we were not allowed to go into the commentary box until after their Lordships had finished 'prayers' – all 'strangers' were excluded from witnessing this event, one of the many peculiarities of Parliament which we had to get used to. So we queued up outside the door to the gallery ready for a Le Mans-type start as soon as the doorkeeper let us in. We squeezed into the tiny commentary box, jammed on the headphones, picked up the microphones and hoped that we and the cameras were in a 'go' condition before the proceedings began.

Once inside the box, the sensation was rather that of the flight deck of a helicopter, hovering over the splendidly colourful scene below, all red leather and gilt. The two commentary positions were side by side, and in between, the senior doorkeeper, 'Chippy' Carpenter, crouched uncomfortably to identify peers rising to their feet during questions.

On the 'windscreen' in front of me, just in my eyeline, was a splodge of what looked unpleasantly like blood – as if some previous broadcaster had managed to collide with a squall of flying peers.

But there was no collision this time. There had been a

contrast of cultures: some more traditional peers had viewed the broadcasters as if we were a band of invading Visigoths. But in the polite, genteel manner so characteristic of the Upper House, the differences had been resolved. I had made a number of appearances, along with representatives of the BBC, before a House of Lords select committee chaired by the urbane Lord Aberdare, to discuss the terms under which the experiment would be held. These often took place in the Moses Room, so-named because of a large and distracting fresco on the wall of Moses on Mount Sinai. The select committee moved ahead with considerable dispatch, establishing ground rules satisfactory to both sides. These were days when the cameras in the chamber had to be manned, and the cameramen were asked to be as inconspicuous as possible and always wear jackets and ties. It was left to the broadcasters to choose which days they wished to televise – a so-called drive-in system which is hard to imagine now in the days of gavel-to-gavel coverage. In fact, the coverage soon became more or less continuous, with ITN cameras providing the pictures for the BBC and other broadcasters.

Most important was the agreement on what the cameras should be allowed to show. This was admirably clear: the cameras should be able to show what the public could see if they were sitting in the galleries. And it was up to the broadcasters to decide how they used the televised material. Editorial control and selection should be left to them, subject to the overall control of the House. This was ground which had to be fought all over again when the issue came to the Commons.

At this stage, I was taking time out from my job as political editor to help to manage the televising of the Lords. So it was a logical progression when the issue of televising became my full-time job. And just as well, because around this time we started producing a late-night round-up of the day's proceedings in the Lords for Channel 4. To initiate the small production team into what they should expect, I contacted an expert on parliamentary procedure, a clerk in the House of Commons called Paul Silk. It turned out that he lived in Cwmdu, just a few miles from my parents' home in Brecon, and later was to become the first clerk to the new National Assembly for Wales and Chair of the eponymous Silk Commission on devolution. We became good friends.

We produced *Their Lordships' House* out of a portable office in Black Rod's Garden, which was by no means as romantic a spot as it might sound. There were few who believed we could make a credible programme out of the Lords' proceedings, which varied considerably in interest from day to day. But the fifteen-minute slot attracted something of a cult following, if only from shift-workers and insomniacs.

By 1986, the Lords had voted to make the televising experiment permanent. There had been grumbles – with peers complaining about the cameramen going home before debates had ended and broadcasters complaining about the quality of the lighting which sometimes seemed to leave their Lordships in vestigial gloom. But overall, it had been judged a success, even though some peers voiced their suspicion that the broadcasters were just using their House as 'the key to the door' to televising the Commons. It was a suspicion that was to some extent justified. We had demonstrated successfully the basis on which a debating chamber could be televised. But nobody in the Commons was taking any notice. In the eyes of MPs, the experience of the Lords was irrelevant.

So the campaign for televising the Commons had effectively to start from scratch. We were aware that another substantive vote on televising would not take place until after the next general election, which was expected in 1987. But well before that, we sought to create a small, informal grouping of MPs and broadcasters to establish a better grounding for the case for televising. This developed rapidly into the parliamentary all-party group for televising the proceedings of the House. The group's secretary was Austin Mitchell, who, as a former broadcaster himself, was passionately in favour. Together with the BBC, I provided all sorts of papers on different aspects of televised parliaments around the world. The group staged an exhibition, got an early-day motion going, and, above all, put pressure on the government to find time for a fresh debate.

One gambit proved particularly productive, and that was the decision to go and talk to backbench groups of MPs. One of the fears about televising was that it would all be hogged by the party front benches. But it was clear to me that televising would be immensely useful to the regional programmes on BBC and ITV, and that was where backbenchers would find themselves on air. So we offered to talk to the regional groupings of Labour and Conservative MPs. The meetings, particularly with the Conservative MPs, were often tough going and attendance varied wildly. But there was some evidence it was worth it; at least two MPs who had been opponents turned up as key supporters later on.

Nevertheless, the general expectation remained that, because the Prime Minister was so strongly opposed, the vote was likely to be lost again. Our soundings, however, showed that the intake of MPs from the 1987 general election were better disposed towards televising than their outgoing counterparts. Perhaps, because they were new to the Commons, they had yet to become steeped in the club-like atmosphere that prevailed. It was also the case that the Labour leader, Neil Kinnock, was strongly in favour, and concerted efforts were made to persuade doubtful Labour MPs that televising would advantage their party.

The debate took place in February 1988, by which time we felt that the vote might at least be close. A Conservative MP, Anthony Nelson, moved the motion, urging the House to take this 'modest but historic' step. And that is what they did, by a margin that surprised everybody. The majority in favour of televising was fifty-four votes, enough to put the principle of televising beyond doubt. Quite a few drinks were bought for me in the Press Gallery bar that night.

If we now thought that we were home and dry, then we were

soon to be seriously disabused. What the broadcasters had proposed was a six-month experiment beginning in November that year, a target which was missed by a mile. It was not until May that we began to give evidence to a Commons select committee about how the experiment would be conducted, and we quickly got bogged down. MPs on the committee who were opposed to televising gave us a hard time. I remember in particular trying unsuccessfully to explain why a camera needed more light than a member of the public watching from the gallery, until I was rescued by an engineering colleague. Of all the broadcasters involved, it was the calm, reassuring voice of the BBC's chief political adviser, Margaret Douglas, which was most helpful. And an awful lot of reassurance was required.

For one thing, a new generation of more light-sensitive cameras was only then being introduced and the technology involved in small, unobtrusive remote-control systems was still being developed. So it was difficult to be too specific about how it would all work, not least how much extra light would be required. And MPs were very sensitive about what many of them predicted would be the heat and the glare. In an attempt to quell some of these doubts, the broadcasters staged a demonstration of cameras and lighting in the chamber itself.

About eighty MPs assembled on the Opposition benches ready for the demonstration. Many of them were ostentatiously wearing sunglasses, so it was not hard to guess their views on the matter. It looked more like a meeting of Mafiosi than a gathering of British politicians. The broadcasters had combined to produce a carefully-scripted performance, and it fell to me to stand at a lectern set up at the bar of the House and describe the different forms of lighting and cameras we had on display. One of the brightest of the lights looked more like a fish tank, and I knew this was going to be a hard sell. But it rapidly descended into a shambles, triggered by the Labour MP Andrew Faulds, who, despite his career in acting, was violently opposed to televising.

Because of fears that the cameras slung under the galleries would be too intrusive, we had mocked up a sort of 'hide' to match the wood panelling of the chamber. Not wishing to knock holes in the panelling to fix the hide, which in any case looked absurd, it had been left on the floor. Andrew Faulds demanded to know why the hide had not been put up around the camera. I muttered to the BBC engineer standing next to me:

'Why isn't the hide up there?'

'Because it's too heavy,' he whispered back.

'Because it's too heavy,' I announced.

At which point, Andrew Faulds got up from his seat, marched across the chamber, lifted the hide above his head and shouted: 'Look, you see, they are all liars.'

The broadcasters had made a number of tactical errors, not least in allowing the running of the televising experiment to get tangled up with the accommodation which would be required for the staff to make the TV and radio programmes which would arise from it. There was talk of hundreds of extra staff, predominantly for the BBC, who would need housing somewhere within, or adjacent to, the parliamentary precincts. I shuddered when I saw a BBC memorandum which suggested mooring a boat close to the House or building double-decker portable buildings on Speaker's Green. We were doing ourselves no favours.

But the key battle was over control of the signal – in other words, who should determine what the cameras should be allowed to show. There was an overriding fear among MPs, irrational on the basis of the experience in the House of Lords, that TV producers would make them look ridiculous or trivialise their work. The Conservative majority on the select committee were determined that the broadcasters should not be allowed to control the cameras. There was a widespread distrust on the Conservative benches of the BBC, a distrust which was grinding the negotiations into the ground. The committee now chose to invite applications from independent companies which it was thought might be more efficient than the broadcasters, and, above all, more amenable to the wishes of the House. In its application, British Telecom, which was believed to be strongly backed by Norman Tebbit, volunteered to do as it was told by the Commons authorities.

Things got so bad that at one stage I held talks with British Telecom to see if there was any common ground, talks which were fortunately unproductive. It was around this time that the select committee just hit the buffers. It wanted to give the contract to an independent company, but it was the broadcasters who were offering to pay the costs of the experiment and they could not square the circle. The Shadow Leader of the House, Frank Dobson, said it was 'taking longer to put a few cameras into one room in Westminster than it took to organise the Normandy landings'.

In January 1989, the select committee chairman, John Wakeham, decided to cut the Gordian knot. If any further progress was to be made, it was going to be made outside the forum of the committee. The broadcasters would negotiate directly with committee officials, led by John Grist, who was to become the first Commons supervisor of broadcasting. And the basis of the negotiations would be a sort of compromise: a company funded by the broadcasters would contract an independent operator to originate the signal.

'Look,' said John Grist, 'the assumption is that we are all broadly on the same side, but the broadcasters won't end up with their fingers on the sensitive bits like deciding the shots.'

This caused a lot of difficulty among the broadcasters on whose behalf I was doing the negotiating. It felt as if we were being asked to pay for something over which we were to have no control. But we proceeded on the basis of assurances that the ground rules of the experiment would not be 'manifestly unreasonable'. The organisational side of things was eventually sorted out with a complex arrangement to set up a company funded by the broadcasters, which would also provide and install the equipment, but the operation of the cameras would be contracted out to a separate independent operator. Both broadcasters and MPs would be represented on the board of the joint company, which became known as HOCBUL (House of Commons Broadcasting Unit Ltd).

There were still some very sticky times. One such moment came when we sought to put the agreement between the company and the Commons on a contractual basis – as you would in the real world. But this was not the real world. The advice from the Speaker's counsel declared that the House of Commons was a sovereign body which had no corporate legal personality and so could not enter into a legally binding contract. In words which I still treasure, he said that the 650 MPs 'could no more sign a binding contract than a chance group of passengers on the 8.10 from Guildford'.

Eventually, it looked as if we were near the finishing line. The indications were that the rules of coverage, governing what the cameras could show, would be sufficiently relaxed to satisfy the broadcasters. Paul Mathews, ITN's deputy chief executive, with whom I was working on this, had set out the guiding principle: that a television viewer 'should be able to follow the proceedings in the same way as a spectator in the public gallery'. But John Wakeham had other ideas. At the last minute, in order to win over opponents in the Commons, he drastically tightened up the rules. The standard format was to be head-and-shoulders only of the MP who was speaking. There were to be no reaction shots, no cut-aways, no panning shots – nothing more than a stilted progression of talking heads which would give the viewer only a limited understanding of what was going on.

There was consternation among the broadcasters. On the ITV side, it was felt that it amounted to little more than a Commons corporate video. We were funding and organising a form of television coverage which we would not transmit ourselves. I myself was caught on the wrong foot, having passed on the generalised assurances that the rules would be more relaxed than this. For a period, it looked as if some broadcasting organisations might pull out of the experiment, and Channel 4 actually dropped its earlier plans for regular live coverage of the Commons.

John Wakeham refused to bow to the protests of the broadcasters, calculating that we would not want to take the blame if the experiment collapsed. I myself took the view that, whatever the level of our disquiet about what the public would be allowed to see, we should not go into reverse gear at this late stage. Each broadcasting organisation issued strongly-worded press statements to coincide with the publication of the select committee's report, with resulting headlines like: 'MPs tune in for Commons show – but you won't see the naughty bits' (*The Sun*). The experiment would now begin in November 1989 – eighteen months after the Commons had voted for it.

In the event, what the public did get to see was livelier and more interesting than the broadcasters had predicted. There were crucial limitations: during the closed-circuit rehearsal period, prior to going live, Nigel Lawson made a statement to the Commons on his sudden resignation as Chancellor of the Exchequer. One of the cameras on the government side picked out an emphatic profile of Mrs Thatcher turned looking intently at him. It was a shot which the director was now unable to select because it was against the rules. But those rules, based on the infamous 'head-and-shoulders' shot, were interpreted flexibly under the aegis of John Grist, and were relaxed a little further after another submission from the broadcasters. After a matter of months, viewers were able to see most of what was going on in the chamber.

The select committee report in July 1990, which led to the experiment becoming permanent, said the broadcasters could legitimately claim to have made 'a praiseworthy attempt to deliver what they promised'. After all the brickbats over the previous two years, that was something of an accolade.

In retrospect, the broadcasters, myself included, were too slow to realise what was going to be the simplest way forward – that televising the Commons should be subcontracted to a third party, thus establishing a kind of cordon sanitaire between the broadcasters and the politicians. That compromise, though cumbersome, lasted well, with the Lords joining the Commons in an integrated remote-controlled system, until eventually Parliament took over responsibility for funding the televising operation from the broadcasters. When parliaments and assemblies were set up in the devolved nations, it was axiomatic that they too would be televised.

Chapter 18

Lives at risk

THE EDITOR OF ITN suddenly looked up at the bank of monitors above his desk. One of the screens was showing the latest feed from Baghdad. Stewart Purvis watched in growing amazement at the sight of an American Cruise missile only a couple of hundred feet up in the air heading for its target. He could see it make a turn, following the computerised directions with which it had been programmed. Then, as our reporter Brent Sadler stood underneath it giving a running commentary, another missile approached. Stewart grabbed a phone and issued swift instructions to prevent the pictures being pirated by a rival station. We had seen the missiles being fired from the US warships in the Gulf, but this was the first time we had seen them arriving at their destination.

The Gulf War, or – as we should now refer to it – the *first* Gulf War, had been underway for just over two weeks. I had been drafted into the editor's office to help draw up the company's policy on reporting the war. The aim was to respond as quickly as we could to events as they happened, and respond quickly also to the political and public pressures which our coverage of the war would inevitably generate.

Brent Sadler had only just managed to get back into Baghdad from Amman when he filed his report on the Cruise missiles. It was the first of many reporting exclusives by ITN during the war, which was the biggest logistical operation that we had faced as a broadcaster, with more staff abroad than ever before. We had been first on air at the start of the war with the bombing campaign against Baghdad, and we were the first British broadcasters into Kuwait City after what was left of the Iraqi army had retreated.

For a public service broadcaster like ITN, however, coverage of a war cannot just be about scoops, great pictures and great reporting. It has to be set in the context of its time. It was almost a decade since the last significant conflict, the battle for the Falklands, and the world had moved on. In the South Atlantic, the geographical isolation of the fighting meant that the Ministry of Defence had control of all forms of communication, and therefore had a large measure of control over the flow of information.

But circumstances were now very different. There were many more sources of information available for the war in the Gulf, not just because of its geography but because so many countries were involved, not least the United States and its vociferous media. And, unlike a decade previously, satellite technology was there to be exploited, bringing instant pictures from the front.

Just a few days before the beginning of the conflict in January 1991, the Ministry of Defence issued guidance on what information about British forces could be used in the media. Given the predictability of the war, this was absurdly late (it was, after all, months since the invasion of Kuwait), and the guidance absurdly restrictive. After a storm of protest from the media, the status of the document was heavily downgraded. The National Union of Journalists also produced a set of principles and guidelines which was far too gung-ho. None of this was going to absolve us from setting our own guidelines for our own reporting.

The central tenet of our own policy was clear: that we would report the war as comprehensively as possible, but that we should not broadcast information 'which might place at risk the lives of Allied forces or jeopardise their operations'. Reporters 'embedded' with Allied troops, for instance, always took care not to reveal their position. But achieving that balance when events are moving very quickly was always going to be a challenge. Within twenty-four hours of the outset of the war, I made a note that one guideline was not holding: 'Flood of material from all sources meant it was totally impossible, as predicted, to check everything with the MoD.'

Within forty-eight hours, we issued a reminder to staff that all reports in our war coverage should be sourced as precisely as possible, whether it was an Allied announcement, an Iraqi claim, a wire service report. And any claims about Allied losses should be matched by a response from Allied military sources. We struggled constantly with how to report any British losses, such as the downing of the Tornado aircraft. It was our aim not to broadcast reports of any casualties without adding that the next of kin had been informed, in order not to alarm the families of other servicemen. But it was sometimes the case that news of any losses was leaking out before confirmation from the MoD that the families had been informed.

The biggest controversy was over our presence in Baghdad. With Brent Sadler back in Baghdad and, for a while, the only British television reporter permitted use of the CNN satellite dish, ITN was able to provide an independent eyewitness account from inside Iraq. But that is not how some Conservative MPs and some of the tabloid press saw it. The *Daily Star* went the furthest, with the headline: 'Lord Haw Haw lives again – scandal of Saddam's propaganda in our homes.' Conservative backbenchers seemed to focus mainly on the BBC, at least one calling the organisation the 'Baghdad Broadcasting Corporation'.

The controversy came to a head over the Allied bombing of the Amariya bunker, with many civilian casualties. Although we ensured that our reporting included the Allied statements that the shelter was a command and control base for the Iraqi military, the toll of the dead and the pictures of the injured lent credence to the Iraqi version of events. In a world of global media, there was no point in trying to pretend that the British public alone could be kept in ignorance.

To help counter the charge that we were the unwitting victims of Iraqi propaganda, we had ensured that a warning was included in the introduction to every report from Baghdad to the effect that it was 'subject to Iraqi censorship'. In fact, attempts by Saddam's regime to censor foreign reports became increasingly erratic, but we said it anyway. But this then raised another problem: how can we fairly distinguish between different forms of restriction on our journalism? It is censorship if it is the enemy doing it, but you do not like to call it censorship if your own side is doing it. In fact, there were gradations of restriction, some of them, of course, self-imposed. In reports from Saudi Arabia and the Gulf, we included, where relevant, the phrase: 'certain operational facts have been omitted for reasons of military security'. In reports from Israel, which was subject to Scud missile attacks, we used the word 'censorship' – which in retrospect was a little unfair.

All this fine-tuning of our approach to covering the war cut little ice with those who thought we simply should not be in Baghdad. The Conservative MP, Nicholas Soames, told the Commons that the BBC and ITN were being 'grotesquely disloyal' in their reporting of the war. The Leader of the House, John Macgregor, replied (I suspect, off the cuff) that representations had been made to the broadcasting authorities about the views that had been expressed. No formal representations were made to us by the Government, but privately they were. Tim Bell, unofficial public relations adviser to the Prime Minister, rang Stewart Purvis – in a 'call that never happened' – to tell him how angry Downing Street was that Brent Sadler was in Baghdad. It was not pressure, however, to which we were likely to succumb.

I like to think, partly because Stewart and I worked closely together during those weeks, that ITN was able to respond rapidly to any problems and complaints. Not only did we constantly adjust the implementation of our policy to meet the changing events, we also tried to head off any criticism as quickly as we could. We would reply to complaints from politicians and others within hours, if we could, and we were not afraid to admit that now and again, in the rush of news, something could have been worded a little better. Compared with the BBC, which can sometimes behave like a lumbering elephant, it kept us more or less out of trouble.

But not completely. David Nicholas, by this time ITN chairman, volunteered to talk to the members of the Independent Television Commission, the body regulating ITV at the time. He was so buoyed up by what he rightly saw as our reporting successes that he wanted to share them with the ITC, and I accompanied him. But we reckoned without Lord Chalfont, one-time minister in Wilson's Labour government in the 1960s and now a member of the ITC. Lord Chalfont's trajectory from the left to the right of the political spectrum had been something of a spectacle over the intervening decades, and it showed in this meeting.

To our consternation, he compared ITN's reporting from Baghdad to reporting from Berlin during the Second World War. It would have been unthinkable then, he said, to be reporting the Nazi version of events and was unacceptable now to be reporting Saddam's. Regardless of the multiple anachronisms in his argument, he was difficult to shake off, and we were fortunate that his argument had little purchase with the other members of the commission. In the end, we got away with a minor recommendation on improving our coverage.

The real answer lay in the public reaction to the war, which remained overwhelmingly supportive. There was no evidence from the public response to ITN programmes that they wished to be deprived of information which was available to viewers in other countries.

That public support was based on a number of factors. There was no issue about the legality of this war in the Gulf: Saddam's invasion of Kuwait put that beyond doubt. And the first President Bush understood the importance of keeping allies involved, including Arab allies. Above all, he was right to stop the war when he did, without embarking on an invasion of Iraq. It was a wisdom which did not last through into the next decade.

My role at ITN at this time was the rather pompously sounding one of 'controller of public affairs'. In fact, what was missing was any element of control. I was responsible for a range of issues, from press relations and public affairs, to editorial policy, compliance with the regulatory authorities and legal matters. In the BBC, the same issues were handled by several different departments.

I was lucky in that the press office at ITN was run by an affable Welshman, Huw Roberts, who had an engaging enthusiasm for all things ITN, and I could safely leave the day-to-day relations with the press to him. ITN, and particularly *News at Ten*, was a high- quality and highly recognised brand name which was not difficult to promote. It baffles me still, therefore, why the ITV companies were so insistent on trying to shift *News at Ten* from the slot with which ITV was so identified. At the first attempt, I helped to mobilise political opposition to the change, with a meeting attended by MPs in the Commons. With the support of the Prime Minister, John Major, among others, it was seen off. But the ITV bosses came back into the fray, determined (wrongly, as it turned out) to maximise their potential audience by running films until 10.30 p.m. They eventually got their way, sacrificing the *News at Ten* brand for an illusory increase in viewers. Little wonder that the BBC jumped into the slot, and ITV was thereby seriously weakened.

I was lucky, too, in the quality of legal advice that I received, primarily on libel law. It was not uncommon to receive calls from highly-paid lawyers pressuring me to ensure an item was not run because of some presumed damage to a client. One such call, which bordered on the offensive, arose because his client had watched the lunchtime news while in the dentist's chair and had presumed that the name of his product, a particular wine label, was being traduced in some way. He had got it completely wrong, but it took hours to get the lawyer to go away. On another occasion, I had to send the editor to the High Court to try and stop an *ex parte* injunction which would have prevented us broadcasting an item due on the early evening news less than an hour away. Fortunately, the injunction had been thrown out before he got there.

My time in the job coincided with a traumatic period in the life of the company. ITN's budget had been constantly growing, not least because of expanded foreign coverage such as the Gulf War, and new commercial realities were now sweeping in. The ITV companies were being obliged to sell off half the company, and ITN had to change, and change quickly, from an in-house news provider to a commercial entity which could compete not just for its ITV contract but also other business. Under the aegis of Bob Phillis, newly arrived as chief executive, a wholesale review of ITN's operations was undertaken from the ground up. The news programmes were the primary output of the company, so what kind of management, departmental and corporate structure did they need to support them? The result was a radical shake-up, so radical that at one stage it looked as though there would be little corporate management left.

There is no question that it had to be done for the company to survive. But the cost in human terms was heavy. It was quite deliberate that the cuts in management came first, but that did little to temper the anger and anguish of the staff who found themselves redundant – nearly 200 overall, almost a fifth of the company. The turmoil inside ITN was mirrored by the newspaper coverage, which I was supposed to be handling. Those made redundant included some well-known faces, and this put us right at the top of the Fleet Street agenda. When you have the whole of Fleet Street gunning for you, it is a bit like being hit by a plague of locusts. There is little you can do except put your jacket over your head and wait for it to pass. Then perhaps you can try and get your side of the story across to more effect.

The tabloids in particular were ringing everyone they could and raking up a lot of out-of-date material. One such two-page feature in the *Today* newspaper made a series of allegations about ITN's finances and laid the blame at the door of one executive who had only recently retired. Our lawyers were confident that Hugh Whitcomb had been libelled. So I rang Hugh to tell him, expecting him to be dismayed. Not a bit of it.

'Oh, goody, goody,' he said.

And he was right. I am sure he could have bought a new family car on the proceeds of that settlement.

But the truth was that I was getting withdrawal symptoms. I missed the journalism, and the withdrawal symptoms were made worse by the knowledge that I was missing one of the most riveting political crises of the century. The fall of Mrs Thatcher as Prime Minister was theatrical, and I no longer had a ringside seat. Outside Parliament, on College Green, broadcaster after broadcaster was camped, waiting for the latest developments. I went down there, wandering around rather disconsolately and soaking up the atmosphere.

Eventually, I managed to wangle my way back into political reporting, and in 1992 I went back on the beat at Westminster, this time with the title of chief political correspondent – Mike Brunson was by this time the political editor. Times had changed in the five years I had been away. For a start, there seemed much more coverage of politics on the news programmes. This was partly due to the televising of the Commons which had given it more immediacy. But it was just as much to do with the way John Major's government began to disintegrate after the 1992 election. The withdrawal from the ERM and the rows over the Maastricht Treaty fatally weakened the Prime Minister. I was bemused at the sight of the Conservative Eurosceptics parading in front of the cameras in open defiance of their government. At the height of the divisions inside the Labour Party in the 1970s, I could remember nothing quite like this. I could never really understand how an obsession with the European Union and its treaties could so outweigh everything else worth fighting for in political life. Westminster politics for a while may have seemed a little like the Mad Hatter's tea party, but what was surprising was how John Major continued to survive it and serve a full five-year term.

One of the problems was trying to work out what John Major actually stood for in political life. I have a completely unfair image of him from a trip to Sweden for a series of talks with the then Swedish Prime Minister, Carl Bildt. John Major was looking for any friends he could make in the European Union, and he thought he had found one in Bildt. After a meeting in Stockholm, the two men travelled to the Swedish Prime Minister's summer home in the archipelago of islands around that coast. It was late summer, the weather was muggy and overcast, and the island was plagued by midges. John Major wandered aimlessly around, looking rather lost.

The small group of journalists accompanying the visit were transported to the island in a torpedo boat provided by the Swedish navy. This was a trip for which we were seriously under-dressed, not least because of what was about to happen. Encouraged to stay on deck, we were expecting to be driven sedately to our destination. Instead, the torpedo boat went into a series of aggressive manoeuvres, twisting to left and to right as if avoiding an attacker. The spray was coming over the gunwales, and the Downing Street press officer was hanging on for dear life and calling for her mother. It later transpired that the captain had a grudge against journalists because of a recent documentary on Swedish television alleging abuses in the Swedish navy, and he decided to take it out on us.

Such was the unpopularity of the Major government at this time that it suffered some spectacular by-election defeats. Among the most spectacular was the result at Newbury in 1993, the first by-election since the forced withdrawal of sterling from the ERM and the financial crisis of 'Black Wednesday'. I could tell from the way the campaign was going that the Liberal Democrats had a good chance of capturing the seat from the Conservatives, who had held it for the previous seventy years. On the night of the poll, I was due to do a live piece from Newbury into *News at Ten*, but still was not quite sure how to call it.

An hour before transmission, I managed to get in to see the Liberal Democrat agent, Chris Rennard. He told me that he expected to win with a majority of around 3,000, which would have been a convincing victory, and that was the steer I went with. I was as gobsmacked as everybody else when, in the small hours of the morning, the Liberal Democrat majority turned out to be 22,000 – more than seven times the estimate I had given *News at Ten*. Chris Rennard told me later that he had been cautious in what he told me. His canvass returns were predicting a win by about 9,000 votes, but he too had underestimated the size of the swing against the government. John Major was always going to lose the next general election – the only question was by how much.

The greatest political loss at this time was the death of John Smith, the best Prime Minister Labour never had. He had become a cabinet minister right at the end of the Callaghan administration, and his experience showed as Leader of the Opposition where he constantly got the better of John Major. He was arguably too cautious in his reforms of the Labour Party, but he would undoubtedly have won the ensuing general election, if with a smaller majority than Tony Blair. I visited him in his Barbican flat to do a relaxed interview on oratorical styles in the Commons, and we swiftly retreated into anecdotes about political figures of the past, most notably Tony Crosland. He had appeared in good health and good humour, but only a few weeks later suffered his fatal heart attack. It was a privilege for me to represent ITN at his funeral in Edinburgh.

It is usually a mistake to go backwards in your career, and it was probably a mistake for me to go back to political reporting for ITN. Such was the level of demand for political stories on a reduced number of staff that I was spending less time talking to politicians and too much time in the editing booth. A seminal moment came for me when I was producing a piece for the lunchtime news. It was to be the lead story, and with ten minutes to go I was still running down the road with the videotape in my hand. I rushed into the edit booth in our Millbank studios, threw the cassette at the VT editor, Dave Chisholm, tried to explain the sequence of shots and scribbled a script on the nearest bit of paper. With thirty seconds to spare, I was still recording my track, and there was less than five seconds to go when the cassette was in the 'gate' and ready to play into the programme.

'That was close,' I told the programme editor afterwards.

'What's the problem?' he replied. 'You made it.'

But I was approaching fifty years old, and there would come a time when I would not make it.

I did have an ulterior motive in going back to reporting politics. I thought it would make it easier to achieve my next ambition – to return to live in Wales. For politics in Wales was about to get interesting. The Labour Party, which looked a betting certainty to form the next government, was committed once again to implementing devolution and creating a directly-elected Welsh Assembly, and I was keen to follow this political battle. For me, it became a double gamble: an odds-on gamble that Labour would win the election and a more speculative gamble that there would be a Yes vote in the subsequent devolution referendum. But gamble I did, managing to negotiate my way to becoming political editor for BBC Wales in 1994. After a minor squabble over titles, I was back in Wales.

CHAPTER 19

Green grass of home

THE FLIGHT SOUTH from Buenos Aires took two hours. We were heading for *Y Wladfa*, the Welsh settlement in Patagonia. Except that it is only a small part of Patagonia really, and completely unlike Wales. That must have come as a surprise to the emigrants who had come all the way across the Atlantic on the *Mimosa* in the nineteenth century, and it still surprised me.

When we touched down at the small airport at Trelew in Chubut province, the ministerial party was ushered into the VIP lounge to meet the regional governor. This was the first visit by a senior government representative from Britain for fifty years or more, and it required a few formalities. Thus it was that Rod Richards, junior minister at the Welsh Office, found himself in a tiny room, barely big enough to hold a few armchairs, shaking hands with the Argentine governor for the benefit of the photographers. But when they began talking to each other, the realisation dawned. Between them they spoke three languages, but not one in common.

There was a long and embarrassing pause while officials searched for someone who could translate. After what seemed like an age, an old lady in her seventies, wearing a coat that had seen better days, emerged through the crush of bodies in the small room. Courteously, but very slowly, she translated the

Welsh spoken by Rod Richards into the Spanish spoken by the governor. The irrelevant language was English.

As far as the Argentine government was concerned, Rod Richards was a representative of the British government in Wales. But for the descendants of the Welsh settlers, the presence of a Welsh-speaking government minister meant more than that – a direct link with the land of their fathers. Only a few thousand still spoke the language with any degree of fluency, but there was a new enthusiasm for learning it, just as there was in Wales. Indeed, the language classes felt and sounded much the same as the equivalent language classes back in Cardiff, as the pupils recited the Welsh words and phrases. But it took some time to get used to the fact that the other language they were using was not English but Spanish.

The Patagonia of Welsh dreams was in fact a string of settlements in the Chubut Valley, where the Welsh emigrants had carved out a hard living, enduring deaths and disasters along the way. Beyond the narrow strip of irrigated land either side of the Camwy river, the desert surrounded them. Majestic in its colours, but desert nonetheless. It was strange seeing trucks kicking up the dust as they passed a Welsh chapel, where the inscriptions on the gravestones were all in *yr hen iaith* (the old language). There had been nothing but desert there before the settlers came, but they had survived, and the language had survived.

And that made me feel guilty. We were entertained to a typical Welsh high tea in Gaiman, the town with probably the highest proportion of Welsh-speaking residents. As we tucked into the ham and the scones, I could not fall back on English when my stuttering Welsh collapsed. But I understood one question put to me by the old lady next to me.

'You say you are Welsh, and you live in Wales, so why can't you speak Welsh? After more than a 100 years here, away from the homeland, and we still speak it. So why can't you?'

It was a question to which I had no answer. Or rather, the answer would have amounted to a succession of excuses.

In truth, many of the Welsh settlers had gradually intermarried with the local Spanish-speaking farming families, and few of the younger generation now spoke the language with any fluency. At one reception, I found myself talking to three elderly women, who had all married local Spanish-speaking men. I asked them how that had happened.

'Oh, we ran out of Welsh boys,' they said.

On the night before the flight back to Buenos Aires, a concert was staged for the visiting party at an address I still treasure – St David's Hall, Belgrano Avenue, Trelew. It sounded like any concert of Welsh songs, recitations and dances back in Wales. But although only a minority of the younger people taking part were now fluent in Welsh, it was heart-warming to witness their eagerness to maintain the customs and traditions that went with the language, and the willingness of some, at least, to learn it afresh.

My return to Cardiff, where I had begun my journalistic career, was a change of culture in a number of different ways. The *South Wales Echo*, for which I had worked all those years ago, ran a brief story with the headline: 'Green green grass of home for warhorse.'

That did not exactly encapsulate my feelings about it, because I had in reality to adapt to a very different environment. I was leaving a tightly-run outfit like ITN for an organisation with multiple departments and multi-layered management. The newsroom was the most complex I have ever seen, serving radio and television in two languages. I could only admire my bilingual colleagues who had to produce four different versions of the same report. I shared a room with colleagues such as Vaughan Roderick, Miles Fletcher, Julie Barton and Bob Humphrys, the brother of John Humphrys. I went for a drink after work with Vaughan and Miles as often as I could, so that, rather selfishly, I could catch up on what had been happening in Wales in the twenty-five years I had been away.

Joining BBC Wales allowed me to branch out into other forms of programming rather than just news. As political editor, my main focus was to report for the daily news programme, *Wales Today*, but I was also able to present the weekly political programme, which at that time was called *Welsh Lobby* and produced for much of my time there by the talented Cath Allen. It was a studio-based programme recorded on the day of transmission, in which I got to do extended interviews with senior Westminster politicians such as Geoffrey Howe and Donald Dewar, as well as items more specific to Wales. And then there were the documentaries, which perhaps I enjoyed most of all, like the one which took me to Patagonia.

One thing which struck me immediately was the need to adjust my political focus, compared with the state of political debate at Westminster. There is a requirement for impartiality on broadcast journalists, but what that means in any particular context has to be a matter of judgement. When coming to Wales, that judgement meant moving one or two steps to the left. With a Conservative government in power, the centre of debate at Westminster was between those who espoused the free market – if in a less strident fashion than under Mrs Thatcher – and the increasingly Blairite policies of the Labour Party. In Wales, the policies associated with Mrs Thatcher were regarded as anything but mainstream, and the Welsh Labour Party was being dragged along some way behind the Blairite reforms. With the other two parties with elected representatives in Parliament also to the left of centre, the middle ground of Welsh politics was one or two steps to the left of the middle ground at Westminster.

This was something which John Redwood must have understood, but refused to accommodate. The Secretary of State's own constituency of Wokingham, where I filmed on several occasions, was a world away from the south Wales still suffering from the closure of the mines and other heavy industry. But he deliberately refused to pander to Welsh sensibilities, as his predecessors, Peter Walker and David Hunt, had been quite prepared to do. It was not just that John Redwood refused to spend a night in Wales, taking the train back every night across the border. That was merely symptomatic. It was that he gave every appearance of refusing to believe that the economy of Wales, or its public services, required any different treatment from the economy of, say, the south-east of England.

The most notorious example of this insensitivity came when in 1995 he grandly announced that almost a million pounds of Wales's block grant had been handed back to the Treasury in London at the end of that particular financial year. This was seized on by the opposition parties as John Redwood giving away Wales's money. In fact, every government department had to hand back its under spend at the end of every financial year because no government department could plan its spending that accurately. John Redwood's problem was that the under spend was rather larger than usual and he chose to boast about it.

In fact, John Redwood was a good chief executive. I filmed him on one occasion in Gwydyr House, the home of the Welsh Office in London. He was on a video-link to Cardiff for a briefing from civil servants there in preparation for questions in the Commons. He quickly spotted an error in their calculation of the latest unemployment statistics and casually made mincemeat of them. Sitting either side of him were two people who were later to emerge in different roles. One was Ffion Jenkins, his private secretary, later to marry John Redwood's successor as Secretary of State. The other was his political aide, Hywel Williams, who was later to write a scathing account of what he called the collapse of conservatism.

John Redwood had his own agenda, which was not necessarily all bad for Wales. He was in favour of keeping open small, older and rural hospitals. He was quite tough on the quangos, or at least some of them like the Countryside Council for Wales which he thought was wasting money. I watched his modus operandi at one meeting of the Further Education Funding Council. The council members had been planning their presentation for weeks and were rather nervously waiting for him to arrive. As the Secretary of State took his seat, the chairman came round the table to welcome him and shake his hand. By the time the chairman had got back to his own seat, John Redwood had taken over the meeting and was telling them not to focus so much on closing or merging smaller institutions.

John Redwood and Hywel Williams could sometimes be a mischievous pair. I can see them now, sitting in the Secretary of State's office in Gwydyr House, Redwood in an armchair, Hywel Williams on the sofa, giggling together over what looked like the back of an envelope. I surmised that they were working on the calculations that they were soon to announce on the likely cost of Labour's new Assembly for Wales. They probably saw it as a bit of political knockabout when they predicted the cost would be in excess of £120 million per year. But it was a lot more realistic than the assessment made for BBC Wales by the Cardiff Business School, which put the annual cost at less than £15 million, with a ludicrous estimate of only £8 million for the building itself.

John Redwood's unsuccessful bid for the Conservative leadership in June 1995 left a vacancy at the Welsh Office, which was filled by a very different figure. William Hague was quite prepared to try and smooth ruffled Welsh feathers. For a start, he made a point of spending quite a few nights in Wales, and he, unlike his predecessor, did not make an issue about signing letters in Welsh. I filmed him having breakfast in the ministerial flat at the Welsh Office in Cardiff – a moment I remember particularly because the kitchen table was made of glass and the cameramen lay on the floor and shot from underneath the table as the new Secretary of State was eating a banana and reading a Welsh morning newspaper. And of course he married the girl who taught him how to sing the Welsh national anthem. Redwood accused him later of trying 'to blend in with the Welsh establishment'.

There was one issue that William Hague was not prepared to 'blend in' with anybody about, and that was Europe. During a dinner in Cardiff one night in 1996, where our conversation was almost drowned out at times by a neighbouring table of rugby supporters, he made clear the depth of his Euro-sceptic views. He had not been happy with the Maastricht Treaty, but did not regard that as a resigning issue. But he would resign from any cabinet which agreed to join the euro. This hostility to the euro emerged during the 2001 general election, when Hague's leadership of the Conservative campaign degenerated for much of the time into a campaign to save the pound.

In some ways, the real politics during this period in Wales was taking place in the Labour Party. The opinion polls had been pointing to a massive Labour win for some time. It mattered, therefore, what Labour was planning to do in power, and what was causing most controversy was how it was planning to devolve power from Westminster to Cardiff. Unlike in Scotland, where there had remained considerable cross-party consensus on the desire for a Scottish Parliament, devolution policy in Wales was being thrashed out inside the Labour Party. For a generation or more, there had been a fault-line running through Labour in Wales dividing the pro- and anti-devolutionists. The divisions had been there for all to see during the referendum campaign back in 1979, but the Labour leadership this time was working hard to avoid it happening again.

For the Shadow Secretary of State for Wales, Ron Davies, it had to be a process of compromise, much as it irked him. The anti-devolutionists had dropped their public opposition to a Welsh Assembly, but only because there had been an agreement to limit its powers. Ron Davies admitted in an interview with me that proposing greater powers might cause such divisions in the party that the plan might 'fall at the first fence'. But there was still a rearguard battle going on over how the Assembly should be elected. In early 1996 this was being played out in the policy commission Labour had set up to try and get the different factions to agree.

There were those, like Ron Davies himself, who wanted the Assembly to be elected by proportional representation to avoid giving the impression that they were trying to set up another Labour fiefdom – a massive Labour majority was at that time predicted to dominate the Assembly. But an angry meeting of Welsh Labour MPs showed the divisions over PR had the potential to re-ignite the whole devolution debate inside the party. The veteran Labour MP, Ray Powell, for example, told me that he was prepared to accept an Assembly, but no way was he going to accept PR. Ken Hopkins, the chairman of the policy commission, told me that the policy of the party was going to be conventional first-past-the-post elections for the new Assembly.

In just a few months, there was a complete about-turn, and the about-turn was triggered by the party leader. Tony Blair had decided that, in order to make the party's devolution policies more publicly defensible against Conservative attack during the coming election campaign, they should be made subject to referendums. This had not been the policy before that moment, and indeed, the Welsh Labour Party had been against a referendum in case it exposed the same kind of devolution wounds that were caused back in 1979. But it was not the situation in Wales which prompted Blair's about-turn, but the situation in Scotland, where Blair was worried that giving the Scottish Parliament tax-raising powers might undermine his own pledge not to raise income tax at a UK level. Ron Davies saw his chance. If the policy on a referendum was to be changed, so could the policy on proportional representation. He persuaded Blair, who probably did not care too much about the issue, that the Assembly should be elected by the additional member system.

Those in the Welsh Labour Party against PR could live with this volte-face because of the chance that the whole caboodle would disappear in a No vote in the referendum. But they were also told, rather fraudulently, that the AMS system was not going to be a full-blown system of proportional representation. Because there would be forty constituency Assembly members elected in the usual way, and only twenty additional members elected proportionally, it could be portrayed as still mostly a first-past-the-post system. When I reported the announcement, saying (rightly) that this *was* a system of proportional representation, I was rung up by the party general secretary, Anita Gale, and told that I was wrong – there was only 'an element' of proportionality in the election system. I had known Anita for many years, since she was a Labour agent in my local constituency in Surrey, and for her to ring up and complain meant this was a sensitive point. But it was a deliberate misunderstanding which was to continue to cause problems in the party for a number of years.

For Tony Blair, however, it was all about winning that election after so many years in the political wilderness. He was a superb communicator, by far the most professional of all the party leaders I had interviewed during my career. Unlike John Major, who would still fuss about everything, Blair made the whole business of television interviews seem effortless. There was a convention at Labour Party conferences that the party leader gave interviews to the 'regional' TV stations all in one go, usually towards the end of the conference. So Blair would do about a dozen interviews on the trot, not moving from his seat while political correspondents would drop in and out of the chair in front of him. You would get a maximum of about three minutes before dramatic arm signals from Blair's officials would tell you your time was up. Then it was out of the chair, grabbing the videotape from the pooled crew before you were out of the room and it was the turn of the next interviewer.

None of this seemed to faze Blair at all; he would switch on his concentration just a few seconds before the interview began and was rarely caught out. In 1996, I did manage to extract a promise that Ron Davies would be Welsh Secretary in a Labour government, which had been by no means a foregone conclusion. Judging by the reaction of Ron Davies when I told him, Blair had told me before he had told the man himself.

John Major seemed to believe that Labour's devolution plans would unravel during the general election campaign. But the Labour Party in Wales deliberately stayed low-key on the devolution issue – it was not going to win them a lot of votes and they wanted to minimise the risk of any divisions in the party coming to the surface. When the issue was raised, they could point to the referendum as the time when it could all be debated. Instead, the main battles were all in the marginal seats such as Brecon and Radnorshire.

On one fine April day, I accompanied John Major on his only visit to Wales during the 1997 election campaign. He arrived at Cardiff airport with his entourage and accompanying press party, where I joined them. The cavalcade of three coaches, led by the Prime Minister's battle bus, left for Brecon as the press opened their lunchboxes and levered open their half-bottles of white wine. A party official came on the intercom to ask everybody to hang onto their lunchboxes as the roads were likely to undulate a little – presumably a reference to the Brecon Beacons.

The unseasonal sunshine helped to create a festive air in the main square in Brecon, and as the party's cheerleader worked up cries of 'Major, Major!', a steel platform was eased out from the side of the battle bus from which the Prime Minister could address the crowd. John Major seemed to be enjoying himself, bantering with the crowd, in particular with a heckler in Mohican garb and bright orange cockscomb. But there were plenty of people in the crowd with rival party stickers, and he was deluding himself if he thought this was effective campaigning. He then paid a visit to the local hospital, which seemed to be a compulsory stop for every politician in the area. My father, now in his eighties, was there on one of his periodic hospital stays. A lifelong Liberal, he asked the nurse to close the door to his ward to ensure he would not have to speak to the Prime Minister. The following day, he was helped from his hospital bed to be taken to the polling station to make his vote count.

After a night of extraordinary election results, I arrived home at five o'clock in the morning, with the mist lying heavily in the fields. I had not really believed the lead which the opinion polls had been giving Labour for so long, and I was stunned by the scale of the swing. The Labour talk about winning a Tory-free Wales had turned out to be true. In the television studio, where I had been anchoring the election night programme, Glenys Kinnock could not contain her glee when Rod Richards was knocked out at Clwyd West and Michael Portillo at Enfield. I found myself having to discuss results which were well outside any research I had done. The country did appear to have voted comprehensively for change.

Labour's popularity hung around everything the government did in those first few months after May 1997. It was the party's hope that that popularity alone would be enough to secure a Yes vote in the referendum, now scheduled for September, as soon after the election as they could realistically make it. Blair and Prescott were applauded in the streets when they visited Wales in the election aftermath. When John Prescott came to Newport during the referendum campaign, there was still genuine pleasure among the shoppers in the town centre at meeting him. But when he had gone, I walked around the corner and asked people how they would vote in the coming referendum. I could not find a single Yes voter.

The 'Yes for Wales' campaign had been well-organised, kicking off even before the general election. The campaign provided a platform on which the political parties in favour of devolution could come together, allowing Plaid Cymru in particular to swallow its objections over the lack of powers proposed for the Assembly and come in behind the government plans. The campaign rolled out lists of celebrities who backed a Yes vote and staged a sequence of media events such as 'Teachers say Yes' or 'Cardiff says Yes'. In retrospect, some of these were rather silly – after all, in the event, Cardiff voted No. Too often, I had the sense that 'Yes for Wales' rallies were the political classes speaking to themselves.

In contrast, the No campaign consisted of a rag-tag and bobtail crowd, a disorganised mix of Labour rank-and-file and Conservatives in semi-disguise. They seemed an eccentric band, and some in the Yes campaign accused the broadcasters of giving them undue status in the name of balance and impartiality. They were personified by two redoubtable women from the Rhondda, Carys Pugh and Betty Bowen, who were determined to carry the rebel Labour banner into what they saw as almost a personal battle against Ron Davies. They may not have had the political firepower of their rivals, but their slogans about the cost of the Assembly and 'jobs for the boys' were repeated in every pub in Wales.

'You watch,' Carys Pugh told me. 'We're going to give Ron a run for his money.'

And they did. As the votes were phoned in county by county to the National Counting Centre in Cardiff on referendum night, the No vote gradually moved ahead. At about half-past three in the morning, all but one of the results from around Wales had been declared and the No vote was about 16,000 in front. One or two in the Yes camp had grimly conceded in public that they were about to lose.

It was at this point that the Secretary of State chose to stage a walkabout in front of the television cameras at the Counting Centre. It was assumed by those who saw it that this was Ron Davies putting a brave face on defeat. He accepted sympathetic handshakes from those who thought they were commiserating with him over such a major political setback. What they did not know, and Ron Davies did know, was that the final result from Carmarthenshire was about to save his bacon. He had received a call from Nick Ainger, his parliamentary aide, that the ballot papers voting Yes in the Carmarthenshire count were piling up in sufficient numbers to turn the whole result around.

But it was a narrow squeak – an overall majority of fewer than 7,000 votes in favour of the new Welsh Assembly. For me personally, the second and crucial part of my gamble in coming back to Wales had only just worked out.

CHAPTER 20

A moment of madness

HE CLOSED THE gate and walked up the path to the front door with something of a swagger.

'Fancy seeing you here,' he said. And then, rather quickly, he added: 'You can ask me anything you like, boys.'

The 'boys' in question were in fact both getting on a bit – Max Perkins, political editor at ITV Wales, and myself, his opposite number at BBC Wales. And there was no surprise at meeting Ron Davies on this particular afternoon. But there was a bit of 'cloak and dagger' about the rendezvous.

Ron Davies had been in hiding for the several days since his sudden and dramatic resignation as Secretary of State for Wales over an incident on Clapham Common and what he called a 'gross error of judgement'. He said that he had been for a late-night walk on the Common and had ended up being robbed at knife-point – a crime which he had reported to the police. But the details of the incident which emerged indicated that there was always more to it than that, and his behaviour had been sufficiently questionable for him to offer his resignation to the Prime Minister the following morning.

Not surprisingly, the media were soon in hot pursuit. Like just about everybody, they wanted the full story of what had happened and why Ron Davies had felt it necessary to resign, if indeed he was merely the victim of a mugging. His political colleagues, as well as the senior civil servants who worked with him at the Welsh Office, were in a state of shock. But they were not getting any explanations, because Ron Davies had disappeared.

Some time afterwards, I learned where he had been. It was not just the erstwhile Secretary of State who was trying to avoid the attentions of the press. His wife and daughter had been whisked away from their home and were hiding out in the anonymity of a Center Parcs holiday village. Not surprisingly, the first priority for Ron Davies was to talk to his family and two of his former assistants drove him to the site. But they realised they had a problem. If they were to leave Ron there with his family, the camp security would see three men going in and only two coming out. As they drove in through the main gate, the man who, until just a few days before, had been a cabinet minister had to lie under a blanket on the back seat to avoid detection.

But now, he had turned up in what we were calling a 'secret location' to give his explanation in two television interviews. The location was in fact the front room of Vaughan Roderick's house in western Cardiff, but it was secret in the sense that the interviews were exclusive to the two Welsh television stations, and we had to ensure the rest of the press (apart from one local photographer) did not find out about it. That was not as easy as it sounds, as the London newspapers were circling around on the lookout, and I had to fend off a number of calls from press photographers who were getting more irritated as the day went on.

The swagger which Ron Davies affected as he arrived in fact belied the emotional turmoil he was going through. In reality, he looked tired and baggy-eyed. On his hand, he had written the single word 'Sorry', although none of us in the room spotted that at the time.

Max and I had tossed a coin, and he was going first with the interview. And as I listened to Ron's answers, he was clearly dodging the central question – why had he decided, late at night on Clapham Common, to accompany a total stranger for a drink and a curry? The speculation in the press had been based on the fact that the area was a notorious gay haunt. A few weeks earlier, I had picked up a rumour that Ron was visiting gay nightclubs, something I had more or less dismissed as absurd. But now it did not seem so absurd. So when it came to my turn, I decided to press the point.

Ron's central answer, the one he had clearly prepared, was that it was a moment of madness for which he had paid a very heavy price and for which he was truly sorry – doubtless thanks to the prompt on his hand. He flatly denied that there was any truth in the allegations about sex or drugs. In that case, it was still hard to see why he had felt obliged to resign as Secretary of State. So I asked him whether he was gay, a point I eventually put to him four times in one form or another because it was a point he constantly evaded. In the end, he said, with tears starting in his eyes: 'Let me say this. I have a very long-standing and loving relationship with my wife, who has been enormously supportive over the last few days. I think you should take that as the answer you want.'

It was a compelling interview, which was played at length on network TV and radio. But it was an interview which got me into some short-lived controversy. Some liberal commentators argued that even in this case, an individual's sexuality should be a private matter and I had no business hounding him on the issue. From the BBC's point of view, it was complicated by the fact that Peter Mandelson had just been accidentally 'outed' by Matthew Parris on *Newsnight* and the ruling had come down that there should be no repetition of such a reference. So how would the BBC management respond in the case of the Ron Davies interview? As it happened, robustly – and without consulting me. A statement was put out that my questions were unavoidable, and the public would have regarded it as very strange if I had failed to mention his sexuality. Ron Davies himself never complained, then or later.

Subsequent events demonstrated that it was indeed a

justified approach. In a conversation with Ron not long afterwards, I advised him to focus on bread-and-butter issues – he was still an MP and likely to be a member of the new Assembly – and political rehabilitation was by no means impossible. Above all, I advised him that it would be against his interests to talk publicly again about the events on Clapham Common. It was advice which he chose to ignore. A lengthy interview with Vincent Kane for BBC Wales put him further in the mire, and an exposé by the *Sun* newspaper caught him in the woods off the M4 allegedly looking for badgers as he was on his way to Westminster. His constituency could take no more, and he ended up without even a seat in the Assembly.

The irony of it all was that Ron Davies had achieved a great deal in the eighteen months he had been in office. After the narrow Yes vote in the referendum, he had got the devolution legislation through Parliament in good time, in fact in advance of the equivalent Scottish bill. And a site had been chosen for the new National Assembly. I followed all this more closely than I had been able to do with any previous government process, because we had been given access to a whole series of ministerial and civil service meetings for a documentary series. Produced by Esther Prydderch, it was the best documentary I was to be involved with, although given the rather uninformative title of *The Office*.

We watched as the civil servants allocated to the devolution bill wrestled with drafting clauses and briefing ministers according to the ever-changing timetable presented by its passage through Commons and Lords. At times, we would see the officials with their heads in their hands as they were told that they had to produce re-drafts or amendments on complicated points in a matter of a few days rather than the weeks they had been led to expect. But the scene I most enjoyed came at a critical juncture for the bill, when one of its most fundamental features was changed.

The kind of Assembly envisaged in the bill as it was first presented to Parliament was not very different from the model presented in the ill-fated devolution legislation of the 1970s. It was based on the local government model of decision-making by committees, but there was pressure in the Commons, which went with the grain of Ron Davies's own thinking, to change it to a Westminster-type cabinet system with a First Secretary with the power to appoint his own ministers. Ron Davies wanted to accept a Conservative amendment to this effect – but he had a big problem.

He had appointed an independent advisory group to make recommendations on the details of how the new Assembly should be run. It was called the National Assembly Advisory Group, or NAAG, and was chaired by a Labour-supporting businessman, John Elfed Jones. The problem was that NAAG was operating on the basis of the original form of the bill, and the change Ron Davies now had in mind would leave this advisory group embarrassingly out of the loop. Ron sent in his political adviser, Huw Roberts, to sort it out (by this time a good friend after our time at ITN together). I sat in the background as John Elfed Jones, suitably tipped off, introduced the subject of a cabinet system, and Huw – despite some questioning as to why he was there – weighed in with some heavy arguments in favour of a change. The independent group accordingly voted, with some disputation, in favour of a cabinet system. The Secretary of State had got his way.

But the issue which got out of hand was where the new Assembly was to be sited. The obvious choice was the City Hall in Cardiff, a stately Edwardian building in the centre of the city which was little used now that the council had a new headquarters in Cardiff Bay. But Ron Davies had not reckoned with the stubbornness of the Cardiff Council leader, Russell Goodway, who refused to sell the City Hall at the price which the government's valuers had put on it. The dispute became acrimonious, with neither side willing to back down, despite the fact that both were senior figures in the same political party. BBC Wales decided to devote its current affairs programme, *Week in Week Out*, to what the press described as a live TV 'showdown' between the pair – the venue, appropriately, the City Hall itself.

It was going to be my job to chair this confrontation, with Russell Goodway perched on a chair which looked more like a throne in the old council chamber, and Ron Davies on a video link from Westminster. With half an hour to go, I went to meet Russell Goodway who told me in no uncertain terms that the Secretary of State would not be turning up for the programme. As I had telephoned Ron Davies only a short while before to confirm the arrangements, I did not take much notice of what he said and continued with my preparations. When Ron came through on the video link, I noticed the look of surprise on Russell Goodway's face.

It was some years later when I was told what had happened. The Cardiff council leader had rung 10 Downing Street, where he had a particular contact, to get them to put pressure on the Secretary of State to cancel his appearance – on the grounds that to argue in public would reflect badly on Labour. He had clearly believed, as a result of this conversation, that Ron Davies would be forced to withdraw. But if such pressure was put on Ron Davies, it was to his credit that he ignored it.

The live debate served only to entrench positions, and with negotiations behind the scenes also going nowhere, the City Hall receded rapidly as a viable option. The alternative strategy, quickly devised, was to canvass alternative sites for the Assembly across the whole of Wales. Welsh Office officials went house-hunting for the Assembly from Wrexham to Merthyr Tydfil to Swansea, with the bid to place it in Swansea's Brangwyn Hall regarded as particularly strong and cost-effective. For myself, I always regarded this exercise as something of a charade; there was little political logic in putting the nation's new democratic body outside the capital city. And if that was the reality, the growing clamour from Swansea was going to get embarrassing.

As the dilemma over the Assembly site became more and more acute, it rapidly became the centrepiece of the documentary being filmed inside the Welsh Office. I was not present for all the filming because there was an agreement that the information gleaned thereby could not be used on news programmes and would only be made public at the time of the transmission of the documentary series. And I was busy reporting in the meantime for *Wales Today* and other bulletins. But when we came to put the documentary together, it transpired that the decision-making about the site for the Assembly had been anything but straightforward.

By March 1998, it was already past the deadline for an announcement. A meeting was held with a range of advisers and officials to make the final decision, with a press conference scheduled for the next morning. Contrary to the original agreement, our cameras were excluded from that meeting, which ran late into the night. Behind closed doors, the argument was shifting towards a private finance initiative scheme based in Bute Square (now Callaghan Square) just south of the main Cardiff railway station. A new-build scheme there involving a public-private partnership looked like being the cheapest option in the long run. Almost at the last minute, however, a civil servant brought in a message from the Treasury that some key aspects of this plan would not be permissible.

The Secretary of State and his officials were forced to backtrack. The announcement the next day would now be a provisional one only – a new-build scheme somewhere in Cardiff. The press department of the Welsh Office had been having a nightmare time, preparing alternative press releases and display videos for different outcomes. And the announcement at the packed press conference hardly satisfied the pent-up demand for clear answers. It was now going to be a choice between the Bute Square scheme and a site in Cardiff Bay adjacent to an office block already leased by the Welsh Office. With the Welsh Office's own procurement officials in favour of the site next to Crickhowell House in Cardiff Bay, it was in that direction the momentum swung. Ron Davies eventually bought the vacant waterfront site with a symbolic £1 coin.

When permission had been given for the documentary series, there was a proviso that the Permanent Secretary, Rachel Lomax, should be permitted to view a 'rough-cut' of the programmes, a courtesy that would allow her to make comments or factual corrections. Editorial control remained absolutely with the BBC. When the Permanent Secretary saw how much of the programme's focus was on the arguments over the site, and how much information we seemed to have, she exploded. Her rage shook the small viewing room. This was not what the filming was supposed to have been about, she said. We queried whether there was anything factual she thought we had got wrong – but that was not the point.

It later transpired that she was, she thought, protecting her Secretary of State. But Ron Davies needed no such protection. At a function shortly afterwards, I found myself sitting not far behind him. He turned round and said:

'Did you get all the information you needed?'

I indicated that I had.

'Good,' he said – and that was that.

The fall of Ron Davies led to his replacement as Secretary of State by my former journalist colleague on the *South Wales Echo*, Alun Michael, who was by this time a junior minister in the Blair government. Alun had the reputation of being a workaholic, beavering away into the small hours of the morning. Indeed, when I was interviewing him at one critical juncture, he looked particularly baggy-eyed – so I asked him how much sleep he'd had the night before. He admitted that he had not been to bed at all.

Alun never managed to shake off the reputation of being Blair's man in Wales. He always protested that this was unfair, and I had some sympathy with that. He had been brought up in north Wales and spoke creditable Welsh, which was more than I did. But there was an obvious alternative candidate in Rhodri Morgan, who had earlier lost against Ron Davies for the leadership, and was already beginning to acquire his 'man of the people' image. For reasons dating back to their days in opposition, the Prime Minister did not trust Rhodri. Downing Street put its troops into action to stop Rhodri becoming Labour's leader in Wales.

It was a major mistake, and one which Tony Blair subsequently acknowledged. It was a mistake because it demonstrated that he still did not really 'get' devolution and the idea that the Welsh Labour Party should be allowed to make its own decisions. And it was a mistake because it was no longer acceptable to use the trade union block vote in Labour Party elections. It was left up to each union whether it wished to allow its membership to vote, but a number of union leaders, such as George Wright of the Transport and General Workers' Union, had no intention of doing so. They were going to cast their unions' votes the way that Downing Street was asking them to.

I have rarely caught out a Prime Minister in a blatant mis-statement of fact. On a flying visit to Cardiff during the leadership election campaign, Tony Blair held a press conference in the Welsh Office, where he reiterated that this was a one-member-one-vote election. When I tried to point out that that was not what was happening on the ground, he overrode the question as if it was an inconvenient fact he preferred not to recognise.

The party leadership had put in Peter Hain as Alun Michael's campaign manager, but even his efforts – and he was the best campaigner they had – could not prevent support for Alun Michael slipping away. I told him at one stage that trade union support was not going to be as solid as expected, despite the best efforts of the big union bosses. When it came to the result, announced rather oddly in one of Cardiff's poshest hotels, it was a close-run thing. Rhodri had won the membership section very comfortably, but Alun had narrowly won the trade union section and, with his votes from the MPs' section, it was just enough to give him the leadership.

The battle had, however, done Labour lasting damage. The party had always presumed, because of its historic strength across Wales, that it would win an overall majority in the new Assembly. The introduction of proportional representation, in this case the additional membership system, was only expected to make that victory appear a little less overwhelming. But Labour lost ground in those first Assembly elections, and as the newly elected Labour Assembly Members gathered in Cardiff Bay, they faced the prospect of having to form a coalition with the Liberal Democrats.

The Lib Dems were busy briefing that their discussions with Alun Michael about a coalition were on the verge of success, and that was the line the whole BBC newsroom in Cardiff was taking. But calling round some of the new Labour AMs convinced me that was not their mood. In the brave new world of Welsh devolution they preferred to go it alone, and Alun Michael formed a minority government.

The formal opening ceremony for the new democratic institution in 1999 took place without the dressed-up pageantry of Westminster, but was all the better for that. The Queen, the Duke of Edinburgh and Prince Charles, with his smattering of Welsh, were there to do the honours. The new Presiding Officer, Dafydd Elis-Thomas, despite his republican leanings, understood only too well that this royal attendance would serve to entrench the new institution as part of the British state.

For me, however, there was a moment of farce.

The BBC had set up a small studio on wasteland opposite Crickhowell House, from which a live programme about the opening ceremony was to be broadcast. It was a tiny studio, just big enough to fit in the cameras, a table and four chairs. Huw Edwards had been brought in to present the programme, and – joining him as commentators – Sara Edwards, the *Wales Today* presenter; Jenny Bond, the BBC's royal correspondent, and myself, sitting between them. We had done all the necessary tests and rehearsed the introduction, when – with a few moments to go before transmission – Huw suggested to me that the others were looming over me a little and I might like to raise my seat. I reached for the lever, and my seat promptly sank to the floor so that my head was approximately at the height of the breasts of the two women. And there I stayed. Try as I might, I could not shift the seat back up. With transmission approaching, Huw watched with mounting anxiety as a technician crawled under the table and levered the seat back up to where I had been in the first place.

That night, there was a magnificent celebratory outdoor concert in Cardiff Bay, organised primarily by BBC Wales, with performances by Welsh greats like Tom Jones and Shirley Bassey. Infuriatingly, I was late for it. Having completed my report for *Wales Today* at 6.30 p.m., I moved on to compile a piece for the network news at nine o'clock. This could have been completed comfortably by eight o'clock, but was repeatedly delayed. There were too many network news producers trying to complicate things, and the network video-editor lost the link between sound and picture at a crucial juncture. My report was eventually fed to London with just a few seconds to spare as Peter Sissons read the introduction to it. It was ample evidence that not everything was necessarily better done by network centre.

One of the advantages of getting a bit long in the tooth in a job is that you work with colleagues who seem to be younger every day. By this time, I found myself working with some who turned out to be the children of the contemporaries I had started out with back in the days when I was on the *South Wales Echo*. In satirical acknowledgment of my senior status, the *Wales Today* newsreader, Jamie Owen (who I was amazed to discover had lived in the same street as myself in Pembroke Dock, although at a different period), used to refer to me as 'uncle'. This badinage was picked up one day in the BBC cafeteria by some people on the next table.

'It's disgusting,' one said, 'this nepotism in the BBC.'

The problem faced by any minority government is that the opposition parties can rarely resist an opportunity to bring it down. And so it proved for Alun Michael. There was a succession of crises as the new Assembly sought to find its feet and tested its powers and procedures. Within the first six months, there was a successful attempt to pass a motion of censure against the agriculture minister, Christine Gwyther, who struggled to overcome the fact that she was vegetarian. Alun Michael looked increasingly pushed around by events, instead of being in charge of them.

What did for him in the end was the arcane issue of European funding for the poorer parts of Wales. So-called Objective One funding was seen as crucial in lifting Wales out of its position of having just about the lowest gross domestic product per head in the United Kingdom. When the president of the European Commission, Jacques Santer, visited Wales to assess its eligibility, I had the chance to interview him at a stopover in Caernarfon. Plaid Cymru's Dafydd Iwan was among those there to lobby him, and he urged me to use the interview to 'speak up for Wales'. I decided to rely on the more customary rules of fairness and impartiality.

What came to embarrass Alun Michael was that at least some of the Objective One funding that Wales had secured was dependent on matched funding from other sources. This was an incredibly complex issue which the opposition parties tended to over-simplify. Their charge was that the Treasury in London was refusing to come up with extra funding and was therefore putting in peril some of the European money which Wales would otherwise get. Whatever the rights and wrongs of this, what Alun Michael needed was some gesture from the Chancellor, Gordon Brown – something he failed to get.

As the issue headed towards a showdown motion of censure against the First Secretary, I followed it all, not just through news coverage, but also with a documentary series for Radio 4, produced by Mark Palmer. With the opposition parties in the majority, the motion was likely to be passed and Alun Michael would have to resign. The night before the vote, Labour tried to put pressure on the Liberal Democrats to abstain, inviting them to a meeting in Alun's office. With a bottle of wine on the table, the Labour ministers waited. But they waited in vain. Without an assurance of extra funding, the Liberal Democrats had instead decided to go out for a curry.

With his fate therefore sealed, Alun Michael tried to anticipate events, using his speech in the Assembly debate to announce his resignation as First Secretary with 'immediate effect' – and putting his resignation letter on the presiding officer's desk. He told me afterwards that he had not consulted his colleagues beforehand and, although he had talked to Tony Blair, he had not told him precisely what he was going to do. Indeed, Tony Blair was caught in mid-flow in Prime Minister's Questions in the Commons by the news of the resignation. It was a bizarre way to leave office. It did not even stop the motion of censure against him from going ahead.

Rhodri Morgan had fought and lost two battles for the leadership, and now, as he said himself, it fell into his lap. He was to achieve what Alun Michael had not been able to – a stable government through coalitions with first the Liberal Democrats and then Plaid Cymru. Above all, by becoming a highly-visible public figure, he was able to personify what devolution was all about and help cement it into the culture and society of Wales.

A staple part of my job had been to present the weekly political programme, which had a small but remarkably loyal audience, but increasingly suffered from a lack of resources (it was moved out of the studio and onto videotape) and erratic scheduling. One day in early 2000, I returned from a brief holiday to discover I was no longer the presenter.

It never ceases to surprise me how badly the BBC management handles these things. The head of news and current affairs, Aled Eurig, who was my line manager and had been instrumental in getting me the job in the first place, said he had known nothing about it. It turned out that it was Dai Smith, at that time head of English-language programmes, who had decided the programme needed a fresh, and prettier, face to present it. I was to be succeeded by Bethan Rhys Roberts, an able and charming broadcaster, and it was not her fault that the programme continued to languish in the ratings.

With a significant chunk of my job taken away from me, I decided I had no wish to continue as political editor for BBC Wales. I had no regrets. I had achieved my ambition to follow the devolution process and the creation of the National Assembly. The BBC had given me that opportunity and I was grateful. After a transitional period managing public affairs for BBC Wales, I left broadcasting behind me.

CHAPTER 21

Trusty and well-beloved

IT WAS NOON on a warm July day in the year 2000, and I was standing in a nondescript room at the Home Office looking out of the window and desperately trying to collect my thoughts. I was waiting to be summoned to an interview for appointment to the Electoral Commission, a brand-new body being set up to supervise a number of different aspects of the electoral process. The trouble was that I had been on an unaccustomed night out with some Welsh friends in London, and I was having trouble focusing my brain. When I had woken up that morning, I could neither speak nor think. By midday, I had just about got my voice back, but thinking was still beyond me. When the Permanent Secretary, the softly-spoken Sir David Omand, invited me in, I feared the worst.

One member of the panel was Elizabeth Filkin, who had acquired a reputation during her time as Parliamentary Standards Commissioner as someone who, when they got their teeth into somebody or something, was disinclined to let go. Most of the interview passed in a blur, apart from the several occasions when I conspicuously failed to answer Ms Filkin's questions. Nobody was more surprised than I was, therefore, to receive a phone call some weeks later asking, in a slightly roundabout manner, whether I was still available to be nominated as an electoral commissioner.

There was another major hurdle. The appointment was

actually to be made by royal warrant, which in turn would be in response to a formal 'Address' from the House of Commons once the bill setting up the commission had completed its passage through Parliament. In other words, MPs would get the chance to debate the merits of the six appointees – and possibly vote against us. One night in early January 2001, a group of Conservative backbenchers, as part of a filibuster against government business, did indeed decide to debate our merits at great length. The new commission chairman, Sam Younger and I, had both worked for the BBC, which the Euro-sceptic right described as 'institutionally Europhiliac' and argued that we would carry that bias with us onto the commission. The best quote came from Eric Forth: 'Does my Right Honourable Friend wonder how any so-called impartial selection committee could end up with two ghastly BBC people and claim that they were representative of the electorate?'

One of his colleagues went on to argue that too many of the names on the list sounded Scottish – it was by this time well into the early hours of the morning. When the vote was taken, at a more sober time of day later in the week, the motion on the Address to the Queen was carried with only four votes against. The royal warrant, when it eventually arrived, greeted the six of us as 'trusty and well-beloved'.

We were a mixed bunch. Apart from Sam, who had been running the British Red Cross after leaving the BBC World Service, there were two who had been local authority chief executives, Pamela Gordon (Sheffield) and Sir Neil McIntosh (Strathclyde), and had therefore actually run elections. Graham Zellick was a professor of law and at that time vice-chancellor of the University of London, while Karamjit Singh was serving on the Criminal Cases Review Commission. Neil and I were respectively there to represent the interests of Wales and Scotland, although we were not strictly territorial appointments. Over the next few years, we were all to get on remarkably well together, to the extent that virtually every decision was made by achieving a consensus.

While we waited for the Commons to approve our appointments, we met in shadow form in a hotel near Westminster to discuss how we would set about the job. The Political Parties, Elections and Referendums Act had given us a rag-bag of functions based on the recommendations of the Neill Committee two years earlier. These functions fell far short of responsibility for the running of elections – as was the case in Canada and Australia, for instance – but were rather a collection of remedies designed to clean up the bits of the system that had gone wrong. So political parties were to register with the new commission if they wanted to compete in elections and they had to abide by new controls on their income and expenditure, which we had to monitor.

This was the aspect of the work which preoccupied us during the early months. It was not just a learning curve for us, but for the political parties as well. The requirement was for the parties to report to the commission any donations of more than £5,000 (less if it was at constituency level), and any donation of more than £200 had to be checked to ensure it came from a permissible donor – mainly, it had to be someone on the electoral register in the UK. The whole purpose was to make the system of party funding much more transparent, and in that aim it was successful. But political parties are made up of volunteers, and there were soon complaints that it was too much of a bureaucratic burden. I had a lot of sympathy with this complaint and remember arguing with the civil servant who had drafted these clauses that they ground far too small. But I had less patience with those MPs who blamed the commission for the new rules when it was they who had voted the bill through Parliament.

So for the first couple of years, the emphasis was on developing systems to run the new regulations and providing guidance and training for parties and candidates to help them comply. A whole series of seminars and training sessions took place, and I took part in some of those in Wales. It was a couple of years or so before we felt it was right to start thinking about enforcing the penalties against those who broke the rules. And there was one perhaps surprising discovery: contact between the officers of the different political parties rarely took place, and indeed in many cases they had never spoken to each other. Now they found that they had quite a lot in common, not least in getting to grips with the new regulatory regime. The commission set up regular meetings between senior officers from each party to keep them abreast of all the developments likely to affect them. Chairing the political parties' panel in Wales was a productive part of my role.

The first few months of the life of the commission involved a frenetic effort to get the basic systems in place in time for the general election expected in the spring of 2001 – an election which was eventually held in June after a month's delay because of the outbreak of foot-and-mouth disease. What was most striking about the election was not the result but the turn-out, which at just fifty-nine per cent was the lowest for a Westminster election since the advent of universal adult suffrage, and twelve points down on the figure for 1997. There was considerable dismay in the political world about this, and improving voter turn-out was suddenly pushed much higher up the commission's agenda. It was arguable that the relative lack of voter interest in 2001 was mainly because the election outcome was so predictable – another victory for Tony Blair. But preliminary research was already showing that the causes were much deeper than that. The commission committed itself to a programme of voter education to try and surmount what seemed to be a growing disconnect between the public and the politicians.

In Wales the concern was even greater because turn-out at the first elections to the National Assembly in 1999 had been even lower, at just under forty-six per cent, and sank to less than forty per cent four years later. The extensive research we did in the run-up to those elections in 2003 was typical of our wider UK research. The disengagement of so many voters was at least in part down to the dramatic decline in party allegiance.

A sense of civic duty about casting a vote was declining, and instead it was being seen as just another kind of consumer choice. Most worrying of all was the percentage of younger adults who did not vote – nearly seventy per cent of those aged between eighteen and twenty-four had not voted in the 1999 Assembly elections.

The evidence was emerging that the cohort of non-voters was moving up the age scale, with the risk that election turnout would continue to decline. In Wales there was an extra factor: a lack of information available to the public about the work of the new democratic body in Cardiff Bay, at least in part because of the structure of the Wales-based media.

Knowing this was one thing, but doing something about it was another. The commission staged a series of advertising campaigns aimed at encouraging people, particularly younger voters, to take part in elections, and some of these campaigns were very effective. Probably the most memorable were the cartoon characters, Tom and Mike, grumbling in the pub about the things they cared about, only to realise that only through politics could they do anything about them. In Wales, we got involved in some PR stunts, not all of which were so effective. At one point, it was decided to photograph the statues of famous public figures with gags around their mouths with the slogan, 'No voice, no vote'.

Against my better judgement, I agreed to be pictured alongside the statue of Lloyd George in Caernarfon, holding the gag around his mouth. This turned out to be more difficult than anticipated. We hired a hoist to get me up there, only to find that the plinth around the base of the statue was in the way and I was left with my outstretched gag-holding hand some feet short of Lloyd George's head. Sizing up the problem, the hoist operator offered to fetch a bigger cherry-picker from the council depot, which after an interval duly appeared. So I was lifted up and, swaying in a rising wind, nearly knocked the great man's nose off. With an inane smile on my face, I just managed to get the gag within range of Lloyd George's mouth before we sensibly gave up. Needless to say, the photograph was not widely used.

The trouble was that the commission was getting identified far too closely with the turn-out issue. My appearances on TV and radio in Wales were usually on this issue, and when turn-out went down again in 2003 we were faced with suggestions that it was the commission which had failed. In reality, of course, our intervention, on the budget we had, was never going to be particularly effective against wider social and political forces. After five years, in a review of our priorities, the commission decided to focus instead on ensuring that as many people as possible got their names on to the electoral register. After all, if you are not on the electoral register in the first place, you cannot cast a vote.

One thing which struck me very early on was how low-tech, even primitive, the electoral process was in Britain. It dated back to the Victorian era and the structure of how elections were run had changed little since. As a political journalist, I had taken no interest in the details of electoral administration. Now I watched elections with a different eye. In the modern computer age, voters still used pencils on the end of a piece of string, and all votes were still counted by hand. Polling stations were often portable buildings – indeed, in the Rhondda in 2001 the steps to some had been stolen overnight so that older people could not get in and their ballot papers had to be brought out to them. The system of electoral registers was so snail-like that, by the time the election was called, it was almost too late to get your name on the register. And it was a registration system based on the household, not the individual elector, with the head of the household, whoever that might be, completing the form on behalf of everyone else.

There was a general perception that the system was run fairly and impartially, but this disguised the fact that it was a rusty old machine that was not keeping up with the pace of events. It was not possible any longer, if it ever was, for local councils to dust off their election files every few years and set up the election process in just a few weeks. What with elections to devolved and European institutions as well as Westminster and local authorities, there were now elections almost every year. And the advent of postal voting on demand had made the whole process much more complicated.

This had been brought in before the commission was set up, and indeed was seen as a way of encouraging more people to use their vote. For the first time, voters could opt for a postal vote, instead of going to a polling station, without giving a reason. The increasing number of postal votes (they doubled in the 2001 election) added huge extra pressure on the system, as I saw for myself, as local councils struggled to cope with the rapid turn-round of applications and ballot forms. And, not at first but gradually, the issue of fraud reared its head. The whole electoral process in Britain has been based on trust. No check on voters' identity is made before casting a vote in a polling station, and there was little greater scrutiny of postal ballots and the accompanying declaration of identity. It raised difficult questions over how to establish the right balance between getting more people to vote and ensuring there was adequate security around the process.

Seeking to modernise the rules on elections took up a great deal of commissioners' time in the first few years. For my part, I chaired a project group on the administration of postal voting, with a panel which included Professor Colin Rallings of Plymouth University. We urged much greater consistency in the way the different local councils promoted and handled postal voting. And we specifically looked at the issue of fraud. Whereas it is an offence to seek to impersonate someone else at a polling station, there was no related offence when seeking a postal vote. We recommended that there should be a new offence of intending fraudulently to apply for a postal or proxy vote. It was one of a number of proposals made by the commission which were passed by Parliament and put on the statute book in 2006.

There was now growing pressure to expand postal voting

to the extent of abandoning polling stations altogether. There had been a number of pilot schemes at local council elections in England testing out all-postal voting, where every voter was sent a postal ballot, and these pilots had resulted in significant increases in turnout. In 2003, the commission recommended that, subject to implementing a number of changes, all-postal voting was ready to be rolled out for all local elections across Britain. We argued that, in order to improve security, the system whereby voters put their names on the electoral roll by household should be replaced by an obligation for each voter to register individually, providing signatures which could later be checked against postal vote applications and ballots. But we did not say strongly enough that this should be a condition of proceeding to all-postal voting. The whole decision was premature.

There was strong support from much of the Labour Party, and from inside the Labour government, for all-postal voting because they felt that it was they who would most benefit from the increased turn-out. And there was equally strong opposition from the majority of Labour MPs to any move to individual registration because they felt, in my view wrongly, that it was 'their' people in poorer and less well-educated families who would fail to fill in the forms and therefore drop off the electoral roll. I had several up-and-down arguments with individual MPs who refused to accept that it had worked satisfactorily in Northern Ireland under tougher rules than were being proposed for the rest of the United Kingdom.

The Deputy Prime Minister, John Prescott, was a particular advocate of all-postal voting and was now proposing that it should be tested out on a much bigger scale. He wanted to use all-postal voting in several English regions in the combined local and European elections in May 2004, and the commission was tasked with recommending which they should be. On various grounds, we decided that only two regions, the North East and East Midlands were suitable, but John Prescott wanted more. He put enormous pressure on the commission to include the

North West in particular, apparently failing to grasp that we were an independent body not susceptible to pressure of that kind. When he insisted on ignoring our advice and including both the North West and Yorkshire and Humberside in the bill, there was a right royal battle with the Opposition which went to the Lords and back several times.

John Prescott won that battle, but he lost the war. It was a huge administrative burden handling so many ballot papers, and hundreds of people were disenfranchised because of delivery problems. More importantly, the perception that the system was open to fraud and abuse increased dramatically, even though actual cases of fraud were confined in the main to inner-city areas with significant ethnic minority communities. Most importantly, it was clear from our surveys that many people resented losing the choice of going to a polling station. The commission now rightly decided that all-postal voting should no longer be pursued for use at statutory elections in the UK. The government refused to agree, but in reality all-postal voting was now dead.

The government also still refused to accede to our ever louder calls for the introduction of individual registration on the basis of individual human rights as well as providing greater security against potential fraud. But with increasing focus on driving up the performance of local authorities in improving the accuracy and completeness of their electoral registers, the climate did begin to change. In 2009, some time after I had left the commission, the government suddenly announced that it was after all going to bring in individual registration over the next few years – foreshadowing one of the most important changes to the electoral process in the United Kingdom for many years.

More disappointing, however, was the failure to move the electoral process into the computer age. I began at the commission with a strong desire to see voting made easier and more accessible for young people in particular, and voting via the internet seemed one obvious way of achieving that. The government had a budget for a variety of pilot schemes at local elections, which tested such methods as voting at an electronic kiosk in a polling station, voting from home via the internet and even text-messaging your vote. I took part in evaluating a number of such schemes, most notably in Swindon, and on the whole they proved popular. But these experiments were carried out on a pretty arbitrary basis, depending on which local authorities were keen enough to put in a bid, usually at ridiculously short notice.

The first and obvious issue was the extent to which electronic systems could be relied on not to fail during the crucial hours of voting. You cannot have an electoral process which disenfranchises citizens because the machinery has broken down. Although there were some incidents of failure when the pilots were scaled up across the whole of a local authority, that was not the biggest issue. The greatest dilemma was how to guarantee the integrity of an election conducted via e-voting, and demonstrate that it was carried out fairly. In one of the pilots I helped to evaluate, the recording of the votes via the internet was conducted a 100 miles away in a remote office in north London – I am sure with scrupulous honesty. But how do you make that process transparent, compared with physically seeing the paper votes being cast and being counted, so that people know they can trust the system?

The pilot schemes provided few answers to these and many other questions surrounding electronic voting. Above all, the government failed to develop any vision of where it was heading with these experiments, and in fact appeared to have no strategy at all. In the end, the commission effectively told the government to stop wasting money on expensive trials which were going nowhere. In reality, many local councils are having enough difficulty coping with the existing rules and requirements for elections and are obliged to cope with ever tighter budgets. As long as the United Kingdom seeks to run its democracy on the cheap, we are unlikely to catch up with the modern age.

There was one proposal for modernising the electoral system which I was put in charge of reviewing, and it was a proposal designed to address the increasing concerns about the failure of young people to participate in the political process. This was the demand to lower the minimum age for voting from eighteen, where it had been since 1969, to sixteen. The vast majority of western democracies have a voting age of eighteen, but there was increasing pressure by organisations representing young people, and by some political parties, for it to be lowered on the grounds that it was the best way to involve young people once again. I chaired a number of meetings in schools and colleges, we gathered in a wide range of responses from young people, and we looked at evidence from around the world.

Very early on, I was dismayed how deliberately misleading were some of the arguments for change. Campaigners claimed that if you could be married at sixteen, you should be able to vote. In fact you can only get married at sixteen with your parents' consent. They said that if you could join the army and die for your country at sixteen, you should be able to vote. In fact, you can only join the army at sixteen with your parents' consent and British soldiers are only sent to the front line after they have reached 18. They said that if you could pay tax at sixteen, you should be able to vote. It is true that sixteen- and seventeen-year-olds can pay tax, but the figures showed that the number doing so was declining. For me, the defining moment came at a meeting organised by the UK Youth Parliament, where I faced a torrid attack from speaker after speaker, one of whom claimed there would be riots on the streets if sixteen-year-olds did not get the vote. But when one young lady argued that if sixteen-year-olds were regarded as sufficiently responsible to have sex, they were responsible enough to vote, it was an argument too far and the mood of the debate swung round.

In fact, the massive amount of evidence which we collected during 2003 showed that the views of teenagers on the issue were mixed. While some felt they were sufficiently mature to take part in elections, others were not sure they knew enough about the adult world. The responses were often very thoughtful, but at the same time showed there was no clear-cut answer. The expert panel which I chaired came to the conclusion, regretfully in one or two cases, that the arguments for change did not stack up. But that was not how the press saw it. They had become convinced that the commission was taking a lead from Downing Street and that the vote for sixteen-year-olds was going to happen. Both implicit assumptions were wrong: Tony Blair was not necessarily in favour of the change, and the commission was going to make up its own mind, not follow a political lead. What we did recommend, however, was that the minimum age at which candidates could stand for election should be reduced from twenty-one to eighteen, and that far less controversial proposal became law in 2006.

I was immensely lucky during most of my time as commissioner that I had Kay Jenkins as director of the commission office in Cardiff. All the hard work of liaising with parties, candidates and council election officials was done by her and her team, as well as the drafting of the relevant Welsh guidance and reports on electoral matters. Thanks to our recommendation, Wales got itself ahead of the rest of the UK with the establishment of an all-Wales election planning group to coordinate the approach of local authorities to meeting the constantly changing issues. With the National Assembly we coordinated a communications strategy for raising awareness of the Assembly elections, and managed to get a specific power inserted in the Government of Wales Bill to clarify the Assembly's powers in this area.

But our involvement in another part of the Government of Wales Bill was to cause considerable controversy. This was the bill which created further law-making powers for the National Assembly, subject to a referendum. But there was a minor clause, inserted in the bill after pressure from many in the Labour rank and file, which was to change the way the electoral system worked. I have never been a particular fan of the additional member system of proportional representation used for electing Assembly members, but such a mix of constituencies and lists is in common use around the world. The problem was that the Welsh Labour Party had been mis-sold the system in the first place as having 'only an element of proportionality', and there was a tendency to regard the list members as less legitimate than those elected for constituencies. Labour Party workers were particularly annoyed when they saw rival candidates who had been beaten in a constituency appearing in the Assembly because they were high on their party's list – so-called dual candidacy – and the Labour government was now proposing to ban it.

The Secretary of State for Wales, Peter Hain, subsequently argued that we should never have got involved in this argument and that we should have left it to the politicians. I did not agree with that view then, and I do not agree with it now. It came firmly within our remit, and the commission would have appeared to have been ducking a major controversy if we had not intervened. In fact, our intervention was low-key, contained in a submission to the government which was subsequently made public by them and not by us. And we avoided public debate in order to minimise the element of confrontation.

But the evidence for us was clear. All the countries that used equivalent AMS systems permitted dual candidacy and to ban it would put Wales outside international democratic norms. There had been no evidence in the extensive research on public attitudes which we had undertaken to show there was any public concern on the issue of dual candidacy. From the responses we received, it was also obvious that the other parties were against such a ban, which was widely seen by the media and independent observers as partisan. In evidence to the Welsh Affairs Select Committee in the Commons, I said that the AMS system was in operation around the world and no other country had sought to ban dual candidacy in the way the government was proposing, and it was legitimate for the Electoral Commission to point that out. Rhodri Morgan followed us and roundly rubbished our evidence, which then became something of a shuttlecock between the parties in the Commons debate on the bill. I was startled, when switching on the live coverage, to hear my name being mentioned more than once. In the end, of course, Labour's majority won the day and the ban became law.

It was ironic that, contrary to expectations at the time, it was Labour Assembly members who suffered just as much from the ban in the 2007 elections. But that does not detract from the fact that the international consensus remains that bodies elected by AMS, and the parties taking part in those elections, need the flexibility which dual candidacy gives them. It is encouraging to see signs now that the ban might be reversed.

The elections to the National Assembly in 2007 had shown a slight increase in turn-out, as indeed had the general election two years earlier. But Labour's loss of seats, and gains by Plaid Cymru – leading to a coalition in Cardiff Bay between Labour and Plaid – had left Labour MPs at Westminster in a very bad mood. They had a number of grievances about the way the campaign had gone, some of them justified. There had been some cases of candidates like John Marek standing as Independents without resigning from the party they had hitherto represented, but there was nothing in law we could do to stop that. And three Plaid MPs had used House of Commons allowances to take out advertisements during the campaign that, as we were to say, were clearly election expenditure.

At a meeting of the Welsh Labour Group in the Commons that summer, Kay and I had a torrid time. One colleague afterwards described it as a bear-pit. The mood was set early by Don Touhig, the MP for Islwyn, who called for the commission to be abolished – not the first time he had done so. The commission was getting the blame for all the things the Labour Group did not like about the electoral process, from the complexity of the postal vote to the slowness, in some cases, of the count. The truth, as we said in our election report, was that returning officers were managing to cope with such changes as the requirements for signature and date of birth on postal vote applications and ballots. But, as one returning officer put it: 'It was all right on the night, but only by the skin of our teeth.'

As I left the commission at the end of 2007, we called for a complete overhaul of the way elections are run. We summarised it thus: 'Electoral administration is at a crossroads: it is under closer examination than ever before, but it is inconsistently managed, under-resourced and under-supported.'

For too much of my time as a commissioner, vital aspects of the electoral process had been like a football kicked around between the parties for perceived political advantage. The country really needs a modern structure for running elections, based on cross-party agreement about what is best for our democracy.

But the most difficult part of the commission's work was always going to be the regulation of party finances – and this came to a climax as my time at the commission came to an end. We had given the parties time to get used to the new rules, but from 2003 onwards we gradually began to contemplate enforcement action against those who broke them. The rules covered party accounts and expenditure, but the most controversial decisions invariably seemed to come over the permissibility of donations made to political parties. It was up to party treasurers to check whether the donor was on the electoral register, and with no central register for the whole of the UK this was not necessarily an easy task, and they sometimes failed to do it. Gradually, parties found themselves having to forfeit donations which were found to be impermissible – unfortunately to the Treasury and not to us. One or two of those cases, such as a massive donation to UKIP, ended up being fought over in the courts. And when it became clear that parties were taking loans, which they did not have to report, instead of donations, the law had to be changed to make them reportable too.

What was surprising was the extent to which it was the

governing party which got itself into trouble. Too often, Labour Party officials showed an impatience with, or unawareness of, the rules governing party finance, with sometimes dramatic results. One general secretary, Peter Watt, was forced to resign after Labour had accepted donations worth hundreds of thousands of pounds from a businessman through third parties, without reporting that the businessman was the original donor. This was manifestly against the rules, which were after all, designed to achieve greater transparency in party finance. This was taken out of the commission's hands by the Metropolitan Police, but despite their lengthy investigation, no prosecution resulted.

Even more sensitive was the fact that the rules on donations and expenditure applied also to internal party elections, as Peter Hain was to discover to his cost. When he announced his candidature for the post of deputy Labour leader, the commission wrote to him, as well as all the other candidates, reminding him of the rules with which they were obliged to comply. But in the last few weeks of 2007, it became public that the cabinet minister, by this time Work and Pensions Secretary, had failed to report more than £100,000 worth of donations to his campaign. When he realised what had gone wrong, he requested a meeting with officials at the Electoral Commission, where he reported his own mistake. Unfortunately, that did not absolve him from what was clearly an offence against electoral law.

I met Peter Hain by chance at a dinner in Cardiff soon after the initial news had broken. We both said it was probably inappropriate that we should be discussing the matter, but he was understandably preoccupied by it. He said that he'd had no time to attend to issues around the financing of his deputy leadership campaign, because he was at the time both Secretary of State for Northern Ireland and for Wales and he was too busy with the work of government. I said that I did not doubt his personal integrity, but that was not the point. In fact, because I had known Peter Hain for many years, I had a great deal of sympathy for him. Subsequent information showed that those working for him had failed to control the funding of his campaign, but the law, rightly or wrongly, held him responsible.

The key moment came just a few days before I was due to end my time as commissioner, after seven years in the job, at my last full meeting of the commission. Senior officials, led by the director of party and election finance, Lisa Klein, came in direct from a meeting with the Metropolitan Police. The message was clear: if there was to be an inquiry, it was the police who would do it. They did not want us to start an investigation which, with our limited powers, might have to be handed over to the police at a later stage. Given the sheer scale of the money involved, there was no way an investigation could be avoided, and the die was cast.

In fact, the final decision was made immediately after I had left. Peter Hain was given an hour's prior notice of the decision to refer him to the police, and his resignation from the cabinet was inevitable. The police inquiry then dragged on interminably – I just could not understand what was taking them so long – only for the Crown Prosecution Service to decide once again to take no action. Some time later, the commission was given sufficient investigatory powers to handle such cases itself and so avoid the stigma of referring them to the police.

It was a dramatic way to end my role after seven years as an electoral commissioner, for my second term of office had run out. It was only then that I received the royal warrant for my re-appointment to the job I had just left, delivered more than two years late. It confirmed my view that the monarchy seemed to live in a different time zone from the rest of us.

Chapter 22

The picture in the attic

The kitchen smelled of fresh earth, which was not really surprising because there was no floor and we were standing on the red Brecon soil. Looking upwards, we could see all the way to the rafters two storeys up. The builders, led by Gary Prosser who was known unnervingly as 'Slammer', had knocked a large hole in the kitchen wall and dug up the floor with a mini-JCB. There was a point around this time when we wondered whether we had taken on a little too much.

I had finished working at BBC Wales and started my time at the Electoral Commission. But since I was no longer tied into full-time employment, my wife Ann and I could choose where to live, as long as it was in striking distance of Cardiff and London. I had met Ann while working at the BBC, where she was the senior director on the evening news programme, *Wales Today*. When I was reporting to camera complete with earpiece, it was her job to tell me what to do and in particular when to stop talking. The standing joke is that is what she has continued to do ever since.

Our relationship was a welcome contrast to a brief and unhappy marriage which I had contracted while still working for ITN. I had been hoping for some domestic stability after the death of Sian, but that is not what I got. That marriage did not survive the transition back to Wales.

Ann and I had our wedding in 2000, and the following

year, complete with nine-month-old baby Hannah, we were attempting to renovate a Victorian house which was in a considerable state of dilapidation. But above all, Ann and I felt it was an ideal place to bring up Hannah – and so it proved. Just like my grandfather and my father before me, I was returning, relatively late in life, to live in the town of Brecon. It was not a pattern of behaviour I was deliberately repeating, but some of the factors we had in common. It was an area for which I felt a strong tug of affection and there were the familial links to different parts of the landscape. And my father, now well into his eighties, was living on his own and in increasing need of care.

The purchase of Harddfan, meaning 'beautiful place', had been fraught with the usual problems of the house-buying chain, but the family we bought it from patiently waited for us to be ready to buy it. Their mother, who had died, had known my grandmother, and that local link epitomised one of the reasons for moving there. The main part of the house was a Victorian villa built in the 1880s and stitched on to a small cottage which was considerably older. It was constructed with whatever the local builder could lay his hands on, not least lengths of railway line acting as RSJs. They still hold good to this day.

But the purchase was based on instinct rather than common sense. Nothing had been done to the house since the early 1970s and in at least one room the wallpaper dated back to the 1920s. The surveyor's report had grossly underestimated the problems, not least the extent of the damp at the rear of the house. The back garden was such a jungle that you could not open the back door. The garden walls at the front were overgrown with ivy, and over it all loomed a sixty-foot lime tree which cut off the house from its natural view of the mountains beyond the town. The first night we were there, camping in the kitchen – Belfast sink in the corner – and trying to confine the baby to the less grimy parts of the floor, there was a sudden howling noise from the front of the house which had our hearts leaping with a primeval kind of fear. I tracked it down, I think, to the wind coming in through the large keyhole in the front door.

Eventually the house took shape, with a new kitchen, lounge and bathroom, and eventually a new slate roof. At the top of the house, we knocked down a lath and plaster wall dividing a bedroom from the attic to create a large study. Here, I could sit at my desk, out of earshot of the rest of the house, and pretend to work while actually gazing at the panoramic view (once the lime tree had been cut down). Brecon remained a town relatively unchanged, hinged on the bridge over the Usk and enfolded in the hills which surround it. The cattle market had been banished to the outskirts and replaced by a supermarket. There was a big new theatre by the canal basin and a controversial inner relief road was soon to be created. But it was still the town I had known as a child.

As a sign of the times, Brecon now had a Welsh-medium primary school with up to 150 children attending. You do not hear a lot of Welsh spoken on the streets of Brecon, although you used to hear more on market days when the farmers came in from the countryside around. The town lies on a kind of linguistic border. To the west, an increasing amount of Welsh is spoken, but to the east the sound of Welsh is rarely heard. The majority of parents at Ysgol y Bannau (Bannau is the Welsh name for the Beacons) are monolingual but value the opportunity for their children to be brought up in the Welsh language. For Hannah, it proved to be a happy environment, and I made my contribution as chair of the school governing body. Hannah then moved on to Christ College, where she promptly immersed herself in the full range of activities on offer.

Hannah has the advantage of a Welsh-speaking mother and the disadvantage of a father who has struggled to learn the language at various times without a great deal of success. I managed in my fifties to achieve a GCSE in Welsh, enough to follow much of what is being said, but never gained any fluency. So it is a mixed-language household, with my wife and daughter speaking Welsh and with me often replying in English, simply because it is quicker. But whatever language we speak, for me it is wonderful to have a second chance at fatherhood. At home and available far more than I was the first time around, I have a greater sense of involvement. I have quickly forgotten any difficulties there may have been over caring for a young baby – were there really sleepless nights? Time moves on so fast.

There was so much going on, shipping my daughter back and forth to school, to music lessons, to eisteddfodau and to what are misleadingly called 'sleepovers' with friends. The town proved to be rich in cultural activities, and especially in music. And that is not just a reference to the well-known jazz festival in the town each year. Learning to play the cello was made more exciting for Hannah by being able to play in orchestral groups organised by a group called South Powys Youth Music, a group of volunteers dedicated to getting young people involved in playing music.

With Ann has come a connection to north Wales which I never had before. She was born and brought up in a Welsh-speaking household on Anglesey, before going to work at the BBC in Cardiff, and her parents, Meurig and Doris, were very welcoming. Visits to Llangefni were now frequent, and a chance to discover the beaches where she had played as a child. The small beach at Porth Nobla, not far from Rhosneigr, had been the family favourite, and there she had spent long hours with her childhood friend, Ann Ellen. Born just a few days apart, they had played together since they were babies, and have stayed firm friends ever since – an admirable longevity of friendship. To complete the circle, her daughter Alys is now friends with Hannah. And there are coastal views on Anglesey which, I am forced to admit, almost rival some of those in Pembrokeshire. The walk along the beach to Ynys Llanddwyn, with a view all the way down the Llŷn Peninsula as far as Ynys Enlli, is hard to beat.

Kyffin Williams, the most celebrated artist in Wales, was a friend of Ann's parents. Meurig had persuaded Kyffin to paint a seascape for him many years previously, and they had kept in touch. It was this connection which enabled me to sort out an issue I had with a picture I had bought more than thirty years previously from the Howard Roberts Gallery in Cardiff when I was working on the *South Wales Echo*. It had been my first big art purchase, a landscape in pen and ink by Kyffin, which I had bought for just £50. I am not sure I was especially aware of Kyffin's growing reputation at the time – I just loved the stark and evocative drawing of chapel and mountains. The gallery, long since disappeared, told me that it was a place called Cesarea, a slate-quarrying village on the northern slopes of Snowdonia.

We decided to find the location so we could compare it with the picture. It was a surreal journey, stopping and asking the way a number of times. We managed to find it only after realising that, mysteriously, the name of the place had been changed from Cesarea to Y Fron. The chapel was there, disused and boarded up, but somehow it did not look right, particularly the shape of the mountain behind. So I wrote to Kyffin, who replied that the drawing, done in the late 1950s, was in fact of an entirely different place. It turned out to be a ruined chapel at Gerlan, near Bethesda, which we then tried to find. By the time we got there, it had been demolished.

Kyffin continued with his typical dry humour: 'I have always liked Cesarea and have worked up there a lot. There is a bench outside the chapel with "Llandudno Junction" on it, put there presumably during the war to confuse the Germans. I write "is", but I fear it should be "was", as someone has nicked it. Maybe, in the next war, it will find itself in front of a chapel in Tonypandy to fool the Iraqis.'

Ann had always had a love of art and had been collecting Welsh paintings since she was eighteen years old. With the help and advice of Kyffin Williams, she started up an art gallery in Brecon, specialising in the work of artists from all over Wales, which she ran for seven years. It is a challenge setting up a business on your own, and I did what I could to help with securing the premises, preparing business plans and establishing a website. I especially enjoyed visiting artists in their studios, sometimes in scenic locations, finding out how they worked and what made them tick. The studio was often a garden shed or a garage stacked with canvases and frames and with an easel or desk multi-coloured with disused paints. Sometimes, as with Donald McIntyre at Tregarth, you were only allowed into the inner sanctum after a number of apprenticeship visits. There, untypically, he used to have the work of other artists hanging on the walls, especially the Scottish colourists who had strongly influenced him.

It was while helping out in Ann's gallery that I received another lesson in the transience of television fame. Now and again I still get a flicker of recognition from people, usually older people, who vaguely recall me from the days when I appeared on screen. This time it happened as a couple came into the gallery as I was going out. The man turned and asked Ann:

'Do you know that man?'

'I should do,' she said, 'because he's my husband.'

'I know I've seen him before somewhere,' he said. 'I remember. He's that undertaker from Abergavenny.'

My father's health had by now become more fragile, as you would expect of someone approaching ninety. My mother would have been surprised how well he had coped on his own since her death. But the level of care he required was gradually increasing. It was no longer enough for someone local to go in once or twice a day and make his meals and do the housework. I ended up organising a rota of Zimbabwean women to stay for months at a time – such was the collapse of the Zimbabwean economy that they were coming to Britain just to earn some hard currency. But my father never gave up. As my niece Lowri said: 'He didn't know how to give up.'

In the last years of his life, he agreed to set up a fund for a literary prize in his name, with the aim of celebrating Welsh writing in English. The prize was awarded for those aspects of writing in which he had been most engaged – poetry, of course, but also short stories, Welsh history and literary criticism. I chaired the panel of judges, all of whom knew more about these forms of literature than I did, and we had enjoyable times, and occasional arguments, deciding who should get the award. At the time of writing, the Roland Mathias Prize lives on as the poetry award for the Wales Book of the Year.

My father was almost ninety-two when he died, in the early hours of an August morning. He was uncomplaining to the end, content in the knowledge, I think, of a life of achievement behind him. I rarely tried to compare myself to him – we lived our lives in very different ways. I still attend the Plough chapel, but I have never, for instance, managed to match the strength of his religious faith. In one of his poems, he asks the rhetorical question: 'Is the old witness done?' and seeks to answer it himself:

... Each on his own must stand and conjure
The strong remembered words, the unanswerable
Texts against chaos.

*

I was still working part-time and had become something of a poacher turned gamekeeper on behalf of Ofcom, the regulator of the UK's communications industries – which included broadcasting. In 2007 I became a member of Ofcom's Welsh advisory committee, where I could only admire the level of technical expertise of colleagues with backgrounds in telecommunications. It was a robust committee which made itself heard. One of its notable successes was to persuade Ofcom of the need to respond to emergencies in remoter parts of the countryside by obliging the mobile phone companies to allow emergency roaming – now if you dial 999 you will pick up a signal from any of the mobile companies, not just your own. In all this work, the advisory committee benefited from the support of the small team in the Cardiff office of Ofcom, led by Rhodri Williams.

On the broadcasting front, it was the labour of Sisyphus. There was growing concern at the reduction in television programming targeted at Welsh viewers, in particular English-language programming. At one stage, there appeared to be a significant danger that ITV would pull out of 'regional' programming altogether, including news programmes, on the grounds that the company could no longer afford to provide it. That could have meant that there would no longer be any alternative to the programmes provided by BBC Wales in the English language (the crisis over the funding of S4C came later). In any democracy, and particularly in the fledgling democracy created by the devolution settlement for Wales, a plurality of media voices is essential for democratic debate to thrive.

For Ofcom, there had seemed no alternative to accepting the decline in ITV's programming obligations, a stance which attracted some controversy along the way. Now the issue had reached a different level, and in 2009 Ofcom recommended that the UK government should consider an 'alternative model' for providing television news to the devolved nations and English regions. This would involve independently-funded consortia providing an alternative source of news to the BBC, but broadcast in the slot where ITV news programmes had previously been transmitted. The Labour government at Westminster accepted this analysis and decided that the concept would be tested in three pilot areas across the UK – in Wales, Scotland and the north-east of England – at a cost to public funds of £6,000,000.

The following January, I was surprised to receive a call asking me to sit on the panel that was going to select what were called 'preferred bidders' for the three pilot areas. The call came from Richard Hooper, a former deputy chair of Ofcom, and now to be chair of the selection panel. I was never quite sure how such things operated, but I had been heavily involved in writing submissions to Ofcom's reviews of public service broadcasting.

The panel was immediately plunged into a fast-moving procurement process set against a demanding timetable. We all knew that a general election was due in a few months' time, and that the Conservatives – who were expected to win – had announced they would abandon the IFNC project. But if there was always an element of unreality about the work of the panel, it was not allowed to show. There was a detailed evaluation of the rival bids and meetings around the country with the rival bidders. And it was about more than just replacing the regional ITV news: it was intended to be a multi-platform approach using a variety of media with newspaper and radio partners – a forerunner, perhaps, of things to come.

The decisions were not easy, and in Wales they were the hardest of the lot. The ultimate decision was to name a consortium led by UTV as the preferred bidder for the Welsh pilot. A leading factor in that decision was the offer of a harder-edged news service, based on a strong track record in Northern Ireland. Despite the fact we had chosen an outsider over two rival bidders from Wales, it was a decision which received widespread, if not universal, support. Peter Hain, now back as Secretary of State for Wales, improvised a press conference in Cardiff to announce the result, even though he had nothing to do with it. I was given a walk-on part.

Reality finally broke in. The new Conservative Culture Secretary, Jeremy Hunt, duly cancelled the whole project on the basis that it was not an appropriate use of public money. That was hugely ironic, given that he then promptly twisted the arm of the BBC into providing a considerably larger sum out of the licence fee to provide start-up funding for his own pet project, local television stations around the UK. There were many doubts as to whether local TV would ever be sustainable or worthwhile in Britain outside the biggest cities, but it was Ofcom's job, as the regulator, to implement the government's legislation and there were a surprising number of people bidding for the licenses. It was doubly ironic that – as the wheel turned – I ended up on Ofcom's broadcast licensing committee ploughing through mountains of application forms while helping to decide who should be awarded the local TV licences. I wait with interest to see how local television fares in this country.

It was not just government policy which changed. ITV's own assessment of the financial viability of its regional programming changed as well, partly because of resurgence in its advertising income. When it became time to seek renewal of its licence in 2012, the company was much more positive about maintaining its level of programming for the following ten years. And it agreed to replace its cross-border licence for Wales and the West of England with a separate licence for Wales. It was another small mark of political progress.

*

Particularly interesting in this so-called 'portfolio' of roles has been the opportunity to apply whatever skills I have acquired in different directions. The most intense period of work I have ever undertaken was a review of the work of the Local Government Boundary Commission for Wales, which the Welsh Government was demanding should be completed in three months. It led to the dismissal of the three commissioners and the passage of legislation through the National Assembly to put the whole system on a more up-to-date legal footing. And at the time or writing I am fortunate to be involved with Dŵr Cymru, the not-for-profit water company which has no shareholders and – as an example to other utilities – is run for the benefit of its customers. Instead of shareholders, it has fifty or so members to hold the company to account, and I act as chair of the Membership Selection Panel.

One thing I have had to live with all my life – it may or may not have been an advantage – is the fact that I have always looked younger than my age. From my school photographs onwards, I have never looked the same age as my contemporaries. Perhaps this was something of an obstacle in climbing up the professional ladder, but being thought of as younger than I was helped me to disregard the passing years.

Those of my friends with a literary bent would sometimes make cracks about 'the picture in the attic', a reference to the novel by Oscar Wilde about a young man, Dorian Gray, who kept a portrait of himself in the attic. Dorian Gray had sold his soul to ensure his portrait would disfigure with age rather than himself. There are aspects to this tale of hedonism which I would prefer to believe do not apply to me, but the theme of unseen disfigurement has a touch of truth about it.

The psoriasis from which I had suffered for more than thirty years was spreading around my body and was increasingly difficult to ignore. Twice flare-ups landed me in A&E. As it got worse, I was persuaded to take a succession of drug treatments which never succeeded in healing it, but the side-effects of the treatments invariably affected me badly. That is not true for all sufferers from psoriasis, for the specialists in this field never really know how any particular treatment will impact on any individual patient. I gradually became aware of an international samizdat community of refugees from the medical profession advocating alternative therapies. The only one which worked for me involved lying in the sun on the shores of the Dead Sea in Israel until the skin had healed. The psoriasis always came back.

But I have been fortunate. I have otherwise survived in good health when others around me have not, and I can still walk the local mountain tops with Ann and manage to pant no more than our big, black labradoodle. I have been one of the lucky post-war generation, going from a fully grant-funded university degree into continuous employment, which took me all the way through my career until the point I decided to leave it. I had a ringside seat at the political theatre at Westminster during some tumultuous years, and worked on what I still think was the best and sharpest news programme of them all – ITN's *News at Ten.*

The last fifteen years or so have been particularly happy. Perhaps with advancing years comes a greater serenity, but it is more than that. It is being part of a loving family and seeing my children grow up and make their own way in life. Megan, after a first-class degree at Southampton University, becoming a management consultant, and Mathew as a marine instructor making a career out of his love of the sea. And I have just seen my grandson, Max, bouncing on the trampoline outside the kitchen window, and I can hear Hannah practising her cello.

I can sit at my desk, look out at the mountains and put the span of my life in its rightful context.

And maybe I can just raise the faintest of echoes from the past.

Acknowledgements

MY INTEREST IN writing this book began a few years ago when my cousin Gareth turned up at my front door with a bunch of old letters he had found in the attic of his mother's house. My Aunt Ogwen had recently died, and he was clearing her house. The letters, some in fragments but in a beautiful copperplate handwriting, were from my grandfather Evan sent to his mother and brother living in Sennybridge, just a few miles from Brecon in mid-Wales. Although serving abroad as an army chaplain, he was assiduous in keeping in touch with the rest of his family. It prompted me to find out more about his military career, about which I had known very little.

After the death of my father Roland in 2007, I was able to find out more from the amorphous pile of paperwork he had left. For further information on life in Shanghai in 1927, I am grateful to the Imperial War Museum in London.

There was also a period in my father's life about which I knew little, mainly because he never spoke about it. I had known that he had been a conscientious objector and had served time in prison during the Second World War, but little more than that. He had sent the bulk of his papers to the National Library of Wales in Aberystwyth, so I spent several enjoyable days ploughing through a large number of boxes. The official printed letters and documents were easy enough to find, but the letters from my grandmother Muriel were a tougher challenge. Her appalling handwriting had clearly baffled the archivist, so I was fortunate in being able to remember how to decipher it.

For information about life in the valley above Talybont-on-Usk before it was flooded, I owe a great deal to *The Talybont Saga*, by David Tipper and published by Dŵr Cymru. It is an invaluable account of the building of the reservoir in Glyn Collwn and the loss of a community. But my father also kept files on the different farms that were lost, and I was able to use those also.

The extracts from my father's poems are all taken from *The Collected Poems of Roland Mathias*, edited by Sam Adams and published by the University of Wales Press (2002).

As to my own life and times, I have relied primarily on my memory. I have kept diaries only infrequently, and much of what I thought important at the time was rarely so important in retrospect. For the more distant years, I sometimes had to check details in what are now history books – a grim realisation in itself. Much of ITN's video archive is available online to universities, and I am grateful to Russell Deacon, then at Cardiff Metropolitan University, for access to it. BBC Wales was generous in allowing me to view some of my old material at its video library. Some interesting additions of fact became available simply through the device of 'Googling' myself.

Several people kindly read through an earlier draft of the book. My sisters, Mary and Ceinwen, read through the chapters relating to our family and childhood. Stewart Purvis checked through the chapters relating to my time at ITN and gave some helpful advice along the way. Huw Roberts gave me his thoughts on my time at BBC Wales; Sam Younger read through the chapter on my time at the Electoral Commission, while Rhodri Williams advised me on the references to Ofcom. My sister Ceinwen gave me a great deal of assistance with my syntax and punctuation, and Lefi Gruffudd and Eifion Jenkins at *Y Lolfa* encouraged me throughout. I am indebted to all of them, but any mistakes of fact, any omissions or any events misremembered are all my own work.

I am especially grateful to my wife Ann who had to put up with my preoccupations in writing this book. Without her support, I would not have been able to do it.

GM, April 2014

A Haven from HITLER

"Kate Bosse becomes a figure of huge moral and symbolic significance."
– Simon Brooks, *Planet*

A young woman's escape from Nazi Germany to Wales: the story of Kate Bosse-Griffiths and her family

Welsh Book of the Year 2013

Heini Gruffudd

y Lolfa

£9.95

Richard Lewis

out of the VALLEY

The Autobiography of a Media Man

£8.95

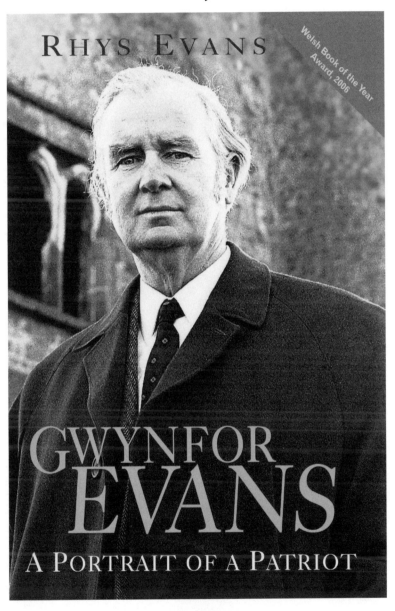